BARRON'S

PAINLESS

Spanish

Second Edition

Carlos B. Vega, Ph.D.
Illustratred by Michele Earle-Bridges

Dedication

This book is dedicated to the Spanish teacher in particular, and to the teaching profession in general, the noblest and hardest of all human endeavors. We cannot imagine a world without teachers, as we cannot imagine a world without a sunrise or a tree without branches and leaves. Hail to the teacher, for he or she brings light to what otherwise would be a world of darkness.

All inquiries should be addressed to:
Barron's Educational Series, Inc.
250 Wireless Boulevard
Hauppauge, New York 11788
www.barronseduc.com

ISBN: 978-0-7641-4711-1

Library of Congress Control Number: 2011921051

PRINTED IN THE UNITED STATES OF AMERICA
9 8 7 6 5

CONTENTS

Lección 6: Estudiamos para mejorar nuestra condición humana/We study to become better people   97

Lección 7: Sin economía no hay país/ The economy is vital to every country   129

Lección 8: Cuatro ruedas para todo/ Four wheels for everything   155

CONTENTS

Lección 9: No hay mejor educación que el viajar/Traveling is the best education 175

Lección 10: Con buen gobierno avanzan los pueblos/Nations advance with good government 195

Lección 11: El arte es maravilloso/ Art is wonderful **229**

Lección 12: Deportes para todos los gustos/Sports for all tastes **253**

Lección 13: La naturaleza es vida/ Nature is life **271**

Appendix A

Appendix B

Appendix C

Appendix D

Appendix E

Appendix F

Appendix G

Index

INTRODUCTION

The book you are holding in your hands promises one thing: to teach you Spanish if you make a true effort to learn it. We have worked diligently to teach it to you, and you should work as diligently to learn it. No excuses, no games, no shortcuts.

The kind of Spanish you will learn here is real Spanish, the one people speak with the same fluidity and spontaneity as you speak English. But we have taken it a step further. Not only will you be learning real Spanish, but we will also expose you to the real Hispanic world, to its culture, history, and writing. In other words, you will be submerged in real, authentic Spanish in all of its wonderful aspects. Let us say this—if a person wants to learn English, the best you can do for that person is to use the kind of English we all speak, meaning it is not a matter of just words but how words are used and in what context. For example, I can learn such common words as "life," "people," "year," "place" by reading Jefferson or Lincoln or a tabloid. The words are the same, but the contexts in which they are used differ greatly. One context has vigor, punch, meaning; it teaches not only the language but the soul of a people. The other has no meaning, and it teaches nothing worth learning. You would also want to expose that person to some basic aspects of U.S. history and culture so as to instill in him or her a broader understanding and appreciation of what this country stands for. You never can separate the language from the people who speak it and what they represent.

Of course, the best and most effective way to learn a language is by using it and hearing it, not sporadically but constantly in a country of origin. But this is not your situation. Therefore, you must not only try to speak it and hear it as often as you can but understand it as well, which is where grammar comes in. If I am here in the United States, I don't need to be taught the difference between "I speak" and "I spoke" because soon enough I will pick it up. But, if I am not here, it would take me an eternity to learn the difference between one and the other unless it is explained to me.

This book has a total of 13 lessons. In each one you will learn an important aspect of the Spanish language and of the Hispanic culture, the information you really need to learn the language and become acquainted with the culture and history of the 400 million people who speak it. You will also learn to read and write proper Spanish, and to express yourself in a basic yet effective way.

Each of the 13 lessons is divided into 9 main parts or sections, with titles given in both Spanish and English, as follows: **Part 1.** The lesson opens with a main theme, which serves as the basis for most of the lesson; **Part 2.** Piénsalo bien/Think it through. Basic grammar; **Part 3.** Más es mejor/More is better. Additional vocabulary; **Part 4.** Habla popular/Everyday speech. Common idioms, expressions, and sayings; **Part 5.** Bien vale la pena/It's well worth it. General information of interest; **Part 6.** Dilo como yo/Say it like I do. Basic pronunciation of Spanish sounds; **Part 7.** Alma hispánica/Hispanic soul. Reading of classic Hispanic authors; **Part 8.** Pluma en mano/Pen in hand. Composition practice; and **Part 9.** Así somos/This is who we are. Cultural aspects of the Hispanic world. Bilingual titles, as shown above, are also provided within the texts of every lesson.

This book has been designed in a way to fit any if not most teaching methods. Although it is meant primarily to be used at the introductory level for middle-school students, it can also be useful for the intermediate or even the advanced levels, for review purposes, and for self-teaching. Each of the 13 lessons could be covered in one week for a total of 13 weeks, or roughly an academic semester. However, some lessons may take a bit longer because of the complexity of the grammar, such as lessons 5, 6, and 10; thus, a longer time frame may be more realistic.

Regarding the grammar, it is not relevant whether you like it or not. It doesn't really matter whether you like math or biology. You have to do whatever is necessary in order to achieve your goals. Bad medicine, perhaps, but you have to take it. We can try to make it easier, perhaps a bit sweeter, but you have to take it regardless.

Throughout each lesson you will find numerous attention grabbers and brain ticklers that we have titled: ¡Ojo! (Watch out!), ¿Te acuerdas? (Do you remember?), ¿Cuánto sabes? (How much do you know?), and ¿Sabías que? (Did you know?).

Each lesson provides abundant examples and exercises in each of the subjects covered.

We congratulate you on your decision to learn Spanish. No doubt it will broaden your perspective of life and the world, and also be a great asset in your future career endeavors.

¡Adelante y manos a la obra!

La familia es nuestro sostén y reposo

The family is our support and comfort

El núcleo familiar es *por lo general* muy extenso y lo forman, *básicamente*, los *padres e hijos*. En mi familia, por ejemplo, tengo a mi padre, madre, y a mis hermanos Jesús, Manolo, Leticia y Emilia, *es decir*, que tengo dos hermanos y dos hermanas. Esta es mi familia inmediata, *la más allegada* pero *también* hay muchas otras personas, como mis abuelos, tíos y primos. Por parte de padre tengo dos abuelos, e igual número *por parte de madre*. Tíos, por parte de padre tengo cuatro, y por parte de madre, seis. Primos son muchos, por ambas partes, más o menos unos quince en total. Mis abuelos y padres, así como mis tíos, son de España, y quitando a mis dos hermanos *varones*, que también son españoles, los demás *nacieron* en Estados Unidos, o sea, que son norteamericanos. Mis padres se llaman Félix y Consuelo, y los quiero mucho por ser tan buenos y amables. Mi padre es ingeniero, y mi madre trabaja como *enfermera* en un hospital. Mis abuelos están *jubilados* y viven en la Florida. Uno de mis hermanos, Jesús, es *médico*, y una de mis hermanas, Emilia, es *abogada*. *Tengo suerte* de tener una familia tan bonita, *tan unida*, y tan inteligente.

Vocabulario básico

por lo general	generally
básicamente	basically
padres e hijos	parents and children
es decir	that is to say
la más allegada	the closest
también	also
por parte de madre	on my mother's side
varones	males (*hembras*, for females)
nacieron	they were born (*nacer*: to be born)
enfermera	nurse (female)
jubilados	retired
médico	medical doctor, physician
abogada	lawyer (female or woman)
Tengo suerte	I am lucky (*tener suerte:* to be lucky)
tan unida	so close

¡Ojo!*—Watch Out!

When you combine *padre y madre* (father and mother) you say *padres* (parents), and the same for *hermano y hermana* (brother and sister), *abuelo y abuela* (grandfather and grandmother), etc. In other words, in the plural, the masculine form takes precedence. However, keep in mind that the plural form can mean also fathers, brothers, grandfathers, etc.

(*) **¡Ojo!** in Spanish means *Watch out!*, *Look up!*, *Pay attention!* Learn this word well as we will be using it throughout this book.

BRAIN TICKLERS
Set # 1

Ejercicios **(This word means exercises in Spanish. Try to learn it as we will use it repeatedly in this book.)**

A. Fill in the blanks with the correct Spanish word or words:

   1. (On my mother's side) _____ tengo cinco tíos.

   2. Mi padre (is) _____ norteamericano.

   3. (My grandparents) _____ todavía trabajan.

4. No (have) _____ hermanos pero sí hermanas.*

5. (Our family) _____ es muy numerosa.

*In question 4 above, notice that the *no* or negative is placed in front of the verb. This is how it is always done in Spanish, regardless of whether the verb is at the beginning of the sentence or in the middle.

B. Give the Spanish for the following words (make sure you spell them correctly and include the definite article for each noun):

1. mother _____
2. many _____
3. number _____
4. retired _____
5. to live _____

C. Unscramble these sentences and phrases, putting each word in the right order. Use capital letters where needed.

1. madre mi es bonita.
2. es nombre mi _____ .
3. su es familia grande.
4. son España de.
5. y tíos tías

Answers are on page 18.

¡Ojo!—Watch Out!

The word *español* can be used in different ways. It can be a noun or an adjective, depending on how you use it. If I say: *Roberto es español* (Robert is Spanish), it is an adjective, but if I say: *Me gusta el español* (I like Spanish), it is a noun. *Español* refers to the country in which Spanish is spoken, or *España* (Spain). In some Hispanic countries, Argentina, for example, they use another word for Spanish, *castellano* (Castilian), which refers to the region of Castile where the language originated and was formed. Which of the two words should you use? "Español" is by far the most common.

PIÉNSALO BIEN
THINK IT THROUGH

About the Spanish language

Spanish is a very old language, at least 1,000 years old. It is
called a *Romance language* because it originated from Latin,
just as French and Portuguese did. Why? Because for many
years Spain was one of the key provinces of Rome and was
greatly influenced by Rome's language, culture, and customs.
Throughout most of the Middle Ages, Latin was the language
spoken in Spain, until the thirteenth century, when King
Alphonse X proclaimed it the official language of his kingdom
of Castile. However, many medieval writers began to write in
romance, or Spanish, early on, and by the sixteenth century
most writers were already writing in Spanish. The father of
the Spanish language, as he is commonly called, was Miguel
de Cervantes, the author of *Don Quijote*, the one who
largely made the language what it is today. Spanish was also
influenced by many other languages, including Arabic, and, of
course, Greek and Latin. When Spain discovered America in
1492, many of the languages spoken by the indigenous cultures,
such as the Aztecs and Incas, also greatly influenced Spanish,
especially in names of food and plants. Some people think
that there are different kinds of Spanish, which is not really
true. There is only one kind of Spanish, although there are
differences in the use and pronunciation of certain words and
sounds, and in the intonation. However, no matter how many
different equivalents a word may have, there is always one
standard word that everybody knows, which is the one you
should use. For example, in the Caribbean, the word most
commonly used for *bus* is *guagua*, and in Central America
camión. However, the standard Spanish word is *autobús*, or
bus. Either one should be your first choice.

BRAIN TICKLERS
Set # 2

*¿Cuánto sabes?** Try to answer these questions by yourself:

1. Do you know where the region of Castile in Spain is?

2. Can you name two important cities of Castile?

3. Do you know the name of a very important queen of Castile? (Tip: She was the queen when America was discovered.)

4. Can you name the country where the Aztecs were from?

5. Who was Montezuma?

(*) It means *How much do you know?* Learn it well as we will be using it throughout this book.

Answers are on page 18.

¡Sabías que! Do you know the origin of the word *España* and what it means? It comes from *Hispania*, the name given to Spain by the Romans, and it means, literally, *land of rabbits*, due to the abundance of this animal in the Iberian Peninsula.

MÁS ES MEJOR
MORE IS BETTER

In this section we are including additional vocabulary relating to the main theme of the lesson.

Nouns

el hogar	home
el familiar	relative

This is a cognate word with two meanings in Spanish. It can mean a relative, in which case it is a noun, or someone/something who/that is familiar to us, in which case it is an adjective. Let's see these two examples: *Pedro es un familiar* (Pedro is a relative), *Pedro me es familiar* (Pedro looks familiar to me).

el cuñado	brother-in-law
la cuñada	sister-in-law
los cuñados	brothers- and sisters-in-law
el hijo	son
la hija	daughter
los hijos	sons and daughters
el padrasto	stepfather
la madrasta	stepmother
el hijastro	stepson
la hijastra	stepdaughter
el padrino	godfather
la madrina	godmother
el hombre	man
la mujer	woman
el esposo	husband/spouse
la esposa	wife/spouse

Two other names for husband and wife in Spanish are *el marido y la mujer.*

el matrimonio	marriage/married couple
la pareja	couple
el niño	boy/child
la niña	girl
el bebé	baby
el abuelo	grandfather
la abuela	grandmother
el novio	groom
la novia	bride
la iglesia	church

Verbs

ser/estar	to be
tener	to have
llamarse	literally, to call oneself (reflexive verb)

When you say *me llamo* in Spanish, you're saying *my name is* (or I am called). What is your name in Spanish can be asked in two ways: *¿Cómo te llamas?* and *¿Cuál es tu nombre?*
For the first you respond: *me llamo* and for the second *mi nombre es*. Usually, however, for the first you should give both your first and last names, while for the second only the first one.

nacer	to be born
querer	to love/want

Conjugation of the above verbs in the present tense

ser	soy, eres, es, somos, sois, son
estar	estoy, estás, está, estamos, estáis, están
tener	tengo, tienes, tiene, tenemos, tenéis, tienen
llamarse	me llamo, te llamas, se llama, nos llamamos, os llamáis, se llaman
nacer	naces, nace, nacemos, nacéis, nacen (The first person, *I* is never conjugated in this verb.)
querer	quiero, quieres, quiere, queremos, queréis, quieren

¿Te acuerdas?*

Padre means father and **madre** means mother. Do you remember what **padres** means?

(*) This means: Do you remember? Learn it well as we will use it throughout the book.

HABLA POPULAR
EVERYDAY SPEECH

Idioms, common expressions, and sayings

An idiom is a peculiar or characteristic way a language has to express something, and it is essential to learn the idiom. For example, as English uses the verb *to be* when referring to the weather (it is cold, it is windy), Spanish uses *hacer*, which means *to do/make*, as in *hace frío, hace viento*. Obviously, such idioms could not be translated literally for they would be meaningless.

Common expressions cannot be translated literally either, for they are made up of words that lose their individual meaning to mean something else. Look at these English idiomatic expressions:

> dressed to kill
> cute as a button

How would you convey the same meaning in Spanish? Only by understanding what is being said in the whole phrase, and not by the meaning of the individual words. Thus, we would say:

> elegantemente vestido – tan bonita como una flor

Sayings express a long-established truth, such as a proverb or adage. Usually, there is something similar in Spanish. Here are two examples of common sayings:

De tal palo tal astilla.	Like father like son.
El amor es ciego.	Love is blind.

¿Sabías que? How much do you think Christopher Columbus's trip cost Spain? It cost 1,167,542 *maravedís*, or approximately $151,780 in today's U.S. dollars.

9

BIEN VALE LA PENA
IT'S WELL WORTH IT

Nombres y apellidos (first and last names)

Usually, Spanish people have two first names and two last names; one is the father's and the other is the mother's (maiden name). No middle initial is used in Spanish as is customary in the United States. What distinguishes two persons with the same first and last names is the mother's last or maiden name. For example:

Rodrigo González Suárez. González is the father's last name, and Suárez is the mother's last or maiden name. In other words, contrary to what is customary in the United States, the mother's last name is always present in all Spanish full names.

Many Spanish first names are taken from the names of saints, such as Pablo, Juan, Pedro, José, and the same for women: María, Guadalupe, Asunción, Teresa. And many last names end in "ez," as in Fernández, Rodríguez, Hernández. The *ez* stands for *son or daughter of* (Fernando, Rodrigo, Hernando), just like Williamson, Peterson, Robertson, in which the *son* stands for the same (William, Peter, Robert).

Spanish, like English, also uses nicknames, which are called *apodos*, like Pepe for José, Enolé for Manolo, Rafi for Rafael, Lelito for Consuelo (Consuelito), Cachita for Caridad, and even others that are totally made up, like Coqui for María.

Many English common first names have equivalents in Spanish. Here are a few:

English	Spanish	English	Spanish
Charles	Carlos	Anthony	Antonio
Elizabeth	Isabel	Louis	Luis
Emily	Emilia	Philip	Felipe
Robert	Roberto	Christine	Cristina
Mary	María	Anne	Ana
Peter	Pedro	Pauline	Paulina

Paul	Pablo	Regine	Regina
Margaret	Margarita	John	Juan
Susan	Susana	Ralph	Rafael

BRAIN TICKLERS
Set # 3

Ejercicios

A. Answer these questions in English:

1. If you were living in a Hispanic country, how would you write your full name?

2. Do you use an apodo? What is it?

3. The Spanish last name Martínez is a two-part word:

   _____ and
   _____ ,

and it means _____.

4. Do you know the Spanish equivalent for Martha?

5. What distinguishes two persons with the same name in Spanish?

B. Match the English first name in the left column with the Spanish one in the right column:

Michael	Arturo
Jane	Josefina
Sophie	Jorge
Christopher	Rosa
George	Alejandro
Josephine	Sofía
Thomas	Cristóbal
Arthur	Miguel
Alexander	Juana
Rose	Tomás

Answers are on page 18.

¡Ojo!—Watch Out!

Spanish, like English, uses titles for people. Some of the most common are:

Spanish	Abbv.	English	Abbv.
Señor	Sr.	Mister/Sir	Mr.
Señora	Sra.	Madam	Mrs.
Señorita	Srta.	—	Miss
—	Sa.		Ms.
Don	D.	—	—
Doña	Dña.	—	—

Explanations

Señorita refers mainly to an unmarried woman, but also to a young woman.

Sa., as in English, makes no reference to a woman's marital status.

Don was originally an honorary title, but it now applies to a man of status, and also to an older man.

Doña is the same as above but applied to a woman.

When referring to a Don or Doña, always use the title before the person's first name, as in Don Miguel, Doña Consuelo. Sr. and Sra. are used before last names, as in Sr. García, Sra. Suárez.

In a Hispanic country, a married woman takes the husband's last name but always keeps her maiden name, as in: Consuelo Vega de Suárez; Suárez is the husband's last name, and Vega her maiden name. However, today, many married women leave out the *de* (which literally means *of*) and say their name: Consuelo Vega Suárez. Professional titles are also used in Spanish, as in *Dr.* Ramírez (a physician) and *Lic.* Escobar (a lawyer). Feminine forms are *Dra.* and *Licda.* Since Spanish names always have masculine and feminine forms, it is easier to identify the gender of a person's profession; for example, *abogado - a, maestro - a, enfermero - a.* When this is not possible, the article identifies it, as in *el bombero* (fireman), *la bombero* (firewoman.) In some cases, when the noun ends in *a*, as in *policía* (police), the only way to refer to a policewoman is by saying *la mujer policía*, or *el oficial de policía* (police officer) or *la oficial de policía* (also police officer, but a woman). In other words, most nouns can change their gender by the ending, "*o-a*," or by the article, *el*, *la*, while others can't.

DILO COMO YO
SAY IT LIKE I DO

El alfabeto español

The Spanish alphabet has a total of 28 letters or symbols: 5 vowels and 23 consonants, both in upper and lower case. They are

Aa	Bb	Cc	CHch	Dd	Ee	Ff	Gg	Hh	Ii	Jj
a	be	ce	che	de	e	efe	ge	hache	i	jota

Kk	Ll	LLll	Mm	Nn	Ññ	Oo	Pp	Qq	Rr	Ss
ka	ele	elle	eme	ene	eñe	o	pe	cu	ere/erre	ese

Tt	Uu	Vv	Xx	Yy	Zz
te	u	uve	equis	i griega/ye	zeta

Explanations

Underneath each letter is its name. Of the 23 consonants, two are double consonants: *ch*, *ll*, and the *r* can be used either as a single or double consonant: *r* or *rr*. Some people add the *rr* to the alphabet, making it then 29 letters instead of 28.

There is no *w* in the Spanish alphabet, but it is used in all foreign proper names, as in Washington. The same applies to the *k*, which is used almost exclusively in words taken from other languages, such as *kilómetro*, *kilogramo*.

An important word about spelling: Since English has many different sounds for letters, words often need to be spelled out. This is not really needed in Spanish, unless it happens to be a very odd or uncommon word, or there is confusion regarding the pronunciation of certain letters, such as the *v-b* or *s-z*. Therefore, generally in Spanish, words are written as they are pronounced. **Note:** Pronunciation of the letters will be explained in the following lessons.

¡Ojo!—Watch Out!

How many words in English end in the suffix *-tion*? Thousands. Well, in Spanish, that suffix is *ción*, changing the *t* to *c* and adding an accent mark on the *ó*. All of the other letters in both English and Spanish are the same. Also, in Spanish, all of such words are feminine. Here are a few of these:

Inglés	Español
constitution	constitución
revolution	revolución
creation	creación
information	información
nation	nación

There are, however, a few exceptions, but generally the words are the same.

¿Te acuerdas?
How many double consonants are there in Spanish? _____.

ALMA HISPÁNICA
HISPANIC SOUL

You are about to read various passages from some of the finest Hispanic writers of all time. What is truly important for you is to focus on the reading itself and not so much on the meaning of the words. As you come upon each word, take your time and try to pronounce it correctly and don't rush through it—read at a normal pace. In this particular passage, most of the verbs are in the past tense—*se armó* (put on his armor), *subió* (got on), *salió* (he left); the imperfect—*era* (he was); and the imperfect subjunctive—*viese* (seeing him), but don't worry about them at this moment.

Miguel de Cervantes

Cervantes (1547–1616) was a seventeenth-century Spanish novelist, dramatist, and poet. He is considered Spain's best writer and one of the world's leading literary figures. Although he wrote many important works, none compares to *Don Quijote de la Mancha*, hailed as the greatest novel ever written in Spanish. It was published in two parts, in 1605 and 1615, and has been translated into all world languages.

Don Quijote was an old man obsessed with the idea of becoming a knight-errant and undoing all wrongs. He read so many books on chivalry that his brain was affected and one day he set out to follow his quest. At the end of a long journey, he recovered his sanity and returned home, where he died peacefully.

The following passage describes Don Quijote's departure from his town:

Y así, sin dar parte a persona alguna de su intención y sin que nadie le viese, una mañana, antes del día, que era uno de los calurosos del mes de julio, se armó de todas sus armas, subió sobre Rocinante … y por la puerta falsa de su corral salió al campo, con grandísimo contento y alborozo de ver con cuanta facilidad había dado principio a su buen deseo.

PLUMA EN MANO
PEN IN HAND

Fiestas familiares/Family parties

Las fiestas familiares son muy alegres y divertidas. En mi casa, cada año celebramos los cumpleaños, los aniversarios, los bautizos, las graduaciones, el Día de Acción de Gracias, las Navidades, el Año Nuevo, el Día de los Reyes Magos y las bodas (weddings), cuando las hay. En esas fechas (On those dates), se reúne toda la familia y cantamos, bailamos y comemos a reventar. Todos nos hacemos (We give each other) regalos, que son muy bonitos y nos vestimos elegantemente. Como (Since) mi casa es muy grande y amplia, y todos mis parientes son muy simpáticos y entusiastas, nos encanta (we enjoy) tener fiestas a menudo.

BRAIN TICKLERS
Set # 4

After reading the above carefully, do the following:

1. Write in the three columns below five nouns, five verbs, and five adjectives: Answers will vary.

   Nouns   Verbs   Adjectives

2. Using one of these same nouns, verbs, and adjectives, write an original sentence in Spanish.

3. See how many articles you can identify, and write them along with the English equivalents.

4. Write the words you do not know, look them up in the general vocabulary, and give the English equivalent for each.

5. Do you know what the common expression *comer hasta reventar* means? Think carefully.

Answers are on page 18.

ASÍ SOMOS
THIS IS WHO WE ARE

The early history of Spain

Just like its language, Spain is a very old country, dating back to antiquity. There are, however, three main periods of Spanish history: Roman, Visigoth, and Arab or Muslim. All three civilizations invaded Spain and settled there, leaving an indelible mark on its culture. The Romans dominated Spain  for almost 600 years, the Visigoths for 200, and the Arabs (or Moors, as they are called in Spain) for almost 800 years. Do the math and you will see that all three were in Spain for a combined period of 1,600 years. The Romans gave Spain their language, Latin, from which Spanish is derived; the Visigoths initiated the reconquest from the Arabs and proclaimed Catholicism as Spain's religion; the Arabs transmitted their great knowledge in the arts and sciences. A visit to any city in Spain, but especially Toledo, would reveal many traces of the rich and lasting legacies of the three civilizations. A leading figure in Spain's reconquest was Rodrigo Díaz de Vivar, known to history as *El Cid* (the Lord).

Finally, in the fifteenth century, Spain established its own cultural and political identity and became a united nation through the marriage of two outstanding monarchs: Queen Isabella of Castile, and King Ferdinand of Aragon, known as the *Reyes Católicos* (Catholic Monarchs). They both reigned with equal powers, and with their wisdom and vision made Spain the most powerful and influential country in all of Europe as well as half the world.

BRAIN TICKLERS—THE ANSWERS

Set # 1, page 3

A.
1. Por parte de madre
2. es
3. Mis abuelos
4. tengo
5. Nuestra familia

B.
1. la madre
2. muchos
3. el número
4. jubilado
5. vivir

C.
1. Mi madre es bonita.
2. Mi nombre es _____.
3. Su familia es grande.
4. Son de España.
5. tíos y tías

Set # 2, page 6

Cuánto sabes?
1. In the center of Spain
2. Ávila, Burgos
3. Queen Isabella
4. Mexico
5. the Emperor of the Aztecs

Set # 3, page 11

Bien vale la pena

A.
1. Answer may vary.
2. Answer may vary.
3. Martín - ez, son of Martín
4. Marta
5. The mother's maiden name.

B.
Michael—Miguel
Jane—Juana
Sophie—Sofía
Christopher—Cristóbal
George—Jorge
Josephine—Josefina
Thomas—Tomás
Arthur—Arturo
Alexander—Alejandro
Rose—Rosa

Set # 4, page 16

Pluma en mano
1–4. Answers will vary.
5. "eat till you burst"

El amor nos une a todos

Love binds us together

Toda persona siente amor: amor por un ser querido, por el aire que se respira, por una flor silvestre, por los animales que le rodean.

Sentir amor es vivir, *sobre todo* al tratarse de otra persona. Con frecuencia *nos encontramos con alguien* que nos emociona y despierta en nosotros *sentimientos muy profundos* y que llegamos a querer *muchísimo*. Si es la persona ideal, la persona de nuestros *sueños*, formamos pareja como *novio* y *novia* y nos prometemos fidelidad *el uno al otro*. ¿Qué si he conocido yo a tal persona? *¡Desde luego que sí!* Su nombre es María Teresa y es mi compañera en la escuela. Nos vemos *todos los días*, y por la noche nos pasamos *largas horas* en el teléfono. No podemos estar sin vernos o hablar un sólo día. *Al conocernos*, al no más mirarnos, fue *amor a primera vista*, el corazón se nos salía del cuerpo. Realmente nos gustamos y estamos *muy enamorados*. ¡Qué bonito es el amor y qué necesario! Yo para ella soy el Príncipe Azul, y ella para mí la Princesa Encantada. Realmente nuestro romance es como un *cuento de hadas* y estoy seguro que tendrá *un buen fin*.

¡Ojo!—Watch Out!

In Spanish, *to talk **on** the phone* is *hablar **por** teléfono*. Also, avoid the common mistake of writing *telé**ph**ono* instead of *teléfono*. Remember, there is no *ph* in Spanish.

Vocabulario básico

Sentir	To feel (irregular verb)
sobre todo	above all
nos encontramos con alguien	we meet someone

sentimientos muy profundos	very deep feelings
muchísimo	very much
sueños	dreams
novio	boyfriend (also fiancé)
novia	girlfriend (also fiancée)
el uno al otro	to each other
¡Desde luego que sí!	Of course I have!
todos los días	every day
largas horas	a long time
Al conocernos	When we met
amor a primera vista	love at first sight
muy enamorados	very much in love
cuento de hadas	fairy tale
un buen fin	a happy ending

BRAIN TICKLERS
Set # 5

Ejercicios

A. Answer these questions in complete sentences:
   1. ¿Tienes tú novio - a?
   2. ¿Cómo se llama?
   3. ¿Cómo lo - a conociste y dónde?
   4. ¿Cuánto tiempo llevan juntos?
   5. ¿Se quieren mucho?

B. Based on the previous story, say whether *verdadero o falso*:

1. Es humano sentir amor.	V	F
2. María Teresa es la madre del que habla.	V	F
3. Los novios nunca hablan por teléfono.	V	F
4. Al no más conocerse se enamoraron.	V	F
5. Los dos se quieren entrañablemente:	V	F

C. Fill in the blanks with the correct Spanish word or words:
1. Me encanta _____ (to speak) por teléfono.
2. (I feel) _____ mucho (love) _____ por mis amigos.
3. (to fall in love) _____ es maravilloso.
4. Mi novio - a y yo nos vemos (every day) _____.
5. (We are lucky) _____ de estudiar en un buen colegio.

D. Give the Spanish for the following words, and include the definite article for each noun:
1. prince _____
2. princess _____
3. romance _____
4. night _____
5. person _____

E. Unscramble these sentences, putting each word in the right order:
1. novia Luisa llama se mi.
2. teléfono su de número es _____.
3. suerte tengo mucha.
4. estudiar necesario es.
5. quieren mucho ellos se.

Answers are on page 36.

PIÉNSALO BIEN
THINK IT THROUGH

The Spanish language in America: the early years

Spanish was the first European language spoken in America, 100 years before English. Christopher Columbus spoke it and wrote it well, and it was his favorite language. The first native American to speak Spanish was an Arawak Indian who accompanied Columbus to Spain, where he was baptized Diego Colón, Columbus's son and heir. The first North American native to speak it was Francisco de Chicora, of the expedition of Lucas Vázquez de Ayllón to the land of Chicora. He learned Spanish in Spain, where he went with Ayllón.

Right after the discovery of America, Spanish became the leading language of Europe, just as English is today. It expanded quickly throughout the Americas, as Spain established its presence in the Caribbean, Mexico, and Peru. In 1513, Juan Ponce de León brought it to North America through Florida, followed by Álvar Núñez Cabeza de Vaca, Hernando de Soto, Francisco de Coronado, and others. Latin was also used at the time but mainly in writing. Nahuatl, Quechua, and Maya were the main languages of the indigenous peoples of Hispanic America, the Aztecs, Incas, and Mayas, in that order. The Spanish missionaries learned the languages well and wrote many important books about them. The missionaries were also instrumental in extending the teaching of Spanish throughout the continent. One of those missionaries in North America was the venerable Friar Junípero Serra, one of our early Founding Fathers.

¿Sabías que? Friar Junípero Serra is credited with having founded California through the many missions he established in the region. In today's U.S. Capitol's Rotunda there is a statue of Father Serra in honor of his many accomplishments.

BRAIN TICKLERS
Set # 6

¿Cuánto sabes?

1. Do you know in which of today's countries Nahuatl and Quechua were spoken?
2. Can you give the name of Christopher Columbus in Spanish?
3. Do you know the name of the woman who helped finance Columbus's voyage?
4. Do you know the names of the three ships Columbus used in his famous voyage?
5. Do you know the country from which Columbus left?

Answers are on page 36.

MÁS ES MEJOR
MORE IS BETTER

Nouns

el beso	kiss
la caricia	caress
el abrazo	hug
el deseo	desire
el cariño	affection
el amor platónico	platonic love
la chaperona	chaperone
el compromiso	engagement
el idilio	romance
la cita	date
enamorado	in love
la pasión	passion
celoso	jealous

Verbs

amar/querer	to love
desear	to desire, want
gustar	to like
comprometerse	to get engaged
besar	to kiss
abrazar	to hug
tener celos	to be jealous
salir con un amigo - a	to date/go out on a date
enamorarse	to fall in love

Conjugation of gustar in the present:

gustar   *Gustar* is a special verb and is conjugated differently. Here, the subject of the verb is not the person, but the thing or things that are pleasing, and that are expressed by the use of the indirect object pronouns*. Let's look at this sentence:

Me gusta la casa.
(I like the house.)

In English, the thing that you like is the house, or the direct object, while in Spanish *la casa* is the subject. Also, in Spanish, the person who likes the thing is the indirect object, thus the indirect object pronouns must be used before the verb. *Gustar* is always used in the third person, either singular or plural, agreeing with the thing that is liked, as in:

Me gusta la casa/me gustan las casas.
(I like the house/I like the houses, or
The house is pleasing to me/The houses
are pleasing to me.)

Never say *me gusto*, or any of the other conjugated forms, but only the third person singular or third person plural. The *o* ending does not apply to *gustar*. This special conjugation of *gustar* applies equally to all verb tenses: past, future, imperfect, etc. Other verbs conjugated like *gustar* are *faltar* (to be missing), and *encantar* (to love/enjoy).

*The indirect subject pronouns are: *me, te, le, nos, os, les*, and, in the case of *gustar*, they always precede the conjugated verb form.

The other verbs above: *amar, desear, besar, abrazar* are all regular; *comprometerse* is both regular and reflexive, and *tener* and *salir* are irregular.

Spanish love phrases

Te amo./Te quiero.	I love you.
Me gustas.	I like you.
Te adoro/idolatro.	I adore you.
mi amor/mi cielo	
mi cariño/mi alma	
mi tesoro/	
mi bombón/	
mi encanto	my love/darling
papi/mami/	
corazoncito/	
azuquita/	
caramelito	dear/honey

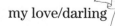

Here is a very popular Spanish song you should learn by heart:

Bésame mucho
Bésame, bésame mucho
como si fuera esta noche la última vez.
Bésame, bésame mucho
que tengo miedo perderte
perderte otra vez.

Do you know what it means? Try to figure it out by yourself. If you get stuck, listen to the song by the Beatles with the same title. Here is a translation:

Kiss me, kiss me with all your heart
as if this night would be the last
Kiss me, kiss me with all your heart
for I am afraid to lose you
to lose you again.
(However, translation may vary.)

¡Ojo!—Watch Out!

One of the most important and common words in Spanish is the adjective *simpático - a*. It is the best compliment you can give to a Hispanic person, and it has several connotations. Basically, it means nice, pleasant, but also lovely, delightful, etc. Its opposite is *antipático*, which no one wants to be, much less to be called.

HABLA POPULAR
EVERYDAY SPEECH

Idioms

tener cuidado	to be careful
de vez en cuando	once in a while
está bien	okay/all right
a veces	sometimes
enseguida	at once/immediately

Common expressions

quererse con locura	to love madly/to death
abrazarse como un oso	to hug like a bear
echar de menos	to miss (someone or something)
salir de parranda	to go out partying/on the town
aventura amorosa	love affair

Sayings:

No es oro todo lo que brilla.	All that glitters isn't gold.

BIEN VALE LA PENA
IT'S WELL WORTH IT

Cardinal numbers 1–99

Counting in Spanish is easy. You may have some difficulty counting from 16 to 19, but not the rest. Let's see first 1 to 10:

uno	one
dos	two
tres	three
cuatro	four
cinco	five
seis	six
siete	seven

ocho	eight
nueve	nine
diez	ten

No big deal, right? However, you need to watch out for *cinco*, *siete*, and *nueve* as you count further. Why? Because the spelling is somewhat different, as you will see later.

11 to 15:

once	eleven
doce	twelve
trece	thirteen
catorce	fourteen
quince	fifteen

Now 16 to 19 (¡*cuidado*!)

diez y seis or dieciséis	sixteen
diez y siete or diecisiete	seventeen
diez y ocho or dieciocho	eighteen
diez y nueve or diecinueve	nineteen

Note: All of the above can be said in three words or one. Literally, what you are saying is: ten plus six, ten plus seven, etc.

20 to 29:

veinte	twenty
veinte y uno or veintiuno	twenty-one
veinte y dos or veintidós	twenty-two
veinte y tres or veintitrés	twenty-three
veinte y cuatro or veinticuatro	twenty-four
veinte y cinco or veinticinco	twenty-five
veinte y seis or veintiséis	twenty-six
veinte y siete or veintisiete	twenty-seven
veinte y ocho or veintiocho	twenty-eight
veinte y nueve or veintinueve	twenty-nine

Note: Also, all of the above can be said in three words or one.

30 to 99:

treinta	thirty
cuarenta	forty
cincuenta	fifty
sesenta	sixty
setenta	seventy
ochenta	eighty
noventa	ninety

Note: When saying thirty-one, forty-four, fifty-seven, sixty-three, ninety-nine, etc., you must say it in three words: *treinta y uno, cuarenta y cuatro, cincuenta y siete, sesenta y tres, noventa y nueve.* Also, remember what we said about *cinco, siete, nueve.* Look at the spelling of *cincuenta, setenta, noventa,* and you will see the difference, especially in the last two (not *sie, nue.*)

BRAIN TICKLERS
Set # 7

Ejercicios

A. Write out these numbers in Spanish:
   1. 18   2. 29   3. 51   4. 77   5. 95

B. Answer these questions in complete sentences, and write out the numbers in Spanish:
   1. ¿Cuántos años tienes?
   2. ¿Cuál es el número de tu casa?
   3. ¿Cuál es tu número de teléfono?
   4. ¿Cuánto dinero tienes ahora mismo*? Cuéntalo**:
   5. ¿Cuántos estudiantes hay en tu clase de español?

   (*) right now.
   (**) Count it.

¿Te acuerdas? *Mario es muy simpático.* What am I saying?

Answers are on page 36.

DILO COMO YO
SAY IT LIKE I DO

Pronunciation of *b, v, p*

Before we start, you should take the pronunciation of Spanish sounds very seriously. You want to say them right and above all, be understood. Although the pronunciation of certain consonants are similar in Spanish and English (such as the *m* or the *n*), there are many others, most, in fact, that are quite different. Since you do not have many opportunities to practice your Spanish, you must read carefully and learn well all the explanations given below.

About the *b* and *v*

First of all, both letters are pronounced identically in Spanish, which is quite contrary to English. In English, for example, you pronounce the *b* using both the upper and lower lips and keeping them tightly together. With the *v*, the lower lip makes contact with the upper teeth. Now say *boy* and *video*, and you will see it clearly.

In Spanish, on the other hand, both the *b* and the *v* are pronounced very close to the *b* in English, but only when either one is pronounced after a pause or before *m* or *n*. Otherwise, they will be pronounced with both lips (upper and lower) slightly open, letting the air flow out. Here are some examples:

bobo   Here, the first *b* is at the beginning of the word, and the second between vowels; the first is pronounced with the lips closed, and the second with the lips slightly open. Now say it: *bobo*.

Other examples: Say each word out loud and explain how both the *b* and *v* are pronounced:

vaca   _____

ave   _____

enviar   _____

bombón _____

la bota   _____

Note: More on the pronunciation of the *b-v* in Chapter 6, but for now it is helpful to know that in all cases, the *b-v* are pronounced the same!

The *p* is similar in both English and Spanish (pronounced with both lips closed), although in Spanish it is not explosive as it is in English, for example, in the word *P*eter. The Spanish *p* is closer to the English *p*, as in *spin*. Practice these words by saying them out loud:

papá   pera   apellido   capa   peso

¡Ojo!—Watch Out!

How many adjectives in English end with the suffix *–able*? Thousands. Well, listen carefully: not only is that suffix the same in Spanish, but in many cases the whole word as well:

Español	Inglés
formidable	formidable
admirable	admirable
indispensable	indispensable
comparable	comparable
inseparable	inseparable

¡Ojo!—Watch Out!

You will never find a double *p* (pp) in Spanish, nor a double *b* (bb), as in *apple*, or *abbreviate*.

ALMA HISPÁNICA
HISPANIC SOUL

Lope de Vega

Lope de Vega (1562–1635) was a Spanish dramatist and creator of Spain's National Theatre. He was a contemporary of Cervantes, who admired him greatly. He wrote many plays and stands today as Spain's greatest playwright. The following passage is from one of his best-known historical plays, *Peribáñez y el comendador de Ocaña*. It is written in verse. You should have no problem making out most of the words, but, again, focus on the reading and on your pronunciation.

Bartolo (one of the characters) speaks:

> Nunca en el abril lluvioso
> halles hierba en verde prado,
> mas que si fuera en agosto.
> Siempre te venza el contrario
> cuando estuvieses celoso,
> y por los bosques bramando
> halles secos los arroyos.

PLUMA EN MANO
PEN IN HAND

La boda de mi hermano/
My brother's wedding

Mi hermano Carlos se casa pronto, el 21 de noviembre de este año. La boda será en una iglesia muy bonita del pueblo donde vive, y la recepción en otro pueblo cercano. Piensan invitar a muchos familiares y amigos, casi doscientas personas en total, cada una de las cuales recibirá una invitación que están a punto de enviar. Hay muchos detalles que les preocupa, como, por ejemplo, la compra del traje de novia, los anillos de boda (ella ya tiene el anillo de compromiso), la decoración de la iglesia, la recepción, el fotógrafo y, claro está, el viaje de luna de miel que lo piensan hacer a Italia y España. La novia es preciosa y el novio, mi hermano, es guapísimo, así que ambos van a lucir de rechupete en ese día; son una pareja ideal. Las dos familias se llevan muy bien, y los suegros son ya muy buenos amigos. Como es costumbre, ambos tendrán sus fiestas de soltero antes de la boda, recordando los buenos y felices tiempos en que cada cual vivía a su manera. Me imagino lo emocionante que va a ser ese día, al llegar la novia con su padre del brazo, la Marcha Nupcial, cuando se pongan los anillos y juren quererse para siempre, cuando desfilen ambos unidos bajo una lluvia de pétalos de rosa. ¡Ay, hermano mío, cómo pasa el tiempo!

BRAIN TICKLERS
Set # 8

Read the previous passage carefully, and then do the following:

1. Write in the three columns below five nouns, five verbs, and five adjectives:

   Nouns   Verbs   Adjectives

2. Using one of the same nouns, verbs, and adjectives, write an original sentence in Spanish.

3. See how many prepositions you can identify, and write them along with the English equivalents.

4. Write the words you don't know, look them up in the general vocabulary, and give the English equivalent for each.

5. Do you know what the common expressions *a punto de*, *lucir de rechupete*, and *a su manera* mean? Think. Give up? Find the answers in the Answer Key.

Answers are on page 36.

¿Sabías que? Sugarcane was introduced in America by Christopher Columbus, who brought it on his second voyage from the Canary Islands. It had been brought to Spain by the Moors who had cultivated it in North Africa. Hernán Cortés was its first grower, and his method was so successful that it has been the only one used since then. Also, the avocado, originally from South America, was brought to Mexico by Cortés. George Washington tasted it for the first time while in Barbados.

ASÍ SOMOS
THIS IS WHO WE ARE

The early history of the Americas

Long before Christopher Columbus discovered America, four major civilizations had flourished to our south: The Aztec, the Maya, the Inca, and also the Chibcha. They were far superior in their accomplishments to any of the ones found in North America, such as the Pueblos. When the Spaniards came and saw for the first time the magnificent roads, majestic cities and buildings, and imposing pyramids, they stood in awe of something they had never before seen in all of Europe. They were particularly struck by the city of Tenochtitlán, the capital of the Aztecs, built on the same site where Mexico City stands today. They were also amazed by many of their customs, their colorful attire, their courtesy, their exceptionally good manners, and their cleanliness. No less amazed were the Spaniards with the city of Cuzco, the capital of the Incas.

¿Sabías que? Did you know that Tenochtitlán was built on an island in a lake? It is the lake Texcoco, and the city was built around 1370 A.D. Why that site? The Aztecs' god, Huitzilopochtli, had told them to build their capital on an island in Lake Texcoco, where they would find an eagle perched on a cactus eating a snake. They found the eagle and built their city there.

BRAIN TICKLERS—THE ANSWERS

Set # 5, page 21

A.
Answers will vary.

B.
1. V   2. F   3. F   4. V   5. V

C.
1. hablar
2. Siento – amor –
3. Enamorarse
4. todos los días
5. Tenemos suerte

D.
1. el príncipe
2. la princesa
3. el romance
4. la noche
5. la persona

E.
1. Mi novia se llama Luisa.
2. Su número de teléfono es

   _____.
3. Tengo mucha suerte.
4. Es necesario estudiar.
5. Ellos se quieren mucho.

Set # 6, page 23

¿Cuánto sabes?
1. Mexico – Peru
2. Cristóbal Colón
3. Queen Isabella of Castile
4. La Pinta, La Niña,
   La Santa María
5. Spain

Set # 7, page 29

A.
1. diez y ocho/dieciocho
2. veinte y nueve/
   veintinueve
3. cincuenta y uno
4. setenta y siete
5. noventa y cinco

B. Answers will vary.

¿Te acuerdas?
Mario is very nice.

Set # 8, page 34

Pluma en mano
1. Nouns: Answers will vary.
   Verbs: Answers will vary.
   Adjectives: Answers will
   vary.
2–4. Answers will vary.
5. about to—to look gor-
   geous—his/her own way

La casa es nuestro hogar y felicidad

WELCOME

The house is our home and happiness

Mi casa es muy hermosa y *acogedora*. En ella vive toda mi familia, un perro y un gato. También tenemos un canario que se llama "Coco". En total, la casa tiene tres *habitaciones*, una *cocina* amplia, *comedor* y dos *baños*. Todas las habitaciones, o cuartos, están en el segundo *piso* y lo demás en el primero. En todos los cuartos hay grandes ventanas *que dan al* patio o al jardín y *se sube* a ellos por una *escalera* muy bonita de unos veinte *escalones*. La casa, por fuera, está pintada de blanco con su puerta principal roja. Tiene su *cerca* alrededor y un *caminito* precioso de ladrillos *que conduce a* la entrada. Los *muebles* son de estilo español y tenemos muchos *cuadros* y libros *por toda* la casa, principalmente en *la sala* y en una pequeña biblioteca de papá. También tenemos muchos *adornos*, la mayoría españoles. La cocina es muy amplia y tiene todos los *aparatos electrodomésticos* necesarios, como refrigerador, microonda, tostadora de pan, lavaplatos, etc. Es nuestro *lugar* favorito y donde nos reunimos a distintas horas del día. *El dormitorio* de mis padres es grande y *con mucha luz* y la cama estupenda. Mamá lo tiene todo muy *arreglado y limpio* y nosostros tratamos siempre de *ayudarla* con uno que otro *quehacer*. A mí, *lo que más me gusta* es el jardín, todo él lleno de hermosas plantas y flores y una fuente en el *centro* con un *chorro de agua* imponente. Me encanta, me apasiona, sueño con mi casa *por dentro y por fuera*; es mi verdadero hogar y donde *paso* mis mejores ratos, *rodeado de* los míos y de muchos *gratos recuerdos*.

Vocabulario básico

acogedora	welcoming/warm
habitaciones	rooms
cocina	kitchen
comedor	dining room
baños	bathrooms
piso	floor/stories
que dan al	that face
se sube	one goes up
escalera	stairs
escalones	steps

cerca	fence
caminito	little path
que conduce a	that lead to
muebles	furniture
cuadros	paintings/pictures
por toda	throughout
la sala	living room
adornos	decorations/ornaments
aparatos electrodomésticos	appliances
lugar	place
dormitorio	bedroom
con mucha luz	well lit
arreglado y limpio	neat and clean
ayudarla	help her
quehacer	chore
lo que más me gusta	what I like best
centro	center
chorro de agua	stream of water
por dentro y por fuera	inside and out
paso	I spend (time)
rodeado de	surrounded by
gratos recuerdos	pleasant memories

¡Ojo!—Watch Out!

Biblioteca in English is *library*. The word in Spanish for *bookstore* is *librería*, often confused with *library*. Avoid making this mistake.

BRAIN TICKLERS
Set # 9

Ejercicios

A. Answer these questions in complete sentences:
   1. ¿Cómo es tu casa de tamaño, grande o pequeña?
   2. ¿De qué color es por fuera?
   3. ¿Cuántas habitaciones tiene?
   4. ¿Tiene patio o jardín? Si lo tiene, descríbelo en dos o tres oraciones.

B. Basado en el pasaje, dinos (tell us) si cada una de estas afirmaciones es *verdadera o falsa*:
   1. La casa tiene tres habitaciones y dos baños.   V   F
   2. Las ventanas son muy pequeñas.   V   F
   3. Los muebles son de estilo francés.   V   F
   4. El lugar favorito de mi familia es la cocina.   V   F

C. Traduce la palabra o las palabras entre paréntesis.
   1. Mi habitación está en el (<u>second floor</u>).
   2. Mi casa por fuera está hecha de (<u>bricks</u>).
   3. (<u>We always help</u>) a mis padres.
   4. En el jardín de mi casa hay (<u>many plants and flowers</u>).

Answers are on page 54.

¡Ojo!—Watch Out!

Hay in Spanish means *there is/there are*. This is a word you should learn well as it is used frequently. And, don't forget that the letter *h* is never pronounced in Spanish. NEVER!

PIÉNSALO BIEN
THINK IT THROUGH

The structure of the basic Spanish sentence

The basic Spanish sentence is made up of two elements: the subject and the predicate. The subject is the person or thing of whom/which we say something. The predicate is what we say about the subject. Every subject may have complements, and so may the predicate. Let's look at this sentence:

> *Juan juega baloncesto.* (John plays basketball.)

If we break it down into its basic elements, we have:

Juan	subject (the person about whom we say something)
juega baloncesto	predicate (what we say about the person)

I could make the sentence longer by adding other elements to it as follows:

> *Juan, el amigo de mi hermana, juega baloncesto muy bien.*
> (John, the friend of my sister, plays basketball very well.)

Here, *el amigo de mi hermana* is a complement of the subject, and *muy bien*, a complement of the predicate. In fact, all that I say about the subject up to the verb is a complement of the subject, no matter how long it is. Thus, the structure of the basic Spanish sentence is as follows:

> Subject + complements of the subject
> Predicate + complements of the verb

In longer, more elaborate sentences, there might also be complements of the verb as follows:

> direct + its complement
> indirect + its complements
> circumstantial + its complements

Keep in mind, however, that a Spanish sentence would rarely have this many elements. Finally, remember that every sentence must have a verb, and every verb forms a sentence.

What is important here is to know that every sentence needs a subject and a predicate, that the subject can be a person or a thing, and that the predicate is a verb that may be used with a variety of complements, just like the subject. No matter how short or how long I make a sentence, the basic structure would not change. Also, the subject can be a noun, or it can express a concept using more than one word to complete its meaning.

BRAIN TICKLERS
Set # 10

Ejercicios

A. Based on the above, underline the subject and predicate in the following sentences:
1. La casa de mis padres está en California.
2. Los edificios de la ciudad son muy altos.
3. El reloj de plata es un regalo de mi novia.
4. Mi maestra de español es de Buenos Aires.

How did you do?

B. Now, rewrite those sentences taking out all the complements of the subject. Try it and see how well you do.

C. Let's take it a step further since we know how smart you are. Write three sentences using a basic subject and predicate, with no complements in either one:

1. _____
2. _____
3. _____

Answers are on page 54.

MÁS ES MEJOR
MORE IS BETTER

Here are other words you should learn. They all relate to the house.

Nouns

el techo	roof/ceiling
la pared	wall
el pasillo	hallway
el sótano	basement
el ático	attic
el cuarto de estar	family room
la calefacción	heat
el aire acondicionado	air conditioning
la lámpara	lamp
la luz	light
la silla	chair
la mesa	table
la bañadera	bathtub
el lavabo	washbasin
el inodoro	toilet
la puerta	door
la ventana	window
la lámpara	lamp
el sofá	sofa
el cuadro	picture

Verbs

vivir	to live
subir	to go up
bajar	to go down
limpiar	to clean
cocinar	to cook
barrer	to sweep
bañarse	to bathe/take a bath
ducharse	to shower/take a shower
descansar	to rest/relax
sentarse	to sit down

¿**Sabías que?** The first trader in North America was a Hispanic by the name of Rodríguez. He traded pots and pans after the purchase of Manhattan Island from the Dutch.

HABLA POPULAR
EVERYDAY SPEECH

More common idioms, expressions, and sayings

a la derecha/izquierda	to the right/left
al lado de	next to/beside
como siempre	as usual
echar de menos	to miss
echar la casa por la ventana	to spare no expense/ all the way
mientras tanto	meanwhile
ir de paseo	to go out for a walk/ stroll, or simply to go out to have a good time
¡De película!	awesome!/wonderful!
Al que madruga Dios le ayuda.	The early bird catches the worm.
Por mejor lo haría Dios.	Everything happens for the best.

¡Ojo!—Watch Out!

Here is a Spanish word almost everybody knows: *siesta*. Literally it means *to take a nap*, and in a way that's what it is; however, it is also a time put aside to be with the family, to have lunch together, to go over what everybody has done and plans to do for the rest of the day. A *siesta* is always taken in the midafternoon, when most businesses close for two or three hours. It is also a time to relax and to digest the biggest meal of the day, which everyone savors with a glass or two of wine. If you, here in the United States, would have such a feast at lunchtime, you would need a *siesta* too, whether taken at home or at work; in other words, you would not be able to function, walking around like a zombie for the rest of the day!

BIEN VALE LA PENA
IT'S WELL WORTH IT

Cardinal numbers 100–1,000

You may think that this is another big hurdle you have to jump, but it is not. The key word here is *cientos*, which literally means *hundreds*. Then, if you know how to count from 1 to 10, you are in good shape. Why? Well, let's count from 100 to 1,000 and you will find out:

ciento	one hundred
doscientos	two hundred
trescientos	three hundred
cuatrocientos	four hundred
quinientos	five hundred
seiscientos	six hundred
setecientos	seven hundred
ochocientos	eight hundred
novecientos	nine hundred

This is what you have to notice:

1. *Ciento*, which means *one/a hundred*, becomes *cien* before a noun, as in *cien libros* (one hundred books).

2. Notice the spellings of 500> **quini**entos (not cincocientos), 700> **sete**cientos (not sietecientos), 900> **nove**cientos (not nuevecientos). Here you have to watch out because in all probability you would tend to make a mistake.

3. *Ciento* and *uno* are variable and may change in gender and number, as in
   doscientos libros (two hundred books, *libros* being masculine/plural), and
   doscientas mesas (two hundred tables, *mesas* being feminine/plural).
   Also, *uno* drops the *o* before a masculine/singular noun, as in *un niño* (never *uno niño*), and would change to the feminine, as in: *una niña*, or in the plural, both masculine and feminine: *unos niños, unas niñas*.

4. In English, both numbers are written separately while in Spanish they form one word.

5. In English, a comma is used to separate thousands from hundreds, as in: *2,147*, while in Spanish a period is used, as in: *2.147*.

6. In English, the word *and* is used between hundreds and tens, as in: three hundred and twenty, but not between tens and units, as in: fifty-seven, four hundred and forty-six. In Spanish, the *and> y* is only used between tens and units, but not between hundreds and tens, as in: *trescientos setenta y cuatro* (three hundred and seventy-four).

7. In everyday spoken English, between 1,000 and 9,999 is counted in hundreds, as in:
   2,700> twenty-seven hundred, 6,946> sixty-nine hundred forty-six. This never occurs in Spanish counting, always in thousands and hundreds, as in: 3,752> *tres mil setecientos cincuenta y dos*.

BRAIN TICKLERS
Set # 11

Ejercicios

A. Answer these questions in English:
  1. In numbers, when do you have to use the *y* in Spanish?
  2. Is this correct or incorrect? 200> *dos cientos*. If incorrect, explain briefly why.
  3. How would you say "five hundred and eight persons" in Spanish?

B. Write three sentences in Spanish using these numbers (make sure you write out each number):

100 _____

544 _____

951 _____

Answers are on page 54.

DILO COMO YO
SAY IT LIKE I DO

Pronunciation of the *d* and *t*

In Spanish, these two consonants are called *dentales* (dentals) because they are pronounced with the tip of the tongue pressed against the back of the upper teeth. The basic difference between the two is that *d* is voiced (vibration of the vocal cords), and *t* voiceless; also, that the *t* is always occlusive (no air passing through), while the *d* can be occlusive and fricative (air passing through). Yes, we know, all this sounds a bit confusing, but it is the only way to learn these sounds properly. Let's explain it further. Let's take this word as an example:

dedo

Here we have two *ds*; the first *d* is at the beginning of the word, after a pause, and the second between two vowels, without a pause. One is pronounced with the tip of the tongue pressed against the back of the upper teeth, with no air passing through (occlusive). The other is also pronounced with the tip of the tongue but slightly separated from the teeth, letting the air pass through. Try to say (we will put the occlusive *d* in bold, and the fricative *d* in italics):

dedo

How did it come out? Did you notice the difference?

It may be a bit difficult for you because the *d* in English is always occlusive, and therefore you would tend to say:

dedo

This would be wrong.

As we said, the *t* is always occlusive, both in Spanish and English. In English, however, it is always explosive in initial position, while in Spanish it is not. Let's see these two words:

Tom – Tomás

Pronounce each one separately and see if you can notice the difference. If you don't, it means that you made both occlusive, which is wrong. Try it again and pronounce the Spanish *t* as in *step*. Got it now?

Ejercicio

Read these words out loud:

adiós	dama	tabla	tesoro
dado	decir	tanto	átono

¿Sabías que? The potato was first harvested in Peru and Bolivia and brought to Europe by the Spaniards, where it became a staple crop. They brought it later to North America. And *maize*, or *maíz* (corn), was cultivated first in Mexico and Central America by the Aztecs and the Mayas. You have them to thank for it.

ALMA HISPÁNICA
HISPANIC SOUL

Santa Teresa de Jesús

Santa Teresa de Jesús, also known as Santa Teresa de Ávila, is one of the greatest figures of Spanish literature, a doctor of the church, and a mystic, a profound, sensitive woman way ahead of her time. Her full name was Teresa Sánchez Cepeda Dávila y Ahumada, born in Ávila, in Old Castile, in 1515, died at Alba de Tormes, 1582. She studied with the Augustinian nuns but due to illness left after 18 months and stayed with her father and relatives. An uncle made her acquainted with the Letters of St. Jerome and she became determined to give her life to God. In the years that followed she became very ill, but survived, and was greatly influenced first by the Dominicans and then by the Jesuits. Among her main works are the *Relations*, the *Book of Foundations*, and the *Interior Castle*, a spiritual biography often compared to the *Confessions of St. Augustine*. In 1562, she founded the convent of Discalced Carmelite Nuns, which rapidly expanded throughout Spain. The province of the Discalced Carmelites was established in 1580.

The writings of Santa Teresa

This is just an excerpt from her book, *Camino de Perfección* (*Way of Perfection*). Here she is talking about the "water falling from heaven" (the rain) and some of its effects:

Excerpt from *Camino de Perfección/ Way of Perfection*

Es la gran otra propiedad limpiar cosas que no limpias. (Si no hubiese agua para lavar, ¿qué sería del mundo?) ¿Sabéis qué tanto limpia este agua viva, este agua celestial, este agua clara, cuando no está *turbia*, cuando no tiene *lodo*, sino que se coge de la misma fuente? Que una vez que se beba, *tengo por cierto* que deja el alma clara y limpia de todas las *culpas*.

---

turbia	muddy
lodo	mud
tengo por cierto	I know it as true
culpa	sin

PLUMA EN MANO
PEN IN HAND

Nuestra casa de Villafranca del Bierzo/
Our house in Villafranca del Bierzo

Villafranca del Bierzo es un pueblecito de la provincia de León, España, con una vieja e ilustre historia que se remonta (dating back) a los tiempos de los romanos. Allí nació casi toda la familia de mi padre, incluyéndolo a él en el año 1906. Nuestra casa, mejor dicho (better yet), nuestro piso, estaba en la plaza, en el centro del pueblo y a poca distancia estaban también las casas de mis tías Consuelo e Isabel. Nuestro piso era pequeño pero muy hermoso, con su balcón en el que nos sentábamos después de cenar a ver pasar a todos los amigos y conocidos. En la parte de atrás (in the back), pasada la cocina, había un patio que cuidaba mi abuela, con una fuente en el medio hecha (made of) de piedra y en la que jugueteaban pececillos multicolores. El suelo era de azulejos (tiles) y las paredes y techo de cal. Las puertas y ventanas eran de gruesa (thick) madera y todos los muebles, los de la sala, comedor y dormitorios de estilo castellano viejo. A la entrada había dos jarrones de cobre (copper) enormes con muchas flores. Por todas partes (everywhere) colgaban cuadros y fotos de la familia, de mis abuelos y bisabuelos y descendencia. Y cuando mi abuela se metía (got into) en la cocina, ¡ay!, sólo el olor de lo que cocinaba nos contentaba los corazones (made our hearts happy). ¿Que si nos gustaba comer? Tres veces al día más las meriendas y el picar (snack) y siempre con nuestra copita de vino. Tiempos felices que guardaré (will keep) siempre en mi alma…

BRAIN TICKLERS
Set # 12

Ejercicios

In the preceding passage you see many verbs, most of which are in the imperfect tense because we are relating a story taking place in the past. We will explain the imperfect tense later, but you should get familiar with it now. This is what we would like you to do:

A. Underline five verbs and rewrite them in the infinitive; then, write what each one means.

B. Now, without translating the entire passage word by word, write in English the gist of what it generally says, what it is all about.

Answers are on page 54.

¡Ojo!—Watch Out!

Do you know what *piso* means? It is the name given in Spanish to an apartment or flat, usually a condo or co-op, a place you own. The word also means floor (also *suelo*, in Spanish) or story, as in: *Ese edificio tiene cinco pisos* (that building has five stories). A *plaza* is typical of every Hispanic city and town, a square, usually with trees, benches, and perhaps a monument or fountain. This word, plus *patio*, are key in Spanish. Learn them well!

ASÍ SOMOS
THIS IS WHO WE ARE

Women in early America

If you look at any history of the Americas
and read about some of the main events
and deeds of people you would hardly
notice any women mentioned, especially
when history was first recorded in the
early sixteenth century. This does not
reflect any disdain toward women in
general, but simply the fact that women,
at that time, were dedicated almost
exclusively to their families and homes.
However, there were many women,
actually hundreds and even thousands of

them, who stood up and contributed in large measure to many
of the discoveries and explorations, side by side with the men.
The fact that they were left out of the pages of history is indeed
an injustice. It should never be forgotten that the person almost
solely behind the discovery of America, the one who really
made it happen, was a woman, one of the greatest figures in
history: Queen Isabella of Spain. Without her vision and
support, no men would have ever crossed the Atlantic, at least
as early as they did. But there were others who followed her
footsteps, and held high positions of leadership, such as María
de Toledo, wife of Diego Colón, son of Christopher Columbus,
first woman governor of the Americas, Isabel de Bobadilla, wife
of Hernando de Soto, first woman governor of Cuba, Isabel
Barreto y Quirós, first and to this day only woman admiral in
the Spanish navy, and many others. But by far, the greatest
accomplishment of all women of the Americas, Spaniards as
well as Native Americans and African Americans, was to help
introduce and solidify Western civilization in the Americas and
to make the Hispanic culture what it is today. Without their
titanic effort, often overlooked, the Americas of today would
be totally different from what we know. Hail to all of these
women, the known and the unknown!

BRAIN TICKLERS—THE ANSWERS

Set # 9, page 40

A. Answers will vary.

B.
1. V   2. F   3. F   4. V

C.
1. segundo piso
2. ladrillos
3. siempre ayudamos
4. muchas plantas y flores

Set # 10, page 42

Piénsalo bien

A.
1. <u>La casa</u> de mis padres—está en California.
2. <u>Los edificios</u> de la ciudad— son muy altos.
3. <u>El reloj</u> de plata—es un regalo de mi novia.
4. <u>Mi maestra</u> de español—es de Buenos Aires.

B.
1. La casa está en California.
2. Los edificios son muy altos.
3. El reloj es un regalo de mi novia.
4. Mi maestra es de Buenos Aires.

C.
Answers will vary.

Set # 11, page 47

Bien vale la pena

A.
1. between tens and units
2. Incorrect. It should be one word.
3. quinientas ocho personas

B.
Answers will vary.

Set # 12, page 52

Pluma en mano
A. Answers will vary.
B. Answer will vary.

El buen comer es un arte

Good eating is an art

En todas partes del mundo hay muchos restaurantes, muchas cafeterías, infinidad de lugares para comer *un bocado*, sobre todo en las grandes ciudades como París, Roma, Madrid, Nueva York. *Así y todo*, para mí no hay nada como la comida de casa, la *comida casera*, la preparada con interés y mucho amor. Triste es que *hoy en día* la gente no tenga el tiempo para disfrutar de un buen plato, de la compañía de familiares y amigos. Todo es correr, correr, y tragar; lo que importa es alimentarse para no morir y, *desde luego*, comer *chucherías* que *no hacen otra cosa* que hacernos engordar y estragarnos el estómago, y esto incluye los refrescos, las sodas, pura agua carbonatada y azúcar. *Claro que* a la gente no se le puede culpar porque es todo lo que *tienen a mano*, o los dichosos lugares de comida rápida, incómodos, bulliciosos, deshumanizados, donde *todo lo que importa* es entrar y salir *a la carrera*. En contraste, piénsese en una mesa con su mantel blanco y bien puesta, con sus buenos platos y cubiertos y adornada con unas flores. Como aperitivos, camarones *rebozados* en salsa verde, unas *rebanadas* de chorizos, papas fritas a la juliana y *aceitunas rellenas*. Como plato del día, *bisté de solomillo a la parrilla*, ensalada de lechuga y tomate y arroz amarillo, mucho pan de barra, cortado en *trozos* y mantequilla y algo bueno de beber. De postre, flan y arroz con leche. ¿Mucho soñar? Quizá; ni tenemos el tiempo ni el dinero para hacerlo ni a nadie que lo haga todo *de agrado*. ¿*De qué valen* todos los cacharros y productos de alta tecnología que tenemos en la cocina? Antes con un modesto fogón, una sartén, y una cazuela u olla se hacía lo que no se hace hoy con todos los *adelantos* y con la super abundancia de comestibles *de toda clase*. Aquí no vale lo de "más es mejor", sino "menos es mejor".

Vocabulario básico

un bocado	a bite (to eat)
Así y todo	Even though
comida casera	home-cooked food
hoy en día	nowadays
desde luego	of course

chucherías	junk food
no hacen otra cosa	they do nothing but
Claro que	Of course
tienen a mano	handy/within reach
todo lo que importa	all that matters
a la carrera	in a rush
rebozados	breaded
rebanadas	slices
aceituna rellenas	stuffed olives
bisté de solomillo a la parrilla	grilled filet mignon
trozos	pieces
de agrado	gladly
¿De qué valen?	What good is it?
adelantos	advances
de toda clase	of all kinds

¡Ojo!—Watch Out!

In Spain and in most Hispanic countries there are three basic meals a day: *desayuno* (breakfast), *almuerzo* o *comida* (lunch), and *cena* o *comida* (dinner.) The main meal of the day is lunch, and dinner is relatively light. Breakfast is also very light—coffee and a roll or something similar. Lunch is usually between 1:30 and 2:30 P.M., and dinner late at night, between 8 and 10 P.M. *Comida* in Spanish can mean several things, including lunch or dinner, and food in general. Throughout Spain, and almost on every corner, there are eating places called *tapas* where people go to have a bite to eat and to have a good time with friends.

BRAIN TICKLERS
Set #13

Ejercicios

A. Contesta estas preguntas en oraciones completas:
   1. ¿Cuál es tu comida favorita?
   2. ¿Qué piensas tú de la comida casera?
   3. ¿A qué hora almuerzas y cenas todos los días?
   4. ¿Cómo es tu desayuno?

B. Basado en el pasaje, dinos si cada una de estas afirmaciones es *verdadera o falsa*:
   1. Los mejores restaurantes están en los pueblos pequeños.   V   F
   2. La gente hoy día tiene tiempo para disfrutar de una buena comida.   V   F
   3. Lo que importa hoy es alimentarse y no el buen comer.   V   F
   4. Las chucherías nos engordan y dañan el estómago.   V   F

C. Traduce la palabra o las palabras entre paréntesis:
   1. Desgraciadamente, yo vivo (in a rush).
   2. (Of course) me falta el tiempo para disfrutar de las cosas.
   3. Siempre hago los quehaceres de mi casa (gladly).
   4. Para mí, (all that matters) es mi familia.

Answers are on page 72.

¡Ojo!—Watch Out!

Aceitunas (olives) *y* (and) *aceite de oliva* (olive oil) are among the main exports of Spain, rivaling those from Italy and Portugal. Leather goods from Spain and Argentina are among the finest in the world, and Chile is the world's largest exporter of copper and copper-made products.

PIÉNSALO BIEN
THINK IT THROUGH

The noun. El nombre o sustantivo

Together with the verb, the noun is the most important part of a sentence. There are basically three kinds of nouns—*common nouns*: horse, sky, tree; *proper nouns*: Madrid, Washington, María; and *abstract nouns*: hate, charity, virtue. In Spanish, all nouns have two genders: masculine and feminine, and must be either singular or plural. There is a fourth class of nouns called *collective nouns*, for even though they are in the singular they represent plurality, such as people, flock, herd. It is of the utmost importance for you to know and realize that, as already said, every single noun in Spanish has a gender, regardless of its nature and that, when a noun is masculine or feminine, every adjective that modifies it must by necessity agree with that gender. We know this is difficult for you because there is no such thing in English as the gender of things. You couldn't care less if a table or a car is masculine or feminine, but in Spanish we do.

> If you want to say:
> the house is red
> you must say in Spanish
> la *casa* es roja

making both the adjective (*roja*) and the article (*la*) agree in gender and also in number with the noun.

And if you want to make that sentence plural, you would have to say:

las casas son rojas (the houses are red)

Using a masculine noun, you would say:

el libro es rojo (the book is red)

and in the plural

los libros son rojos (the books are red)

Usually, a noun ending in -*o* is masculine, and if in -*a*, feminine, but there are many others that end in neither one, in which case only the article determines its gender, as in *la madre, el lápiz.*

There are no ifs or buts in this regard, and no shortcuts. What is, is, and you can't change it. Notice that in English the only change from the singular to the plural is in the noun and the verb, while the article and the adjective remain invariable. In Spanish, everything changes. This is one of the fundamental steps in learning Spanish, and you should take it very seriously and learn it well.

And how do you form the plural of nouns in Spanish?

If the noun ends in a vowel, you simply add -*s*, and if it ends in a consonant, you simply add -*es*, as in:

Vowel

mesa	mesas
hombre	hombres
niño	niños

Consonant

árbol	árboles
mujer	mujeres
papel	papeles

If the noun ends in -*z*, you change it to *c* and then add -*es*, as in:

lápiz	lápices
nariz	narices
pez	peces

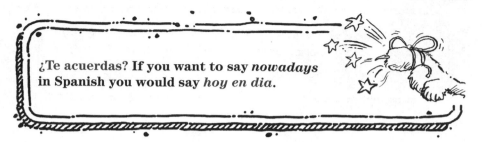

¿Te acuerdas? If you want to say *nowadays* in Spanish you would say *hoy en día*.

BRAIN TICKLERS
Set #14

Ejercicios

A. Indicate whether these two nouns are masculine or feminine and explain why:
   1. pizarra
   2. abuelo

B. Here are five words. We have made them plural, but each one is incorrect. Write each one correctly:

Word	Incorrect plural	Correct plural
1. maestro	maestroes	_____
2. silla	sillaes	_____
3. cruz	cruzes	_____
4. televisor	televisors	_____
5. imagen	imagens	_____

C. Make these two sentences plural:

   1. El estudiante vive en California.
   2. La clase de español es muy buena.

Answers are on page 72.

¿Sabías que? If you like pineapples you have to thank the Spaniard Francisco de Paula Marín, who in 1813 proposed growing them on a large scale in Hawaii.

MÁS ES MEJOR
MORE IS BETTER

Nouns

la servilleta	napkin
el salero	saltshaker
la azucarera	sugar bowl
la sopa	soup
las papas fritas	French fries
el puré de papas	mashed potatoes
la leche	milk
el jugo	juice
el aceite	oil
el pan	bread
la comida congelada	frozen food
el pescado*	fish
la langosta	lobster
el marisco	seafood
la carne	meat/beef
el pollo	chicken
el puerco/cerdo	pork
el huevo	egg
los vegetales/ legumbres	vegetables
el arroz con pollo	chicken and rice
el arroz con frijoles	rice and beans
el sabor/gusto	taste
el café	coffee
el té	tea
la mantequilla	butter
la fruta	fruit
el tenedor	fork

| el cuchillo | knife |
| la cuchara | spoon |

Verbs

poner la mesa	to set the table
quitar la mesa	to leave the table
freír	to fry
asar	to roast
calentar	to heat up
cocer/hervir	to boil
comer	to eat
beber	to drink
masticar	to chew
probar	to taste
preparar	to fix

*¡Ojo! There are two words in Spanish for *fish*. When the fish is alive and in the water, it is called *pez*; when caught and served or eaten, it is called *pescado* (which literally means *caught* in Spanish, derived from the word *pescar* > to fish). In other words, *pescado* can mean the noun fish (caught), or the adjective (caught), or the past participle of the verb *pescar* (to fish, caught). You never eat *pez* but *PESCADO*.

HABLA POPULAR
EVERYDAY SPEECH

Here are more idioms, expressions, and sayings:

a menudo	often
por lo tanto	therefore
además de	in addition to
aún así	even so
dar gusto	to please
en caso de que	in case of
en adelante	from now on
así es la vida	that's life
¡caramba!	good heavens!
¡vete a la porra!	go and take a walk!
No es oro todo lo que reluce.	All that glitters isn't gold.
de tal padre tal hijo	like father like son

BIEN VALE LA PENA
IT'S WELL WORTH IT

Números ordinales (Ordinal numbers)

For now, and at this level, knowing how to count from *first* to *tenth* will suffice.

Spanish	English
primero	first
segundo	second
tercero	third
cuarto	fourth
quinto	fifth
sexto	sixth
séptimo (or sétimo)	seventh
octavo	eighth
noveno	ninth
décimo	tenth

The abbreviated forms in Spanish, which in English equal 1st, 2nd, 3rd, and after that *th* following the number, are formed in Spanish simply by adding a small *o* after the number and a period:

1o. 2o. 3o. 4o. 5o. 6o. 7o. 8o. 9o. 10o.

If they refer to a feminine noun, then it would be *a*, as in *8a*.

Primero and *tercero* drop the *o* before a masculine singular noun, as in:

| el primer mes | first month |
| el tercer año | third year |

The ordinal numbers agree in Spanish in gender and number with the nouns they are modifying, as in:

el segundo piso	the second floor
la segunda parte	the second part
los primeros meses del año	the first months of the year

Above *décimo*, Spanish ordinal numbers are rather difficult and seldom used; for example: *diecisieteavo* (seventeenth), *sexagésimo* (sixtieth).

BRAIN TICKLERS
Set #15

Ejercicios

A. Translate these sentences into Spanish:

I live in a three-story house. My bedroom is on the third floor, and my brother's is on the first.

B. Using the abbreviated form, fill in the blanks with the appropriate ordinal number:

En mi trabajo, mi oficina está en el (fifth floor) **1** _____ _____ y la de mi amiga Dolores está en el (eighth floor) **2** _____. La cafetería está en el (third floor) **3** _____ y la máquina copiadora en el (fourth) **4** _____.

Answers are on page 72.

DILO COMO YO
SAY IT LIKE I DO

Pronunciation of the c, q

The *c* with the vowels *a*, *o*, *u*, sounds like *k*, and so does the *q*, which in Spanish can only be used combined with *ue* and *ui*, as in: *queso, quinto*. Important: In these combinations of the *que* and *qui*, you never pronounce the *u*, never. This is a very common mistake you must try to avoid. In English you do; in Spanish you DON'T. The *c* combined with the other two vowels, *e* and *i*, is pronounced similarly to the *s*, as in *cero, cinco*. The reason for the *que* and *qui* is a simple one: Because the *ce* and *ci* would be pronounced as *s*, not as *k*. Don't forget that the *q* would never be used by itself in Spanish but only followed by *ue* and *ui*. As we said, in English it is different, and that is why Spanish speakers have difficulty pronouncing such words as *quantity* or *question*, because they would not pronounce the *u*.

What is hard for them is easy for you, and vice versa.

BRAIN TICKLERS
Set #16

Ejercicios

A. Take your time; rushing will get you nowhere. Say these words out loud in Spanish:

que	acequia
química	coco
aunque	cesta
cuota	ciprés
carbón	clave

B. Can you write five words in Spanish, two using *que*, *qui*, and the other three *ca*, *co*, and *ce*? Once you have finished, pronounce each one out loud.

Answers are on page 72.

¡Ojo!—Watch Out!

In Spain, the *ce* and *ci* are pronounced similarly to the English *th* in *think*, *three*. This is mainly in the north of Spain, and particularly in the region of Castile. In the south, in the region known as Andalucía, the *c* is pronounced as *s*. Which pronunciation is best? Here in America it is better to pronounce it *s*. In any event, it really doesn't make that much of a difference.

¡Ojo!—Watch Out!

Watch out for the word *cup* in Spanish. The way it is used in English, as in *a cup of coffee*, is *taza* in Spanish, as in *una taza de café*. On the other hand, *copa* translates into English as *glass*, as in:

una copa de vino	a glass of wine
una copa de champán	a glass of champagne

It would make absolutely no sense in Spanish to say *una copa de café*, none whatsoever. The way you say it, again, is *una taza de café*. Keep in mind, however, that glass also translates into Spanish as *vaso*, as in *un vaso de agua* (a glass of water). To be safe, always use *copa* when referring to an alcoholic beverage, especially wine or champagne. A *glass of beer* would be *un vaso de cerveza*. Tricky, we know, but try to learn the difference.

ALMA HISPÁNICA
HISPANIC SOUL

José Martí

Here we have a true giant of Spanish letters, as well as a great patriot and political figure. José Martí was a writer, a poet, and a revolutionary, a man to whom Cuba owes much of its independence from Spain. His father was a Spaniard, but he was as Cuban as a palm tree, even though he loved Spain and spent part of his youth studying there. He was the typical *criollo*, a man born in America of Spanish descent, but longing to be free, to make his country independent and able to chart its own destiny. There is great similarity between José Martí and men such as Thomas

Jefferson, James Madison, or Benjamin Franklin, all three *criollos* as well—great patriots, thinkers, and writers—and for whom Martí professed great admiration. José Martí was determined to see his land free and to that cause gave his life, literally, for he was killed on horseback, fighting, "facing the sun," as history reminds us. Some of the literary figures of the Spanish *Generación del 98*, such as Miguel de Unamuno, had much praise for and greatly admired José Martí as a writer.

He was born in Havana in 1853 and died at Dos Ríos in 1895. In 1869, he published his first newspaper, *La patria libre* (Free Fatherland), for which he was arrested but freed soon after. He went into exile, first in Spain where he published *El presidio político de Cuba* and also studied at the universities of Madrid and Zaragoza. From 1891 to 1895, he resided mainly in New York, where he continued with his writings, returning to Cuba in 1895. In 1892, he founded the Cuban Revolutionary Party. He was a consummate writer of magazine articles, children's books (*La edad de oro*), and poetry (*Versos sencillos*). The great Nicaraguan poet, Rubén Darío, said this of him: "Martí belonged to an entire race, an entire continent." He is called by Cubans "El Apóstol" (the Apostle).

The writing of José Martí

Read and enjoy this poem from José Martí:

Cultivo una rosa blanca

Cultivo una rosa blanca
en junio como en enero
para el amigo sincero
que me da su mano franca.

Y para el cruel que me arranca
el corazón con que vivo
cardo ni ortiga cultivo
cultivo una rosa blanca.

To help you better undestand the poem, *cardo* is a *thistle*, and *ortiga* is a *nettle*. You should be able to figure out the rest.

PLUMA EN MANO
PEN IN HAND

El restaurante "Tío Pepe" de Nueva York/ Tío Pepe restaurant in New York

En la ciudad de Nueva York, como en toda la zona alrededor, hay muchos restaurantes españoles de categoría. Entre ellos (among them), y uno de los más importantes y conocidos (known), y de los más antiguos, es "Tío Pepe" y cuyos dueños se llaman Jimmy y Rocío. Aparte de (Besides) la comida, que es deliciosa y muy variada, lo que más llama la atención (what attracts the most) es el ambiente, sobre todo pasada (past) la medianoche. Allí se reúne gente muy alegre y simpática,  tocan la guitarra, cantan y bailan y hablan por los codos. Al fondo (In the back) del restaurante, hay una especie de jardincito que es un primor (lovely), y donde se puede comer también. La comida es principalmente española pero también sirven muchos platos mexicanos que son para chuparse los dedos. El restaurante, localizado en el Village, en la calle cuatro, lleva allí (it has been there) muchísmos años y se mantiene como el primer día en cuanto a ambiente, calidad y servicio. Todo ello se debe a (All is due to) sus dueños que están siempre allí pendientes de que todo marche bien (goes well). Don Jimmy es todo un personaje en Nueva York, conocido y querido por cuanta persona ha tenido (has had) la suerte de tratarlo. La próxima vez que estés en Nueva York, date una vueltecita por "Tío Pepe", siéntate en la barra y saborea todos los platillos o tapas que se sirven, sin olvidar (without forgetting) tu bebida favorita y, de paso (while there), dile hola a Jaime y a su simpática mujer. Volverás allí muy a menudo (often), te lo aseguramos (we guarantee it).

BRAIN TICKLERS
Set #17

Ejercicios

A. Contesta estas preguntas en oraciones completas:
1. ¿Cómo se llaman los dueños del restaurante?
2. ¿En qué clase de comida se especializa la casa (restaurante)?
3. ¿Cuál es la mejor hora para estar allí?
4. ¿Qué hay en el fondo del restaurante?

B. Here you have three very popular Spanish sayings/idioms. See if you know what they mean. If you get stuck, the answers are provided in the Answer Key.
1. hablar por los codos
2. chuparse los dedos
3. marchar bien

Answers are on page 72.

ASÍ SOMOS
THIS IS WHO WE ARE

"Hello, I am a Hispanic!"

What is a Hispanic? When we think of people south of the border, all the way down to Patagonia, on the very tip of Argentina, excluding Brazil, what do we call them? Is it Spanish, Latins, Latinos, Hispanic Americans, South Americans? Is there a single, proper name that embraces them all? And, if not, what is the proper name that would best apply to them?

To explain this would take a long time. We can, however, point you in the right direction. It can't be Spanish because there are other cultures involved, from ancient times all the way to the present, such as the Aztecs, Incas, Mayas, and others. It can't be Latins or Latinos, because this word, Latin, refers to a culture and a language, not to a people. The country, nation, or empire was Rome, and their people the Romans. It can't be Hispanics because that name comprises only Spain, to which the Romans gave the name of *Hispania*, although at the time it comprised the entire Iberian Peninsula, including Portugal. We are then left with Spanish Americans, or Hispanic Americans, and South Americans. These three names are somewhat proper, but the first two leave out many other modern cultures, such as Portuguese, Italian, German, Asian, and Arab, and even the English in Argentina. Thus, we are left with one single name: South Americans. The problem with this name is that it totally leaves out the European heritage, principally of Spain. The other problem is that South America is not one country but many, which includes the Portuguese-speaking country of Brazil and other non-Hispanic islands and colonies of English, French, and Dutch heritage.

Then, what name to use?

As you can see, there is not really one single historically or culturally correct name applicable to them. But, if we had to choose, we would say South American, which is the name used in Spanish (*suramericano*), in contrast to North American (*norteamericano*), and Central American (*centroamericano*). Finally, we need to say this:

Who are the Americans?

For the United States, it means all its people, and no one else, which is very, very improper. Ask someone from the United States this question: What is your nationality? The answer, inevitably, will be "I am an American." There is no valid justification to monopolize a name that was meant to identify all cultures, all nations, and all the people of the Western Hemisphere. By the way, the name America is really a misnomer, a name given to someone totally undeserving of such recognition. Amerigo Vespucci was an obscure explorer who had nothing to do with the discovery of America or with any of its major discoveries or explorations. His name was printed erroneously on a map and it stuck. When the mistake surfaced, it was already too late to change it. A lucky man indeed!

BRAIN TICKLERS—THE ANSWERS

Set # 13, page 58

A. Answers will vary

B.
1. F 2. F 3. V 4. V

C.
1. a la carrera
2. Desde luego
3. de agrado
4. todo lo que importa

Set # 14, page 61

A.
1. feminine
2. masculine

B.
1. maestros
2. sillas
3. cruces
4. televisores
5. imágenes

C.
1. Los estudiantes viven en California.
2. Las clases de español son muy buenas.

Set # 15, page 65

A.
Vivo en una casa de tres pisos. Mi dormitorio está en el tercer piso y el de mi hermano en el primero.

B.
1. 5o 2. 8o 3. 3o 4. 4o

Set # 16, page 66

A. Pronunciation
B. Answers will vary.

Set # 17, page 70

A.
1. Jimmy y Rocío
2. española y también mexicana
3. pasada la medianoche
4. un jardincito

B.
1. talk 'till you drop
2. finger-licking good
3. to go well

Vestir bien nos ayuda a triunfar en la vida

Dressing well helps us succeed in life

En estos tiempos modernos *cada cual* viste como le parece, *a su manera*, sin importarle *en lo más mínimo* la opinión de los demás. "Soy quien soy y como soy; al que le guste bien, y al que no, *que se fastidie*". Con un pantalón, una camisa o blusa, y unos tenis basta. Los tiempos de los trajes y corbatas, de los vestidos y zapatos de tacones quedaron muy atrás. *Hubo un tiempo* en el que vestir bien reflejaba el buen gusto y elegancia de una persona, *hasta el punto de que* se decía "tal vistes, tal eres", como igual se decía "tal hablas, tal eres". Se comprende que, al vestirse así, *a la ligera*, se ahorra tiempo, trabajo y dinero, razones *que intentan justificar* lo que llamaríamos "el vestirse por vestirse", *sin otro propósito* del de no salir desnudo a la calle, *con todas las vergüenzas al aire*. También se busca, y se insiste, en una sociedad "unisexo", en la que no hay distinción, o la hay muy poca, entre el hombre y la mujer. Pero, como nosotros *pecamos de* tradicionales, de gente a la antigua, *aferrada a* sus buenas costumbres y tradiciones, seguimos prefiriendo el buen vestir, sin importar el sexo o la edad, ni aun la condición económica de la persona, pues el que tiene gusto con *dos trapitos* sabe lucir como un rey o una reina.

De todas maneras, no se puede decir que toda la gente piense igual. Hay excepciones. Un paseíto por la Quinta Avenida de Nueva York, en una reunión de ejecutivos de una gran empresa de la Avenida Madison, o una fiesta en el hotel Plaza nos demuestran *que aún hay* gente que valora la apariencia personal, *que se esmera* por lucir bien. Así, se ven mujeres con vestidos *de alta costura*, cuero, zapatos de tacones altos, muy maquilladas y llenas de finas joyas. *En cuanto a* los hombres, *se les ve* con traje obscuro de tres botones, corbatas de seda, zapatos de finísimo cuero, y abrigos largos de pura lana virgen o cachemir.

Vístase cada cual *como le dé la gana*; sí recomendamos que para la próxima entrevista de trabajo que se tenga se vista uno de forma presentable y digna. *De lo contrario*, ¡adiós trabajo!

Vocabulario básico

cada cual	everybody/each of us
a su manera	to his/her own liking
en lo más mínimo	in the least
que se fastidie	too bad/who cares
Hubo un tiempo	There was a time
hasta el punto de que	to the point that
a la ligera	casually
intentan justificar	try to justify
sin otro propósito	without any other purpose
con todas las vergüenzas al aire	with all the private parts exposed
pecamos de	we are at fault of
aferrada a	holding tight to
dos trapitos	with two rags
que aún hay	that there is still
de alta costura	high fashion
En cuanto a	As far as/Regarding
se les ve	they can be seen
como le dé la gana	as he/she pleases
De lo contrario	Otherwise

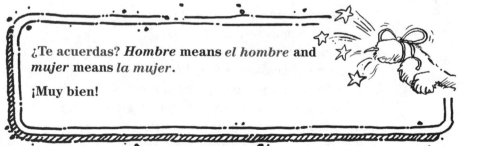

¿Te acuerdas? *Hombre* means *el hombre* and *mujer* means *la mujer*.

¡Muy bien!

BRAIN TICKLERS
Set # 18

Ejercicios

A. Contesta estas preguntas en oraciones completas.
 1. En general, ¿cómo te vistes tú?
 2. ¿Cuál es tu color favorito de ropa?
 3. ¿Estás por lo general de acuerdo con lo que se dice en el pasaje? ¿Por qué sí o por qué no?
 4. ¿Te consideras tú una persona tradicional?

B. Basado en el pasaje, dinos si cada una de estas afirmaciones es *verdadera o falsa*:
 1. En cuanto al vestirse, a la gente de hoy le importa la opinión que de ella tienen los demás.   V   F
 2. La gente de hoy piensa que el vestirse a la ligera ahorra tiempo, trabajo, y dinero.   V   F
 3. La gente de antes no estaba aferrada a sus costumbres y tradiciones.   V   F
 4. Cuando vamos a una entrevista de trabajo debemos vestirnos bien.   V   F

C. Traduce la palabra o las palabras entre paréntesis:
 1. Mi padre siempre (dresses) con traje y corbata.
 2. Mi amiga Rosa tiene (a red dress) precioso.
 3. Para mi jefe, la (personal appearance) es muy importante.
 4. Los (leather coats) son bonitos pero muy caros.

Answers are on page 95.

¡Ojo!—Watch Out!

Lucir in Spanish means *to look*, in the sense of *looking good*—the way you are dressed, your appearance, etc. *Looks* has of late been incorporated into the Spanish language and has the same meaning as in English. A similar term is *sex appeal*, which is now widely used throughout the Spanish-speaking world.

PIÉNSALO BIEN
THINK IT THROUGH

The verb, Part 1. El verbo, Parte 1

Here we are going to cover all that is important and basic about the Spanish verb.

We have aready said that the verb is one of the most important parts of a sentence. It denotes action, movement, just like the engine of a car. There are many similarities in the use of verbs between English and Spanish. Here are a few:

- They form the predicate.
- They are conjugated.
- They have different moods and tenses.
- The conjugation of each verb has six persons, three in the singular and three in the plural.
- They can be both regular and irregular.
- They have present (gerund) and past participles.
- They have active and passive voices.
- They can be transitive or intransitive.
- They can be reflexive.

There are also some basic differences. Here are a few:

Every Spanish verb, in any tense, and referring to any person, has a different ending. This is quite different from English. In fact, verbs in English are much easier than in

Spanish in that sense—let's take a verb, such as "to walk," and conjugate it in English and Spanish:

to walk	caminar
I walk	(yo) camino
you walk	(tú) caminas
he/she/it walks	(él/ella/usted) camina
we walk	(nosotros) caminamos
you walk	(vosotros) camináis
they walk	(ellos/ellas/ustedes) caminan

In comparing both, notice that in English, you form the infinitive (name) of the verb by placing *to* before it. In Spanish, that *to* equals the ending of the verb after it is separated from the root or stem, which is *camin-*. As you can see, each of the endings of the six persons is different, while in English the name of the verb, *walk*, remains invariable with the exception of the third person singular to which we add -*s*. In fact, you conjugate a verb in English by using different personal pronouns (I, you, he, they, etc.). The verb remains the same; the pronouns change. On the other hand, in Spanish, there is really no need to use the personal pronouns since each ending tells us who the person is. But there is more: In Spanish there are three main conjugations depending on the vowel used in the infinitive; those vowels can be *a*, *e*, or *i*, which are followed by the letter *r*; thus: *ar*, *er*, *ir*, as in *cant-ar* (to sing*)*, *com-er* (to eat*)*, *viv-ir* (to live). The verbs ending in –*ar* belong to the first conjugation; in –*er* to the second conjugation; and in –*ir* to the third conjugation. What we have said up to now may seem too difficult for you, and in a way it is, but we can make it easier to understand. Here is how. Let's conjugate the three verbs mentioned above in the three conjugations:

cant-ar	com-er	viv-ir
cant-o	com-o	viv-o
cant-as	com-es	viv-es
cant-a	com-e	viv-e

cant-amos	com-emos	viv-imos
cant-áis	com-éis	viv-ís
cant-an	com-en	viv-en

Look at all the endings and you will notice that the main difference between each lies in the last vowel. With the exception of the *i* form, the vowel for the first conjugation is *a*, for the second *e*, and for the third also *e*, excluding the *we* form and the *you* form in the plural, which is *i*. Notice that all the consonants following each of the vowels are the same for all three. Knowing this, which should be quite clear, you will be able to conjugate any regular verb in the present tense. Just remember the vowels of each conjugation.

Now, to conjugate any verb in Spanish, once you know its infinitive (name), you must first separate the stem or root from the ending, as we did above, and then add to it the corresponding endings of the desired tense. This is for all of them.

BRAIN TICKLERS
Set # 19

Ejercicios

A. Answer these questions in English: What are the three basic similarities between Spanish and English verbs?

B. Now write the most important difference between the two.

C. Conjugate the verb caminar in the present tense. When you are done, explain briefly the steps you took to do it.

Answers are on page 95.

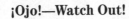

¡Ojo!—Watch Out!

In the previous conjugations you noticed the second person plural, or the *you* (*vosotros*) form. Today, many people leave it out, claiming that it is used only in Spain and that there is really not a need for it. In a way this is true, and you have that option. However, keep in mind that this form is not used only in Spain but also in certain other parts of South America, such as Argentina.

The verb, Part 2. El verbo, Parte 2

Modos (Moods)

There are four moods in Spanish:

Indicativo	Indicative
Potencial/Condicional	Conditional
Subjuntivo	Subjunctive
Imperativo	Command/Imperative

Why four?
Each of these moods has a purpose, a specific function:

- The indicative tells us what is, what is real.
- The conditional tells us what could be or should be.
- The subjunctive tells us what may be.
- The command serves to tell someone to do something.

Of the four, the subjunctive is the one requiring the most attention, mainly because it is used in Spanish far more frequently than in English, and also because it has almost as many tenses as the indicative. The conditional* has only two tenses, and the command only one, which is always in the present. So, the two moods of greatest concern are the indicative and the subjunctive. The indicative has a total of 8 tenses, 4 simple and 4** compound. The subjunctive has a total of 6 tenses, 3 simple and 3 compound. In this lesson, we will cover only the indicative.

The 4 simple tenses of the indicative are

1. Present
2. Past or Preterite
3. Imperfect
4. Future

The 3 compound tenses are:

1. Present perfect
2. Past perfect
3. Future perfect

We already saw the present tense. With the past tense, we have to go through the same process and separate the stem or root from the ending of the infinitive, to which the different past tenses are added. The endings of the past tense for all three conjugations are

cant-ar (to sing)	com-er (to eat)	viv-ir (to live)
cant-é (I sang)	com-í (I ate)	viv-í (I lived)
cant-aste	com-iste	viv-iste
cant-ó	com-ió	viv-ió
cant-amos	com-imos	viv-imos
cant-asteis	com-isteis	viv-isteis
cant-aron	com-ieron	viv-ieron

Notice that the endings of the -*er* and -*ir* verbs are the same. Also, the *you singular* forms end in -*ste* for all three conjugations; the *we* form ends in -*mos*; the *you plural* ends in -*steis*; and the *third plural* ends in -*ron*. In other words, the only difference is in the thematic vowel of the ending—a to i.

(*) Some people make the conditional part of the indicative; others make it a separate mood. We prefer the latter.
(**) In this book we will use only 3, leaving out the Pretérito anterior, which is rarely used.

Ojo!—Watch Out!

A *simple tense* uses one conjugated verb; a *compound tense* uses two verbs, a conjugated one, which is called a helping or auxiliary verb, and a past participle, which is invariable. We will explain it further in lesson 6.

The endings for the imperfect tense are

cant-ar	com-er	viv-ir
cant-aba (I sang)	com-ía (I ate)	viv-ía (I lived)
cant-abas	com-ías	viv-ías
cant-aba	com-ía	viv-ía
cant-ábamos	com-íamos	viv-íamos
cant-abais	com-íais	viv-íais
cant-aban	com-ían	viv-ían

Notice that the endings of the *-er* and *-ir* verbs are identical. Also notice that the endings of the first and third person singular are the same in all three conjugations. The difference is determined in the context.

Looking at the conjugations of the past and the imperfect, you may become confused since both appear to mean the same in English. They do not. Here is the difference:

The past tense denotes a past action, which in the mind of the speaker is concluded, as in

I played basketball yesterday.

Here, the playing of basketball is an action with a definite end—yesterday.

However, in this other sentence

I played basketball when I was in high school.

the playing of basketball in the mind of the speaker is a continuous action with an indefinite ending. In other words, I played basketball for as long as I was in high school. Said differently, the playing of basketball is dependent upon my being in school. I could say it differently this way:

I used to play basketball when I was in high school.

When English and Spanish are compared in terms of the use of the imperfect, the difference is that in English the imperfect is implied, while in Spanish it is expressed by a specific tense that is different from the past tense. In English, the past tense is used for both, as in *played*. In other words, English has no imperfect tense.

Here is how we would say the sentences in Spanish:

Jugué baloncesto ayer (I played basketball yesterday).
Jugaba baloncesto cuando estaba en la escuela secundaria
    (I played/used to play basketball when I was in high
    school).

Many times, both the past and imperfect tenses are used in the same sentence:

While I (watched) was watching television, the phone rang.

Here, there are two expressed actions: one, *I watched/was watching television*, was in progress at the time; the other, *the phone rang*, occurred or took place. In Spanish, we would say

Mientras miraba la televisión sonó el teléfono.

BRAIN TICKLERS
Set # 20

Ejercicios

A. Answer these questions in English.
   1. How many moods are there in Spanish?
   2. For what specific purpose is the Indicative Mood used?
   3. Explain briefly what simple and compound tenses are.
B. Conjugate the verb trabajar in the imperfect tense.

        Answers are on page 95.

MÁS ES MEJOR
MORE IS BETTER

Nouns

los zapatos	shoes
la blusa	blouse
la falda	skirt
el cinturón	belt
los calcetines	socks
las medias	stockings
la ropa interior	undergarments
el sombrero	hat
la gorra	cap
el suéter	sweater
la chaqueta	jacket
las botas	boots
las sandalias	sandals
los guantes	gloves
la bufanda	scarf
la talla	size (*la talla* is applied almost exclusively to clothes; otherwise it would be *el tamaño*)
la tintorería	dry cleaners
la lavandería	laundromat
las zapatillas	slippers
la camisa	shirt
el vestido	dress

Verbs

llevar	to wear
ponerse	to put on
quitarse	to take off
probarse	to try on
abrochar	to fasten/button up
planchar	to iron
peinarse	to comb (one's hair)
cepillarse	to brush (one's hair)
maquillarse	to put on one's makeup

¿**Cuánto sabes?** Do you know what *quedar bien/mal* means? If you do, write it down: _____. If you don't, look it up and then write it down.

El cuerpo humano (the human body)

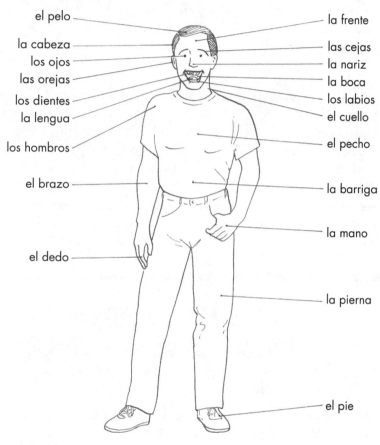

el pelo — la frente
la cabeza — las cejas
los ojos — la nariz
las orejas — la boca
los dientes — los labios
la lengua — el cuello
los hombros — el pecho
el brazo — la barriga
— la mano
el dedo — la pierna
— el pie

la cabeza	head	las orejas	ears
el pelo	hair	el cuello	neck
la frente	forehead	los hombros	shoulders
los ojos	eyes	el pecho	chest
las cejas	eyebrows	el brazo	arm
la nariz	nose	la mano	hand
la boca	mouth	el dedo	finger
los labios	lips	la barriga	belly
los dientes	teeth	la pierna	leg
la lengua	tongue	el pie	foot

HABLA POPULAR
EVERYDAY SPEECH

Here are more idioms, expressions, and sayings.

es decir	that's to say
por encima de todo	above all
siempre y cuando	provided
al contrario	to the contrary
por supuesto	of course
¡manos a la obra!	let's get going!
¡ni modo!	no way!
¡adelante!	let's go!/let's move on!
no sólo de pan vive el hombre	man doesn't live by bread alone
la curiosidad mató al gato	curiosity killed the cat

¿Sabías que? The first European women and children arrived in North America in the expedition of Lucas Vázquez de Ayllón in 1512.

BIEN VALE LA PENA
IT'S WELL WORTH IT

Basic arithmetic

The word for *arithmetic* in Spanish is *aritmética*.

The key words you should learn are

por	meaning times, as in: 5 times 5> 5 *por* 5
más	meaning plus (you could also say *y*, for plus), as in: 5 plus 5> 5 *más* 5 (or 5 *y* 5)
menos	minus, as in: 5 minus 5> 5 *menos* 5
entre	divided by, as in: 5 divided by 5> 5 *entre* 5

All of the symbols are the same in Spanish and English: $\times$, $+$, $-$, $\div$. Other key words are

la multiplicación	mutiplication
la suma	addition

la resta	subtraction
la división	division
igual a	equal to
el total	total
la cantidad	amount
la cifra	number/figure
la unidad	unit
el punto decimal	decimal point
el dígito	digit
es/son	is/are
cuánto	*Cuánto* means how much, in the singular, and how many, in the plural. Used as an adjective, it must agree in gender and number with the noun, as in: *¿Cuántos libros hay en la mesa?* (How many books are on the table?) *¿Cuántas casas hay en esa cuadra?* (How many houses are on that block?) But, *¿Cuánto dinero tienes?* (How much money do you have?)

¿Sabías que? *El sistema decimal* (decimal system) is the one used throughout the Hispanic world and in most countries (except the United States). It is applied to the number system based on decimals or tens.

BRAIN TICKLERS
Set # 21

Ejercicios

A. Write out in Spanish the following mathematical operations, including the numbers:
  1. 15 × 10
  2. 7 + 7
  3. 20 – 8
  4. 30 ÷ 6

B. Contesta ahora estas preguntas en oraciones completas:

1. ¿Cuánto es uno por uno?

2. ¿Cuántos estudiantes hay en tu clase?

3. ¿Cuánto son diecisiete más ocho?

4. ¿Cuántos años te quedan (remain) para terminar tu bachillerato?

C. Dinos si cada una de estas afirmaciones es *verdadera o falsa*:

1. All of the mathematical symbols are the same in English and Spanish.   V   F

2. In Spanish, más is the same as *y* when adding.   V   F

3. For *divided by* Spanish uses the word menos.   V   F

4. Cuántos means "how much" in Spanish.   V   F

Answers are on page 95.

¡Ojo!—Watch Out!

Is there a difference between the Spanish words *aun* and *aún* and *solo* and *sólo*? Yes, there is a difference:

aun, without an accent mark, is an adverb and means *even*, as in: *aun así, lo llamaré* (even so, I will call him).

aún, with an accent mark, is also an adverb, but it means *still*, as in: *aún está trabajando* (he's still working).

solo, without an accent mark, is an adjective and means *alone*, as in: *Me siento solo* (I feel alone).

sólo, with an accent mark, is an adverb and means *only*, as in: *Yo sólo hablo inglés* (I speak only English).

DILO COMO YO
SAY IT LIKE I DO

Pronunciation of the *g, j*

The *j*, in combination with any of the five vowels, is always pronounced similarly to the *h* in *ham*, although not as strong, and without the aspiration typical of the English sound. It is never pronounced like the *j* in *jam* or *jelly*, never, with any of the vowels. Examples of the *j* in Spanish are *jamón* (ham), *jardín*, *jefe, joya*.

The *g* has the same sound as the *j* followed by the vowels *e* and *i*, as in *gente, gigante*. With the other three vowels, *a, o, u*, it is pronounced like the English *g* in *goat*, as in *gato, gota, gusto*. The problem that you are going to be facing all the time when it comes to the pronunciation of Spanish will be not so much with the consonants, although in some cases you will indeed find it challenging, but with the vowels, as the three examples above prove, regarding the *a*, in *gato*, the *o*, in *gota*, and the *u*, in *gusto*. It is, therefore, to your great advantage to practice all you can the pronunciation of the five vowels in Spanish until you feel you have come closer to their correct pronunciation. When the *g* is followed by *u* and the vowels *e* and *i* > *gue, gui*, the *u* is never pronounced, unless it has a diaeresis over it, as in *agüita, güiro*; otherwise it would sound like a *j*. The diaeresis is the two dots placed over the "u" indicating its usual pronunciation.

Pronunciation of the double consonants *ch, ll, rr*

These are the only double consonants in Spanish that cannot be separated. They form one letter and one sound.

The *ch* is pronounced similarly to the English *ch* in *chocolate*, although not as explosive: *noche, chaleco*.

The *ll* is generally pronounced like the English *y* in *yes*. There are variations in Spain and other Spanish-speaking countries (Peru, Bolivia), but that shouldn't concern us at this time. It is never pronounced as it is in English as two *ls*. Examples: *caballo, pollo*.

The *rr* is the pronunciation to watch, but for speakers of English, it is very hard. Nonetheless, even if you mispronounce it, you will be understood, unless it happens to be a word such as *pero* (but), which can also be *perro* (dog), or *caro* (expensive), which can also be *carro* (car), leading to some confusion. The *rr* is always trilled, as in *burro*; the *r* also is trilled at the beginning of a word or following *n*, as in: *rama* and *honra*.

BRAIN TICKLERS
Set # 22

Ejercicios

A. Say these words out loud:
   general   gitano   guitarra joven
   Camagüey góndola guagua ¡irafa

B. Answer these questions in English:
   1. When is the *g* pronounced in Spanish like *j*?
   2. What is the purpose of the *u* in the combinations *gue* and *gui*?
   3. What is a diaeresis?

Answers are on page 95.

¿Sabías que? You will be surprised at the new Spanish word for *blue jean*. Any guesses? It is *bluyín*, a Spanish phonetic transcription based exactly on its English pronunciation. That proves how popular the term has become worldwide! For some it continues to be *vaqueros* (cowboys), but it doesn't even come close in popularity to the other.

ALMA HISPÁNICA
HISPANIC SOUL

Azorín

Azorín was his pseudonym; his real name, José Martínez Ruiz, a great contemporary Spanish writer and essayist, a key figure of the famous *Generación del 98*. He saw the little things in life that are common and ordinary and that we seldom notice or pay attention to, and wrote about them in a wonderful, poignant, and simple style. He was also a penetrating and profound observer of Spanish history and culture and helped us understand it and appreciate it better. He wrote about many of the Spanish classics, including Miguel de Cervantes and his *Don Quijote*, and his essay, *El artista y el estilo* (The Artist and Style) is a must-read for those interested in stylistics. His book *Castilla* describes the landscape, cities, and people of Old Castile, a region of Spain he loved dearly. He was born in Alicante in 1873 and died in Madrid in 1967. If you are interested in knowing and understanding the true Spanish soul throughout the ages, Azorín is the source.

The writing of Azorín

This is an excerpt from his book *Castilla*. Azorín describes in his unique style a little town in Old Castile.

En la plaza de la ciudad se levanta un *caserón* de piedra; cuatro grandes balcones se abren en la fachada. Sobre la puerta, resalta un recio *blasón*. En el primer balcón de la izquierda se ve sentado en un sillón un hombre; su cara está pálida, *exangüe*, y remata en una *barbita* afilada y gris. Los ojos de este *caballero* están *velados* por una profunda tristeza; el *codo* lo tiene el caballero puesto en el brazo del sillón y su cabeza descansa en la *palma de la mano*.

To help you better understand this passage, here is the meaning of some key words:

caserón	big house
blasón	coat of arms
exangüe	exhausted
barbita	little beard
caballero	gentleman
velados	fogged
codo	elbow
palma de la mano	palm of his hand

PLUMA EN MANO
PEN IN HAND

La moda de hoy/Today's fashion

Toda época tiene su moda propia que trata de ser distinta de las demás. La de estos tiempos, tal como la vemos a diario, es la que podríamos llamar a lo que salga (whatever works) y lo más barato y cómodo. Los grandes modistos italianos y las finas telas inglesas son para una minoría selecta, para la gente de posición (people of means) y para los que cuentan con tiempo suficiente. Parte también de la moda actual, al menos (at least) en la mujer, tira a (leans toward) lo natural y lo ligero. Las telas de más uso parecen ser (seem to be) el algodón, la seda y la lana y también el cuero, principalmente en las chaquetas y abrigos. En cuanto a las tallas, las más comunes son las medianas y grandes. Referente a los precios, y como casi toda la ropa está hecha en la China, son por lo general asequibles, aunque siempre hay que saber (one must know) dónde comprar para no gastarse una millonada. Las tiendas de descuento son las más baratas y populares pero no siempre las más atractivas.

BRAIN TICKLERS
Set # 23

Ejercicios

A. Contesta estas preguntas en oraciones completas:
1. ¿Qué piensas tú de la moda de hoy?
2. ¿Cuentas tú con tiempo y dinero suficientes para vestirte bien?
3. ¿Cuál es tu talla en zapatos y pantalones?
4. ¿Qué clase de telas te gustán más?

B. En no más de tres oraciones, describe la ropa que tienes puesta (llevas) hoy.

Answers are on page 95.

ASÍ SOMOS
THIS IS WHO WE ARE

The Hispanic heritage of the United States

To most people, including you, the Western Hemisphere is divided into two main parts: the English to the north, and the Spanish to the south. The one to the north is called America, and the one to the south, South America or Latin America. We already explained this, so we will not dwell on it.

After the discovery of America, and for the next 100 years, America was called the Indies. What is called today a state, such as Louisiana or Florida, was then called a country, an immense piece of land with no known boundaries, and covering a big chunk of North America, extending all the way down to the Strait of Magellan. That vast territory, even Brazil for some time, was under Spanish domain. Then, after those first 100 years, other Europeans arrived—the English, Dutch, and also the French, to the northeast, and the Russians to the northwest. The Dutch left quickly, the French stayed a bit longer, and the British longer than the French. The country that stayed the longest, up to 1812, to be precise, was Spain—almost 300 years. But if we count Mexico, which was part of Spain until it became independent in 1821, and the vast territory it possessed in the Southwest and ceded to the United States in 1848, and Cuba and Puerto Rico, which were also part of Spain until 1898, the Spanish presence in America lasted more than 406 years, counting from the year of discovery.

It stands to reason, then, that not only was Spain the first European nation to arrive in America, but the one that stayed the longest and the one that did the most. It stands to reason also that America's Spanish heritage is far greater than that of any other nation, including ours, the United States. If anything, it should be split in two: the Spanish and the English, with all of the others coming in second place. Food for thought.

¿Sabías que? Some of the Spanish firsts in North America:

- First European flag (Castile and León) carried by Juan Ponce de León in 1513 when he landed in Florida. In fact, it is considered the first U.S. flag.
- First European language, Spanish.
- First colony, San Miguel de Guadalupe, founded in 1526 by Lucas Vázquez de Ayllón, on a site 32 miles from the second colony, Jamestown, founded by the British 95 years later.
- First city, San Augustín (Saint Augustine) in Florida, founded by Pedro Menéndez de Avilés in 1565.
- First printing press established in Mexico by Juan Pablos in 1535, and the first book published in that year by the same person.
- First universities, Santo Tomás de Aquino, founded in the Dominican Republic in 1538, and the University of Mexico, founded in 1551, 85 years before Harvard, and 195 years before Princeton.
- First to discover the Pacific Ocean, the Gulf of Mexico (called earlier the Spanish Sea), and the Caribbean Sea.

BRAIN TICKLERS—THE ANSWERS

Set # 18, page 76

A. Answers will vary.

B.
1. F   2. V   3. F   4. V

C.
1. se viste
2. un vestido rojo
3. la apariencia personal
4. los abrigos de cuero

Set # 19, page 79

Piénsalo bien
A. Answers will vary.

B. Answers will vary.

C.

camino	caminamos
caminas	camináis
camina	caminan

Answers will vary.

Set # 20, page 83

A.
1. 4
2. what is, what's real
3. Single tense uses one conjugated verb; compound tense uses two verbs.

B.

trabajaba	trabajábamos
trabajabas	trabajabais
trabajaba	trabajaban

Set # 21, page 87

A.
1. quince por diez
2. siete y siete
3. veinte menos ocho
4. treinta entra seis

B.
1. uno
2. Answers will vary.
3. 25
4. Answers will vary.

C.
1. V   2. V   3. F
4. F

Set # 22, page 90

A. Pronunciation

B.
1. when followed by "e" or "i"
2. so it doesn't sound as in "ge" "gi"
3. the two dots over the "u"

Set # 23, page 93

Pluma en mano
A. Answers will vary.

B. Answers will vary.

Estudiamos para mejorar nuestra condición humana

We study to become better people

¿Para qué estudiamos? Lo hacemos para aprender, para adquirir *conocimientos*, para ampliar nuestros horizontes, para honrar a nuestra familia y a nuestro nombre, para mejorar de posición y *llevar una vida* más segura y cómoda. Lo hacemos también para humanizarnos, para ser más comprensivos y nobles, para ser más personas. No lo hacemos, o no deberíamos hacerlo, *por el mero afán* de ganar dinero y adquirir y poseer cosas.

Hace muchos años sólo *asistía a* la universidad el que tenía vocación y capacidad en algún *campo del saber*. Hoy, afortunadamente, las puertas de las universidades están abiertas de *par en par* para acoger a toda persona que quiera estudiar sin tener necesariamente una vocación definida. Eso, por lo general, *viene después*, cuando el estudiante adquiere más conciencia de lo que quiere *llegar a ser* el día de mañana, de cuál *habrá de ser* su carrera profesional.

Indudablemente que el *sistema de enseñanza* de Estados Unidos, desde la escuela primaria, pasando por el *bachillerato* y la universidad, es uno de los mejores del mundo, *máxime* al llegar a los estudios avanzados o de postgrado. Las llamadas "Ivy League", *que no pasan de* siete, son centros de enseñanza de primerísima clase, no sólo por la calidad del estudiantado sino también por la del profesorado y por todas las facilidades que brindan. La única *traba* es el costo que sólo está *al alcance* de la gente adinerada, *a menos que* el estudiante sea muy bueno y se gane una *beca*. Los sistemas de enseñanza de Europa son también excelentes y ofrecen universidades que están *a la par* o a veces sobrepasan a muchas de Estados Unidos. Estas son universidades *antiquísimas*, con una tradición que *data de* la Edad Media, como son las universidades de Oxford en Inglaterra, o Salamanca en España.

Vocabulario básico

conocimientos	knowledge
llevar una vida	lead a life
por el mero afán	just to/merely to
Hace mucho años	Long ago
asistía a	attended

campo del saber	field of knowledge
par en par	wide open
viene después	comes later
llegar a ser	to become
habrá de ser	will be
sistema de enseñanza	educational system
bachillerato	secondary school/high school
máxime	especially
que no pasan de	that are not more than
traba	obstacle
al alcance de	within the reach
a menos que	unless
se gane una beca	wins a scholarship
a la par	equal
antiquísimas	very old/ancient
data de	dates from
Edad Media	Middle Ages

BRAIN TICKLERS
Set # 24

Ejercicios

A. Fill in the blanks, choosing the appropriate word(s) from the list below. You must concentrate to do it successfully.

asistir   legar a ser   ganar
estudiar   bachillerato   beca
escuela   costo   estudios

Yo **1** _____ a una universidad en el sur de California. Yo **2** _____ pues quiero **3** _____ un/una maestro/a. Cuando estaba en el segundo año de **4** _____ me gané una **5** _____ de $5,000 de mi **6** _____ Thomas Jefferson. Así el **7** _____ de mis **8** _____ será más económico.

B. The following verbs are all regular. Translate the words in parentheses using the correct form of the present tense:

1. Ellos (estudiar) italiano.

2. Nosotros (aprender) mucho en la escuela.

3. Ella no (ganar) lo suficiente.

4. Yo (llegar) siempre tarde (late) al trabajo.

C. Look at all these academic subjects in Spanish and write the English equivalent. Notice the similarity between the Spanish and English.

1. las matemáticas
2. la arquitectura
3. la ingeniería
4. la sociología
5. el cálculo
6. la historia
7. las ciencias políticas
8. las ciencias sociales
9. la filosofía
10. el arte

11. la medicina
12. las leyes/el derecho
13. la geografía
14. la psicología
15. el comercio
16. la biología
17. la economía
18. la literatura
19. la química
20. la astronomía

Answers are on page 127.

¡Ojo!—Watch Out!

To attend, as you have seen, in the sense of attending school, is not *atender* in Spanish, which means something totally different. In this case, you must use *asistir.* Also, *bachillerato* is the name in Spanish for high school. It is not bachelor. And *colegio* is not college, but school, either primary or secondary. The word in Spanish for college is *universidad.* Campus is *recinto universitario,* although you can use campus in Spanish as well since it happens to be a Latin word, but with a different meaning of open space or field.

PIÉNSALO BIEN
THINK IT THROUGH

The verb, Part 3. El verbo, Parte 3

Here you will learn about the future and conditional tenses and reflexive verbs. We will also explain the subjunctive and the command.

The future and conditional are the only tenses in Spanish formed by keeping the infinitive form of the verbs as is, without removing their respective endings. In other words, here you do not have to worry about the stem or root; you add the future and conditional endings to the whole infinitive, so the endings are the same for all three conjugations.

The endings for the future are

-é, -ás, -á, -emos, -éis, -án.

caminar	vender	escribir
caminaré (I will walk)	*venderé* (I will sell)	*escribiré* (I will write)

Notice how the ending *-é* is added to the whole infinitive of all three verbs. Notice also the accent mark on all endings with the exception of the "we" form.

For the conditional simple, we follow the same process, adding the endings to the infinitive of all three conjugations.

The endings for the conditional are

-ía, -ías, -ía, -íamos, -íais, -ían (which are the same for the imperfect for verbs of the second and third conjugations, as we saw previously).

caminar	vender	escribir
caminaría	*vendería*	*escribiría*
(I would walk)	(I would sell)	(I would write)

You can look at it this way: The future endings correspond to the English *will*, and the conditional endings correspond to the English *would*.

The reflexive verb means, simply, that the subject performs the action and receives it at the same time, as in a boomerang—you throw it and it comes right back to you. Both Spanish and English have reflexive verbs, the only difference being that in

English it is mostly implied, while in Spanish it is expressed. If I say *I wash my hands*, it is implied that I am the one doing and receiving the action. It would be uncommon for me to say *I wash my hands myself*, for it is implied that you yourself do it. In Spanish we would have to say *me lavo las manos*, from the infinitive *lavarse*. The *me* is the reflexive pronoun, and the *se* at the end of the infinitive denotes that the verb is reflexive. However, using that same verb, *lavar*, I could also say *lavo el carro*, in which case I perform the action but it is received by the car, not by me.

The reflexive pronouns in Spanish are

me	myself	
te	yourself	(use for the familiar singular)
se	himself, herself, itself	(also use for the polite singular)
nos	ourselves	
os	yourselves	(also use for the familiar plural)
se	themselves	(also use for the polite plural)

Positioning of the reflexive pronouns

If it is a conjugated verb, put the reflexive pronoun before the verb, *me lavo las manos* (I wash my hands).

If it is an infinitive or a present participle, put it before the first verb or attached to the main verb,
me voy a lavar las manos (I am going to wash my hands), *voy a lavarme las manos* (same)
me estoy lavando las manos (I am washing my hands), *estoy lavándome las manos* (same).

If it is a compound tense, put it before the helping verb, *me he lavado las manos* (I have washed my hands).

The same reflexive pronouns are also used in reciprocal verbs, as in *nos escribimos a menudo* (we write to each other often), *se hablan todos los días* (they speak to each other every day). As we will see later, in the case of the command, all reflexive pronouns are attached to the verb, as in *¡lávate las manos!* (wash your hands!).

The subjunctive

The subjunctive is really the mood of choice in Spanish, and it is used much more frequently than in English. It expresses life as it should be, rather than as it is, as Don Qujote felt it.

The typical use of the subjunctive in Spanish requires two subjects and two verbs. The first verb expresses any of the following: hope, desire, possibility, doubt, preference, request, fear, sorrow, among others, and, when this happens, the second verb is always used in the subjunctive, as in:

> *Espero que Manuel vaya a la fiesta* (I hope (that) Manuel goes to the party).
> *Es probable que Manuel vaya a la fiesta* (It's probable that Manuel will go to the party).
> *Dudo que Manuel vaya a la fiesta* (I doubt that Manuel will go to the party).

All of the three sentences show:

two subjects (Manuel and I)
two verbs (to hope and to go: *esperar* and *ir*)
something that is not certain, but rather a hope, a probability, a doubt
the use of *que*

You could also say that you need two clauses, the second one depending on the first. The first clause takes the indicative, and the second the subjunctive.

This is the perfect formula in Spanish for the use of the subjunctive. Again, let's put it this way: We all look at life in two different ways: 1. what to us is certain, real, factual as in *I see the tree, tomorrow is my birthday*; and 2. what we wished or hoped would be true and real, as in *I hope she loves me, I wish she would look at me*. In English, the subjunctive is expressed in numerous ways; it is rather implied than expressed with specific verb tenses, which is quite opposite to Spanish. In Spanish, we have specific subjunctive tenses and a formula that is easy to follow, as indicated above.

Let's go back to the two verbs, and here is the other formula:

- If the first verb (main clause) is in the present or future, the second verb (second clause) takes the present subjunctive.

- If the first verb is in the preterite, the imperfect, or the conditional, the second verb takes the imperfect subjunctive.

There are other verb tenses in the main clause that would take either the present or imperfect subjunctive, but let's leave that out for now.

Let's give some examples of the first two:

Quiero que María me llame (I want Maria to call me).
Espero que Bernardo salga bien del examen (I hope [that] Bernard passes the exam).

Quería que María me llamara (I wanted Maria to call me).
Esperaba que Bernardo saliera bien del examen (I hoped that Bernard had passed the exam).

This would work both in affirmative and negative expressions, as in

No quiero que María me llame (I don't want Maria to call me).
No espero que María me llame (I don't expect Maria to call me).

No quise/quería que María me llamara (I didn't want Maria to call me).
No esperé/esparaba que María me llamara (I didn't expect Maria to call me).

Finally, the subjunctive is also used with certain expressions not requiring two subjects or two verbs. Some examples are

Es una lástima que no pueda ir (It is a pity I can't go).
¡Ojalá que pueda ir! (I hope/wish I can go!)
Es necesario que Roberto lo haga (It's necessary for Robert to do it).
Es probable que llueva mañana (It's probable that it will rain tomorrow).

Notice that in all of these sentences *que* is also used.

In the previous chapter we said that the subjunctive has a total of 6 tenses, 3 simple and 3 compound. So far, we have seen 2 simple ones: the present and imperfect. Of the compound ones, the only ones that should concern us are the present perfect and the past perfect, which we will cover in the next lesson along with the other compound tenses of the indicative.

Endings of the present and imperfect subjunctive for the three conjugations:

Present

AR	ER	IR
-e	-a	-a
-es	-as	-as
-e	-a	-a
-emos	-amos	-amos
-éis	-áis	-áis
-en	-an	-an

Notice that for the ER and IR, the endings are the same. Notice also that in the AR, the vowel is *e* while in the ER/IR the vowel is *a*. Also notice, as with the indicative, the use of the same letters after the *e* or *a*.

Imperfect

AR	ER	IR
-ara	-iera	-iera
-aras	-ieras	-ieras
-ara	-iera	-iera
-áramos	-iéramos	-iéramos
-arais	-ierais	-ierais
-aran	-ieran	-ieran

Notice the switch of the vowels from the *e* to the *a* in the AR of the present and imperfect, and that the endings of the ER and IR are the same, and so are the letters after the *a* and the *e*.

The command is another troublesome mood in Spanish. First, you have the affirmative and negative command; second, it has only five persons minus the *I* form; third, the only true command forms are the *you* familiar singular and the *you* familiar plural; the other three are taken from the subjunctive, which has only one tense, the present. Let's see an example using the verb *cantar*:

canta	command form
cante	subjunctive form
cantemos	subjunctive form
cantad	command form
canten	subjunctive form

¡Ojo!—Watch Out!

As with many other tenses, verbs in the subjunctive can be regular or irregular. A good tip to remember is that, usually, when a verb is irregular in the first person of the indicative, it will also be irregular in the present subjunctive. Not only that, but the other five persons of the subjunctive will follow the same irregular form. Let's take these verbs as examples, *tener* and *hacer*:

	Present Indicative	Present Subjunctive
tener	tengo	tenga
	tienes	tengas
	tiene	tenga
	tenemos	tengamos
	tenéis	tengáis
	tienen	tengan
hacer	hago	haga
	haces	hagas
	hace	haga
	hacemos	hagamos
	hacéis	hagáis
	hacen	hagan

For the negative command, all of the forms are taken from the subjunctive. The negative *no* always precedes the verb, as in *no cantes*. All pronouns: reflexive, direct, and indirect objects, are always attached to all affirmative forms of the verb, as in

¡Lávate!	Wash (yourself)!
¡Dame!	Give me!
¡Dámelo!	Give it to me!

For the negative command, the order is
negative + pronoun + verb, as in

¡No te laves!   Don't wash (yourself)!

Therefore, in the affirmative, the pronouns are attached to
the verb. In the negative, they are placed between the *no* and the
verb.

All of the negative command forms are taken from the
subjunctive, as in

¡No cantes!	Don't sing!	you, familiar singular
¡No cante!	Don't sing!	you, formal singular
¡No cantemos!	Let's not sing!	we
¡No cantéis!	Don't sing!	you, familiar plural
¡No canten!	Don't sing!	you, formal plural

Note: In most of Hispanic America the *you* formal plural is the
same as the *you* familiar plural; in other words, there is only one
form for both. In Spain they use both forms.

You must also be aware that many verbs in the command are
irregular, especially verbs such as:

ir, hacer, poner, salir, and *ser* in the affirmative informal
both singular and plural, as in

ir
¡Ve!	Go!	you, familiar singular
¡Vayan!	Go!	you, both formal and informal plural

hacer
¡Haz!	Do/Make!	you, familiar singular
¡Hagan!	Do/Make!	you, both formal and informal plural

poner
¡Pon!	Put!	you, familiar singular
¡Pongan!	Put!	you, both formal and informal plural

salir
¡Sal!	Leave!	you, familiar singular
¡Salgan!	Leave!	you, both formal and informal plural

ser
¡Sé!	Be!	you, familiar singular
¡Sean!	Be!	you, both formal and informal plural

The following pointers may prove useful in using the
command forms.

Formal affirmative singular and plural commands

correspond to the same forms of the subjunctive, as in:

¡Hable primero con la maestra! Talk with the teacher first!
¡Vayan después al parque! Go to the park later!

Informal affirmative singular commands

correspond to the third person singular of the indicative, as in:

¡Estudia! Study!
¡Come! Eat!

The *we* form corresponds to the *we* form of the subjunctive, as in:

¡Salgamos a pasear! Let's go out for a walk!
¡Escibamos el ejercicio! Let's write the exercise!

As for the negative, the informal singular and plural forms correspond to the present subjunctive, as in:

¡No corras tanto! Don't run so much!
¡No hagan eso! Don't do that!

BRAIN TICKLERS
Set # 25

Ejercicios

A. Completa los espacios en blanco con el presente de subjuntivo según (according to) el verbo que se da (that is given) en paréntesis:

1. Deseo que Ana (lavar) _____ el carro.
2. No es seguro que mi padre (trabajar) _____ mañana.
3. Te ruego (I beg you) que lo (escribir) _____ ahora.
4. ¡Ojalá que ellos (hablar) _____ con el maestro!
5. Es verdad que hoy (ser) _____ martes.

B. Make five sentences in the subjunctive, using for each sentence one of the verbs/expressions in the list:

querer	esperar	¡ojalá!	es necesario
es posible	creer	es mejor	no hay duda

C. Answer if *true* (V) or *false* (F). The statements are given in English.

1. The subjunctive is used more frequently in Spanish than in English. V F

2. Compared to the indicative, the subjunctive expresses general emotions rather than facts. V F

3. The typical subjunctive construction in Spanish requires only one subject and one verb. V F

4. The subjunctive is used only in affirmative expressions and never in negative ones. V F

5. The relative pronoun *que* is generally used in all subjunctive constructions. V F

D. Translate this brief paragraph into Spanish:

I hope that my mother buys the dress and puts it on for my graduation. I know, however, that she doesn't have the money, but it is possible that she may have it in a day or two. This is what I prefer she would do.

E. Completa los espacios en blanco con la forma correcta del imperativo familiar (familiar command) según se da en paréntesis:

1. Emilio, (study!) ¡_____ para el examen!

2. María, (buy it! – a dress) ¡_____ en esa tienda!

3. ¡Por qué están sentados! (Let's dance!) ¡_____!

4. Josefina y Magdalena, (speak!) ¡_____ con el profesor!

5. Ustedes no tienen que escribir la composición. (Don't write it!) ¡_____!

Answers are on page 127.

The verb, Part 4. El verbo, Parte 4

Now you will learn about compound tenses of the indicative, conditional, and subjunctive, and how to form the past and present participles in Spanish, helping verbs, the active and passive voices, and transitive and intransitive verbs.

The past participle in Spanish, as in English, is used to form compounds of perfect tenses. Again, a compound tense simply means that you are using two verbs instead of one. The first verb is an auxiliary or helping verb, and the second a past participle. All past participles are invariable. In English, you form the past participle of regular verbs by adding -ed to the verb infinitive, as in: *walk>walked*, *work>worked*. That -ed in Spanish has two forms, as follows:

For the first conjugation (AR) you add -*ado*, as in: *caminar>caminado*, *trabajar>trabajado*. For the verbs of the second (ER) and third (IR) conjugations you add -*ido*, as in: *comer>comido*, *vivir>vivido*. We repeat that these are the endings for all regular verbs, which happens to be the vast majority.

The helping verb in Spanish in the active voice is *haber*, which in English is *to have*. So you would form a compound or perfect tense thus:

Spanish
haber + a verb ending in -*ado*/-*ido*

English
to have + a verb ending in -*ed*

Here are some sentence examples:

He trabajado mucho hoy. I have worked a lot today.
Hemos vivido aquí desde 1990. We have lived here since 1990.

The helping verb *haber* is irregular in Spanish. Here is the conjugation in the present tense:

haber			
he	I have	hemos	we have
has	you have	habéis	you have
ha	he/she/it has	han	they have

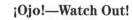

¡Ojo!—Watch Out!

Before we proceed, *haber* is not *tener,* which also means *to have.* So you don't get confused, use *haber* only as a helping verb in compound tenses and *tener* for all other cases.

Past participles can also be irregular both in English and Spanish. Following are some of the most common irregular past participles:

escribir>escrito	to write>written
hacer>hecho	to do/make>made
decir>dicho	to say>said
poner>puesto	to put>put
abrir>abierto	to open>opened
volver>vuelto	to return>returned
ver>visto	to see>seen

The three perfect tenses of the indicative:

Present perfect:	uses the present tense of *to have* plus a past participle
Past perfect:	uses the past tense of *to have* plus a past participle
Future perfect:	uses the future tense of *to have* plus a past participle

The three in Spanish are

Pretérito perfecto:	uses the present tense of *haber* plus a past participle
Pretérito pluscuamperfecto:	uses the imperfect tense of *haber* plus a past participle
Futuro perfecto:	uses the future tense of *haber* plus a past participle

Here are some sentence examples of the three:

He hablado con el profesor.	I have spoken to the professor.
Había hablado con el profesor.	I had spoken to the professor.
Habré hablado con el profesor.	I will have spoken to the professor.

The conjugations of the helping verb *haber* in the three tenses:

Present:	he, has, ha, hemos, habéis, han (irregular)
Imperfect:	había, habías, había, habíamos, habíais, habían (regular)
Future:	habré, habrás, habrá, habremos, habréis, habrán (irregular)

The conditional has only one compound tense, which is formed with the conditional form of the helping verb plus a past participle, as in : *I would have studied, they would have called.* In Spanish, it is also formed by the conditional form of *haber* plus a past participle. Here is the conditional of *haber*:

habría	I would have
habrías	you would have
habría	he/she/it would have
habríamos	we would have
habríais	you would have
habrían	they would have

Here are the two sentence examples above in Spanish:

habría estudiado	(I would have studied)
habrían llamado	(they would have called)

For the subjunctive, we need only be concerned with two compound tenses: the present perfect and the past perfect. Here, you need the present and imperfect subjunctive of *haber*. Here are their conjugations:

Present subjunctive:

haya	that I may have
hayas	that you may have
haya	that he/she/it may have
hayamos	that we may have
hayáis	that you may have
hayan	that they may have

Imperfect subjunctive:

hubiera	that I may have had
hubieras	that you may have had
hubiera	that he/she/it may have had
hubiéramos	that we may have had
hubiérais	that you may have had
hubieran	that they may have had

Here are some sentence examples of both:

Es posible que lo haya visto ayer.
(It is possible that I may have seen him yesterday.)
Es posible que lo hubiera visto antes de que me llamara.
(It is possible that I may have seen him before he called me.)

¡Ojo!—Watch Out!

Past participles can also function as adjectives, in which they are generally used in English with *to be* and in Spanish with *estar*; as in: he is tired>*está cansado*. There is a major difference, however—as an adjective in Spanish, the past participle, now an adjective, must agree in gender and number with the subject, as in: *están cansados* (they are tired—masculine plural), *estamos cansadas* (we are tired—feminine plural).

The present participle is the verb ending in English in *-ing*, as in *singing, dancing*. This is the form used in the present progressive tense, which also takes a helping verb: *to be*, as in *I am singing, they are dancing*. In Spanish, that helping verb is always *estar*. To form the present participle in Spanish, you add to the stem or root the endings *-ando* (AR verbs), *-iendo* (ER/IR verbs). It is the same as the past participle but with an *n*. As with the past participle, the present participle is invariable. You conjugate *estar* (helping verb) and the present participle remains as is. Here are some sentence examples:

Estoy estudiando para el examen de español.
(I am studying for the Spanish exam.)
Estamos escribiendo en la clase. (We are writing in class.)

Of course, *estar* can be conjugated in any tense, for I may be doing something now, was doing something yesterday, or may be doing something tomorrow. It can also be conjugated in any compound tense, as in *He estado estudiando toda la noche* (I have been studying all night). Why is it called present progressive?

Simply because it denotes an action that is in progress, that is happening at the time we say it. If I say, *leo en la clase* (I read in class), it is not the same as saying, *estoy escribiendo en la clase* (I am writing in class). The *leo en la clase* can be at any moment, any day, while *estoy escribiendo en la clase* denotes that I am doing it right now, as I speak. As we said, I could also refer to an action in progress in the past, as in: *estaba mirando televisión cuando mi madre entró* (I was watching television when my mother came in). Here, the watching of television is an action that was in progress when the other action (my mother came in) took place. It is an action in the imperfect but in progress, using *estar* in the imperfect plus the present participle of *mirar* (to watch).

The active and passive voices

In Spanish, the active voice is used far more frequently than the passive, which is not the case in English. The passive voice simply means that the subject receives the action of the verb instead of being an agent of it. In the active voice the subject is the agent of the action but not its receiver. Let's see an example:

Active voice

> *Cervantes escribió "Don Quijote".* (Cervantes wrote *Don Quixote*.) Here, Cervantes is the subject and the agent of the action (*escribió*>wrote).

Passive voice

"Don Quijote" fue escrito por Cervantes. (*Don Quixote* was written by Cervantes.) Here, the subject is no longer Cervantes but *Don Quijote* and Cervantes receives the action of the verb. The passive voice in English is formed with *to be* as a helping verb, plus a past participle. The same is true in Spanish, although *to be* is not *estar* but *ser*. If it were *estar*, as explained, the past participle would function as an adjective. Notice the use of the preposition *por* (by) in this passive construction.

As we said, the Spanish language generally rejects the use of the passive voice as described above. It is much better to do it in a different way, which is by using the pronoun *se* and a verb in the third person either singular or plural, as in:

> *Aquí se habla español.* (Spanish is spoken here.)
> *En esa tienda se venden productos mexicanos.* (In that store Mexican products are sold.)

¡Ojo!—Watch Out!

The use of the pronoun *se* and a verb in the third person also indicates that the action is not attributed to a determined subject, but that it is impersonal, as in *Se dice que el profesor renunció* (It is said that the professor resigned).

Regarding transitive and intransitive verbs, a transitive verb always takes a direct object to complete the meaning, while the intransitive doesn't. Here is an example:

Transitive verb

Compré un vestido para mi madre. (I bought a dress for my mother.) Here, *comprar* (to buy) is a transitive verb because it takes a direct object, which is *vestido* (dress).

Intransitive verb

Juan salió tarde. (John left late.) Here, there is no direct object.

MÁS ES MEJOR
MORE IS BETTER

Nouns:

la clase	class
la sala de clase	classroom
el curso	course
la asignatura	subject
la tarea	homework
el horario	schedule
la prueba	test
el libro	book
el estudiante	student
el maestro	teacher

el profesor/la profesora	professor
el ejercicio	exercise
el examen	exam
el libro de texto	textbook
la nota	grade
la matrícula	tuition/registration
el título	title
el lápiz	pencil
la pluma	pen
el bolígrafo	ballpoint pen
la pizarra	chalkboard
el pupitre	student's desk
el repaso	review
los apuntes	notes

Verbs

aprender	to learn
aprobar	to approve
suspender	to fail (an exam, etc.)
pasar	to pass
graduarse	to graduate
repasar	to review
inscribirse/matricularse	to register/enroll
entender/comprender	to understand
repetir	to repeat
leer	to read
escribir	to write
tomar notas/apuntes	to take notes
explicar	to explain

HABLA POPULAR
EVERYDAY SPEECH

Here are more idioms, expressions, and sayings:

hasta la fecha	up to now
en lo sucesivo	hereafter
de suerte que	so that

dejar tranquilo/en paz	to leave alone/not to bother
con mucho gusto	gladly
a través de	through/throughout
a fin de que	so that
a fin de cuentas	in the final analysis
por si las moscas	just in case
sin ton ni son/sin comerlo ni beberlo	for no reason
Dime con quién andas y te diré quién eres.	You're judged by the company you keep.

BIEN VALE LA PENA
IT'S WELL WORTH IT

Profesiones (professions)

el médico	physician, doctor
el/la abogado/a	lawyer, attorney
el/la arquitecto/a	architect
el/la ingeniero/a	engineer
el/la psiquiatra	psychiatrist
el/la psicólogo/a	psychologist
el/la dentista	dentist
el/la periodista	journalist
el/la publicitario/a	publicist
el/la artista	artist
el/la técnico/a de computadoras	computer technician
el/la programador/a de computadoras	computer programmer
el/la diplomático/a	diplomat
el/la contador/a	accountant
el/la farmacéutico/a	pharmacist
el/la diseñador/a	designer
el/la juez	judge
la/el secretaria/o	secretary
la/el enfermera/o	nurse
el/la maestro/a	teacher
el/la empresario/a	businessperson
el/la ejecutivo/a	executive
el/la bibliotecario/a	librarian

el/la arqueólogo/a	archeologist
el/la científico/a	scientist
el/la astronauta	astronaut
el/la funcionario/a público/a	public official
el/la escritor/a	writer
el/la agente de bienes raíces	real estate broker
el/la editor/a	editor, publisher
el/la modisto/a	fashion designer

Days of the week. Months of the year

Días de la semana (Days of the week)

In Spanish, the week starts on a Monday. Days of the week are usually not capitalized. All seven days are masculine.

lunes	Monday
martes	Tuesday
miércoles	Wednesday
jueves	Thursday
viernes	Friday
sábado	Saturday
domingo	Sunday

Meses del año (Months of the year)

The months are not capitalized either.

enero	January
febrero	February
marzo	March
abril	April (notice the *b* in Spanish, not *p*)
mayo	May
junio	June
julio	July
agosto	August (notice there is no *u* in Spanish)
septiembre	September (you can write it with a *p*, or without it> setiembre)
octubre	October (notice there is no *u* in English)
noviembre	November (notice the *ie* in Spanish)
diciembre	December (notice *di* in Spanish, not *de*)

¡Ojo!—Watch Out!

The date in Spanish. In Spanish, you start with the day of the month, followed by the month, and then the year, as in:

4 de enero de 2011   (January 4, 2011)

The abbreviated form would be:

4–1–11

A mistake here can be very costly, so be careful!
Day of the month + month + year. That's the way it is done in Spanish. If you want to add the day of the week, you can do it this way:

Day of the week + day of the month + month + year>
(*el*) *lunes, 4 de enero de 2011.*

Notice the use of *de* in Spanish before the month. Contrary to English, Spanish uses cardinal numbers for the date, as in

hoy es nueve   today is the 9th

unless it is the first of the month, in which case in most of Hispanic America they would use the ordinal number, as in

Hoy es el primero (1o.) de marzo.
Today is the 1st of March.

Often, the article *el* is included, as in

Hoy es el 17 de agosto.   Today is the 17th of August.

But if the day of the week is mentioned, the article is omitted before the number, as in

Se fueron a Europa el martes 4 de abril.
(They went to Europe Tuesday, April 4th.)

There are several ways of asking the date in Spanish:

¿Qué día es hoy?	What day is today?
¿A cómo estamos?	What's the date?
¿Qué fecha es hoy?	What's today's date?

DILO COMO YO
SAY IT LIKE I DO

Pronunciation of the *ñ* and the *b-v*

The *ñ* is a letter unique to Spanish. Other languages, including English, have pretty much the same sound but not the symbol.

The first thing you have to learn is how to write it. The *n* has a curved (or straight) line or dash right over it, which is called a *tilde* ; it is used in upper or lower case: ñ, Ñ. If you leave it out, it is simply an *n* with a totally different pronunciation and often with a different meaning, as in: *peña* (rock/crag), *pena* (pity/sorrow). Concerning its pronunciation, you should have no major problem since it is quite similar to the English *ni* in *onion*. Your problem is not how to pronounce it, but leaving out the tilde, which often happens. Don't do it! The *ñ* cannot stand by itself, needing always to be followed by a vowel, and never separating the two.

BRAIN TICKLERS
Set # 26

Ejercicios

A. Say these words out loud:
   español   niño   caña   puño
   año   otoño   señal   riña

B. Divide these three words into syllables:
   1. viña
   2. uña
   3. cañón

Answers are on page 127.

More on the pronunciation of the *b-v*

As we said earlier, there is often confusion when writing a word with a *b* or *v* since both consonants are pronounced alike in Spanish. The following tips may help you avoid such a confusion.

Written with a *b*

- All verb infinitives ending in *-bir* and their respective tenses: *escribir> escribo, escribí, escribía, escribiré*; *concebir> concebimos, concebíamos, concebiremos*
- The verbs *deber* and *beber*, and their respective tenses: *deben, debieron, deberán*; *beben, bebieron, beberán*
- All the endings of the imperfect tense of *-ar* verbs: *soñaba, bailábamos, cantaban*
- The imperfect tense of the verb *ir*: *iba, íbamos, iban*
- Words beginning with the syllables *bu, bus, bur*, and the sound *bibl*: *butaca, buscar, burocracia, bibliografía, biblioteca*
- Any word in which the *b* precedes another consonant: *subsistir, admirable, breve*

Written with a *v*

- All adjectives ending in *ave, ava, avo, eve, eva, ivo, iva*: *suave, esclava, cóncavo, diecinueve, nueva, exclusivo, llamativa*
- Following the syllable *ad*: *adversidad, advertir, adverso*
- The present indicative, subjunctive, and command of the verb *ir*: *vamos, vayamos, vayan*

Remember! Both the *b* and the *v* are pronounced identically in Spanish—no difference whatsoever.

The pronunciation of the *d* at the end of a word

There is also some confusion or hesitation regarding the correct pronunciation of the letter *d* at the end of a word. There are generally three different pronunciations:

1. It is totally dropped following a pause, as in: *pared> paré, usted> usté.*
2. It is pronounced similarly to the Spanish *z* in *lápiz.*
3. It is pronounced like the *d* in initial position: *doy, dolor* (dental/occlusive).

Which one is the correct pronunciation?
Either 1 or 2 is recommended as being the most common.

Pronunciation Practice

A. Read these words out loud, paying special attention to
the *b-v*:

avance	abanico	bisonte	verde	a la vez
a lo bestia	embudo	en vano	avestruz	bombero

B. Read these words out loud, paying special attention to
the final *d*:

ciudad	haced	potestad	multitud	Simbad
verdad	soledad	realidad	obscuridad	potestad

ALMA HISPÁNICA
HISPANIC SOUL

Juan Ramón Jiménez

Juan Ramón Jiménez is one of the most gifted writers of
contemporary Spain. Although he wrote for newspapers and
translated several works, he is best known for his poetry and for
his insightful perception of what this art is, of its language and
meaning. Although he spent most of his early years in Spain,
when civil war broke out in Spain in 1936, he left, like many
other Spaniards, to try his fortunes in other lands. He accepted
an invitation to teach at the University of Puerto
Rico, then Cuba, later the United States,
and from here he traveled extensively
throughout South America. He was born
in Andalucía, in the village of Moguer,
Huelva, in 1881, and died in 1958. Juan
Ramón was a prolific writer, and many
of his works have been translated into
various languages. One of his most
precious writings is the story of *Platero y
yo*, published in Madrid in 1914. Platero
was a donkey. Following is an excerpt of
this most beautiful and tender story.

Platero y yo

Platero es pequeño, *peludo*, *suave*, tan *blando* por fuera, que se diría todo de algodón, que no lleva huesos. Sólo los espejos de *azabache* de sus ojos son duros cual dos *escarabajos* de cristal negro.

Lo dejo suelto y se va al prado, y acaricia tibiamente con su *hocico*, rozándolas apenas, las florecillas rosas, celestes y gualdas... Lo llamo dulcemente: "¿Platero?", viene a mí con un *trotecillo* alegre, que parece que se ríe, en no sé qué *cascabeleo* ideal.

Come cuanto le doy. Le gustan las naranjas mandarinas, las uvas moscateles, todas de ámbar; los higos morados, con su cristalina *gotita* de miel...

To better understand this passage, here is the meaning of some key words:

peludo	hairy
suave	smooth
blando	soft
azabache	jet, as in jet black
escarabajo	beetle
hocico	snout
trotecillo	light trot
cascabeleo	jingling
gotita	little drop

Describe briefly what in your opinion is the relationship between *Platero* and the author.

PLUMA EN MANO
PEN IN HAND

La universidad de Salamanca/
The University of Salamanca

La universidad de Salamanca es la más antigua de España y la cuarta más antigua de Europa. Fue fundada por Alfonso IX en 1218 y grandemente organizada por Alfonso X en 1254. El papa (Pope) Alejandro IV confirmó su fundación en 1255. Cuenta, pues, con 787 años de fundada. La universidad se encuentra situada en el noroeste (northwest) de Madrid, en la señera (unique) ciudad de Salamanca en la región de Castilla la Vieja. Cuando Cristóbal Colón andaba gestionando (negotiating) su gran viaje, se presentó ante un consejo (council) de geógrafos de la universidad de Salamanca que le rechazó (rebuffed) su ambicioso proyecto. Uno de los más destacados eruditos (scholars) de España, Antonio de Nebrija, inició allí sus estudios a los 15 años de edad, graduándose cuatro años después. En 1475 regresó ocupando una cátedra (professorship) de retórica (rhetoric). Fue Nebrija el célebre autor de la primera gramática de la lengua española, *Gramática de la lengua castellana*, publicada en 1492, así como de dos diccionarios latino-español.

Hoy, la universidad de Salamanca es una de las principales del mundo, gozando (enjoying) del mismo prestigio que siempre la ha caracterizado. Entre sus múltiples programas se ofrecen cursos especiales para estudiantes extranjeros (foreign students). Si te interesa continuar con tus estudios de lengua española, debes (you ought to) considerar asistir a la universidad de Salamanca. No sólo (not only) aprenderás buen español pero además adquirirás un diploma que te valdrá mucho en tu futura carrera profesional.

BRAIN TICKLERS
Set # 27

Ejercicios

A. Below are three of the verbs you learned earlier in this lesson. Write a sentence in Spanish with each one in the present, and then write another sentence using the same verb in the past. All are regular verbs.
   1. aprender:
   2. estudiar:
   3. asistir:

B. Based on the passage on the preceding page, fill in the blanks:
   1. La universidad de Salamanca es la más antigua de

   _____.
   2. Está situada al _____ de Madrid.
   3. Antonio de Nebrija fue el autor de _____.
   4. Entre sus múltiples programas se ofrecen _____.

¿Cuánto sabes? Can you name two important cities of Spain?

Answers are on page 127.

ASÍ SOMOS
THIS IS WHO WE ARE

Early education in the Americas

After the Spaniards completed their first phase of conquest and exploration, a wave of missionaries from various religious orders (Franciscans and Dominicans at the beginning) made their way to America. They came with one purpose only—to convert the natives to Catholicism and to educate them according to Western beliefs and traditions.The cross and the book spread to all corners of the Americas, changing it forever. Churches, cathedrals, schools, convents for sick and abandoned women, and hospitals sprung up everywhere, laying the foundation of a new civilization. In less than 50 years, houses were built, roads opened, universities were founded, books were written and printed, institutions, libraries, botanical gardens, industries, and arts established, as well as laws enacted, called *regulamientos*. In total, seven universities were founded in the Americas before Harvard.

In North America, the Spanish missionaries led by Friar Junípero Serra founded a string of missions (21 in total) that would later become some of our greatest cities, such as Los Angeles and San Francisco. They taught the native peoples how to read and write, different methods for cultivating the land, and techniques of arts and crafts. Of our present 50 states, Spain discovered and settled almost half of them, and of the original 13 colonies, Spain was the first in establishing settlements in three of them, Virginia, South Carolina, and Georgia; of the others, it was also the first in Alabama, Arizona, Arkansas, California, Florida, Louisiana, Minnesota, New Mexico, Tennessee, and Texas.

¿**Sabías que?** The Spaniards Álvar Núñez Cabeza de Vaca, Hernando de Soto, Francisco de Coronado, and Father Juan Crispi, trekked over 100,000 miles in North America by mule or by foot.

BRAIN TICKLERS—THE ANSWERS

Set # 24, page 99

A.

1. asisto
2. estudio
3. llegar a ser
4. bachillerato
5. beca
6. escuela
7. costo
8. estudios

B.

1. estudian
2. aprendemos
3. gana
4. llego

C.

1. mathematics
2. architecture
3. engineering
4. sociology
5. calculus
6. history
7. political science
8. social sciences
9. philosophy
10. art
11. medicine
12. law
13. geography
14. psychology
15. commerce
16. biology
17. economics
18. literature
19. chemistry
20. astronomy

Set # 25, page 108

Piénsalo bien

A.

1. lave
2. trabaje
3. escribas
4. hablen
5. es

B. Answers will vary.

C.

1. V   2. V   3. F   4. F   5. V

D. Espero que mi madre compre el vestido y se lo ponga para mi graduación. Sé, sin embargo, que ella no tiene el dinero, pero es posible que lo tenga en uno o dos días. Esto es lo que prefiero que ella haga.

E.

1. ¡estudia
2. ¡cómpralo
3. ¡Bailemos!
4. ¡hablen
5. ¡No la escriban!

Set # 26, page 120

Bien vale la pena

A. Pronunciation

B.

1. vi-ña
2. u-ña
3. ca-ñón

Set # 27, page 125

Pluma en mano

A. Answers will vary.

B.

1. España
2. noroeste
3. "Gramática de la lengua castellana"
4. cursos especiales para estudiantes extranjeros

¿Cuánto sabes?

Answers will vary. Sample answer: Salamanca and Madrid.

Sin economía no hay país

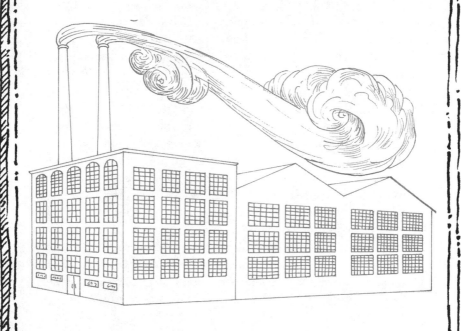

The economy is vital to every country

Todo país depende de su comercio y economía para *mantenerse a flote*, para no caer en *bancarrota*, para el buen vivir de su *ciudadanía*. Unos *sobresalen* por su industria, otros por su agricultura, otros por su técnica y muchos de ellos por sus exportaciones. ¿Qué se *requiere* para que una economía *florezca* y *se desarrolle*? Veamos.

Lo primero es un sistema político estable, democrático y de *libre empresa*; lo segundo, una infraestructura al menos adecuada: *carreteras*, acueductos, buen sistema eléctrico; lo tercero, *recursos naturales* de toda clase: minas, petróleo, gas; lo cuarto, una *fuerza trabajadora* preparada y competente; y lo quinto, organización y buenos servicios públicos y de transporte. Buenos ejemplos *de tal* economía son los Estados Unidos, en primer lugar, seguido de algunos países europeos, el Japón y la China. Hablemos en particular de Norteamérica, de la tierra de Lincoln. José Martí se refirió a ella *como* "la mayor fábrica de trabajadores libres del mundo", *y si así era* hace cien años, mucho más lo es en la actualidad. Las grandes fábricas de todo tipo y las enormes corporaciones multinacionales han alcanzado un desarrollo *nunca visto antes*. Ahora bien, debido al *alto costo de vida* y a los grandes salarios que exige el trabajador muchos negocios se han visto obligados a trasladar sus operaciones manufactureras al *extranjero*, *buscando con ello* ahorrar dinero y mantener sus productos a precios *asequibles* al consumidor. *Así*, mucho de lo que se vende hoy aquí en las grandes *tiendas por departamentos* o de descuento, *está hecho* fuera del país, mayormente en China y países como Indonesia y Guatemala. La calidad de productos es buena y los precios bajos aunque, claro, *el que sale perdiendo* es el *obrero* de esos países, al que se le paga la cuarta parte, *si acaso*, de lo que se gana aquí. O sea, que la gran fábrica a la que se refería Martí poco a poco se va *desplazando* al tercer mundo, donde *la mano de obra* es más barata. En otras palabras, unos ganan y otros pierden, relativamente hablando. La *clave*, como dijimos, es la mano de obra barata, la cual es *imprescindible* fuera o dentro del país, sobre todo para el desempeño de ciertas labores a las que el norteamericano común *les hace asco*, considerando que a su nivel profesional y económico *ya* no le corresponde hacerlas. Entra en acción el emigrante *recién llegado*, *dispuesto*, por necesidad, de *echar mano* a lo que otros *desprecian*, a trabajar en *lo que sea* por lo que se le pague.

Este ha sido siempre el *sino* del emigrante hasta que, pasado el tiempo e innumerables sacrificios, logra *superarse* y llegar a una posición digna, por lo que será siempre *merecedor* del mayor *encomio* y admiración. *El de arriba* disfruta de complacencia y exige; *el de abajo* sueña y se conforma.

Vocabulario básico

mantenerse a flote	to stay afloat
bancarrota	bankruptcy
ciudadanía	citizenship
sobresalen	stand out
requiere	requires
florezca	flourishes
se desarrolle	develops
libre empresa	free enterprise
carreteras	roads
recursos naturales	natural resources
fuerza trabajadora	workforce/manpower
de tal	of such
como	as
y si así era	and if it was that way
nunca visto antes	never seen before
alto costo de la vida	high cost of living
extranjero	overseas/abroad
buscando con ello	looking to
asequibles	affordable
Así	Thus
tiendas por departamentos	department stores
está hecho	is made
el que sale perdiendo	the one who comes out losing
obrero	laborer
si acaso	if (that much)
desplazando	moving
la mano de obra	labor
clave	key
imprescindible	indispensable
les hace asco	finds disgusting
ya	already
recién llegado	recently arrived

dispuesto	willing
echar mano	to grab
desprecian	despise
lo que sea	in whatever
sino	fate
superarse	to better onself
merecedor	worthy
encomio	praise
El de arriba	The one on top
el de abajo	the one under

BRAIN TICKLERS
Set # 28

Ejercicios

A. By looking at these words, you should know what they mean. Write the meaning of each one:

1. político
2. acueductos
3. transporte
4. europeos
5. operaciones
6. relativamente
7. común
8. innumerables

B. Traduce la palabra o las palabras entre paréntesis:

1. Muchas de las grandes corporaciones estadounidenses tienen oficinas en el (overseas).
2. (I have never before seen) tantos automóviles en las (roads).
3. Gran parte de los productos que se compran hoy día (are made) en la China.
4. Cuando mi hermano tiene hambre le (grabs) a lo que sea.
5. Estudio mucho para (to better myself).
6. Mi padre siempre está (willing) a salir con nosotros.
7. En Europa hay muchos (laborers) competentes.
8. (The aqueduct) de Segovia fue construido por los romanos.

9. Muchos países occidentales tienen (political systems) democráticos.
10. (The economy) de Estados Unidos es la más avanzada del mundo.

C. Basado en el pasaje anterior, dinos si cada una de estas afirmaciones es *verdadera o falsa*:
1. Para no caer en bancarrota, todo país tiene que mantener una buena economía.   V   F
2. La estabilidad política es imprescindible para que un país se desarrolle.   V   F
3. La China no exporta sus productos a Estados Unidos.   V   F
4. Norteamérica es la tierra de Lincoln.   V   F
5. Al emigrante recién llegado no le gusta trabajar.   V   F

Answers are on page 154.

¡Ojo!—Watch Out!

The *Inc.* of a corporation corresponds to *S.A.* in Spanish, meaning Anonymous Corporation (the *S.* stands for Society), or stock company, as in: Consumer Products, Inc.> Productos del Consumidor, S.A. A corporation means that the ownership of the business belongs to an entity, not to the individual.

PIÉNSALO BIEN
THINK IT THROUGH

The adjective. El adjetivo

Crucial in any language is the use of adjectives. The function of the adjective is to denote some degree of quality or way of being of a noun.

There are two kinds of adjectives—those that qualify the noun and those that determine it:

Qualifying the noun:

mujer buena   good woman

Determining the noun:

dos lápices   two pencils

As we said earlier, it is of the utmost importance to know that every single qualifying adjective in Spanish *must* agree in gender and number with the noun. If you want to really learn Spanish, this is one of those key things you must forever keep in mind. In terms of its positioning in a sentence, an adjective usually follows the noun in Spanish. In some cases, it may precede the noun, and by so doing, the quality of the subject is highlighted, as in

buena mujer instead of *mujer buena*

or

mal hombre instead of *hombre malo*

But, as we said, such use is infrequent.There are some masculine adjectives that when used in the singular drop their final *o*, such as: *malo, bueno, uno, alguno, ninguno*.

mal hombre	bad man
buen día	good day
un libro	one book or a book
algún año	some or one year
ningún niño	any child

In addition to the ones above, there are other adjectives, such as *grande*, that drop their last syllable before a masculine singular noun, as in:

gran profesor   great professor

Another adjective, *ciento*, as we saw earlier, becomes *cien* before the noun, as in:

cien camiones   a hundred trucks

There are cases in which an adjective can be used as a noun by preceding it with the neuter article *lo*, as in:

lo bello	the beautiful
lo sublime	the sublime
lo necesario	the necessary

Adjectives can also be used to compare the quality of nouns in terms of being superior, inferior, or equal. I can say, for example:

Superior:

Esta flor es más bonita que ésa.	This flower is prettier than that one.

Inferior:

Esta flor es menos bonita que ésa.	This flower is less pretty than that one.

Equal:

Esta flor es tan bonita como ésa.	This flower is as beautiful as that one.

For the superior, we use:

más + adjective + que	more + adjective + than

For the inferior, we use:

menos + adjective + que	less + adjective + than

For the equal, we use:

tan + adjective + como	as + adjective + as

For the superlative, we use:

más + adjective + de preceded by the definite article: *el más, la más, los más, las más*	the + the adjective ending in –est + of
Este edificio es el más alto de la ciudad.	This building is the tallest in the city.
Estos árboles son los más antiguos del parque.	These trees are the oldest in the park.

When no comparison is made in expressing the highest quality of a noun, we can do it by using *muy* or by adding *ísimo–ísima–ísimos–ísimas* to the adjective, as in:

Esta comida está muy buena.	This food is very good.
Esta comida está buenísima.	This food is very, very good.

Notice how the adjective drops the final vowel before adding –*ísimo*.

Tip: *Más* in Spanish for the superior comparison equals the suffix *-er* in English, and *el/la/los/las más* for the superlative in Spanish equals the suffix *-est* in English. Just remember that for the superior you also use *que* in Spanish, meaning *than* in English, and for the superlative you also use *de*, meaning *of* in English. For the inferior comparison, in Spanish you use *menos*, or *less* in English. The *más*, *menos* come before the adjective followed by *que*. The *el/la/los/las más* come before the adjective followed by *de*.

Some adjectives have irregular forms for the comparative and superlative, such as: *mayor* (older, oldest), *menor* (younger, youngest), *mejor* (better, best), *peor* (worse, worst). They all have plural forms. Let's look at some examples:

Carlos es mayor que Juan.	Charles is older than John.
Carlos es el mayor.	Charles is the oldest.
Isabel es menor que Emilia.	Isabel is younger than Emily.
Isabel es la menor.	Isabel is the youngest.
Mi comida es mejor que la tuya.	My food is better than yours.
Mi comida es la mejor.	My food is the best.
Esta película es peor que la otra.	This movie is worse than the other one.
Esta película es la peor.	This movie is the worst.

Mayor and *menor* are only used when referring to age.

¿Sabías que? When you are enjoying that juicy steak, thank the Spanish Franciscan missionaries for it. Christopher Columbus brought spotted Castilian range cattle to America. In 1579, a traveler in northern Mexico reported that some ranches had as many as 150,000 cows. In 1685, Spanish livestock operations had been established in East Texas, Arizona, California, and New Mexico. By 1860, Texas alone had more than three and a half million head of cattle.

BRAIN TICKLERS
Set # 29

Ejercicios

A. Here you will see five nouns and five adjectives. Make up Spanish sentences using one of each:

la nieve   las corbatas   la caja
los caballos   el papel
blanco   cuadrado   largo
pequeño   rápido

B. What is wrong with these sentences? One sentence is correct.

1. La mujer rubio llegó a la fiesta con vestido y zapatos negras.
Write it correctly:

2. El altos hombre llevaba un botas negro.
Write it correctly:

3. Cuando era niño mis padres me compraron una bicicleta roja y blanca.
Write it correctly:

C. The comparative and the superlative. Write two Spanish sentences using: *más que* and *la más de*

D. Now, write two sentences using: *mayor* and *mejor*

E. Traduce la palabra o las palabras entre paréntesis:

1. Yo soy (prettier than) mi amiga Magdalena.
2. Esta blusa es (more expensive than) que aquélla.
3. Mi amigo Manuel es (the tallest) la clase.
4. Esos niños son (the worst) del barrio.
5. Mi padre es (younger than) mi madre.

Answers are on page 154.

MÁS ES MEJOR
MORE IS BETTER

Nouns

el ingreso	income
la nómina	payroll
el valor	value
el pequeño negocio	the small business
el propietario	proprietor/owner
la tasa	rate
el mayoreo	wholesale trade
el menudeo	retail trade
el mercadeo	marketing
la publicidad	advertising
la contabilidad	accounting
la cuenta	account
la factura	invoice
las relaciones públicas	public relations
el banco	bank
la cuenta bancaria	bank account
el embarque	shipment
las finanzas	finances
el anuncio	advertisement
el archivo	file
el reciclaje	recycling
la conferencia	conference
la reunión	meeting
el puesto	job
el cajero automático	ATM
el depósito	deposit
el impuesto	tax
el descueuto	discount
el pago	payment

Verbs

negociar	to negotiate
descontar	to discount
fabricar	to manufacture
distribuir	to distribute
anunciarse	to advertise

valer	to be worth/to cost
delegar	to delegate
opinar	to give an opinion
traer	to bring
permitir	to allow/permit
conferenciar	to have a conference/to hold talks
confirmar	to confirm
aumentar	to increase

HABLA POPULAR
EVERYDAY SPEECH

Here is an important and complicated Spanish verb: *tener* (to have).

Tener is used in very common expressions where English uses *to be*. Hard as it may be to understand, in Spanish you don't say *I am hungry*, but *I have hunger*. Here are some other examples:

Tengo hambre.	I am hungry.
Tengo sueño.	I am sleepy.
Tengo frío/calor.	I am cold/hot.
Tengo miedo.	I am afraid.

When discussing how old you are in Spanish, you use *tener*, as in: *tengo veinte años* (I am twenty years old).

It doesn't help that *tener* is an irregular verb in the present, past, and future indicative, as shown below:

Present	Past	Future
tengo	tuve	tendré
tienes	tuviste	tendrás
tiene	tuvo	tendrá
tenemos	tuvimos	tendremos
tenéis	tuvisteis	tendréis
tienen	tuvieron	tendrán

Another troublesome verb in Spanish is *to be*, which can be either one of these two verbs: *ser* or *estar*. Yes, we can give you some ideas that may come in handy at times, but we can't categorically set you on a path that you can always follow.

Perhaps the best pointer we can give you is that *ser* is generally used to express permanent states, while *estar* is generally used for temporary states, as in:

Soy feliz.	I am happy.
Estoy feliz.	I am happy.

The difference here is that when I say *soy feliz*, I am denoting that I am a happy person, that it is my nature to be happy. On the other hand, *estoy feliz* denotes that I am happy about something that just happened, not that I am by nature a happy person. See if you can tell the difference in this example:

Soy un hombre feliz.	I am a happy man.
Estoy feliz porque mi hijo se casó.	I am happy because my son got married.

This may be the general rule, but there are exceptions, as, for example, when you say:

Él está muerto.	He is dead.

Being the ultimate state of permanency, here you use *estar* and not *ser*.

As indicated, *estar* is generally used with adjectives that are transitory, and also with the past participle acting as an adjective, as in

Estoy triste.	I am sad.
Estoy cansado.	I am tired.

Estar, as we already saw, is also used to form the present progessive, as in: *estoy corriendo* (I am running). *Ser* is also used as a helping verb to form the passive voice, as we saw earlier, as in *La casa fue construida por mi padre* (The house was built by my father). It is important to learn to conjugate these two verbs:

ser	*estar*
soy	estoy
eres	estás
es	está
somos	estamos
sois	estáis
son	están

Notice how irregular *ser* is and that *estar* is also irregular in the first person singular. *Ser* in the past tense is even worse, and it gets confused with the verb *ir*, which is conjugated the same in the past:

Past Tense:	**ser**	**ir**
	fui	fui
	fuiste	fuiste
	fue	fue
	fuimos	fuimos
	fuisteis	fuisteis
	fueron	fueron

The difference, of course, between one and the other is in the context, as in:

Fue una mujer amable.	She was a kind woman.
Fue a Europa el año pasado.	She/He went to Europe last year.

Here is an interesing saying in Spanish:

El que la hace la paga.	Crime doesn't pay.

¿Sabías que? Our dollar symbol ($) is derived from the Spanish *pillar* or milled dollar, the pillar or scroll design on the coin's reverse. It was used by a government clerk in 1788 and it came into general use soon thereafter. Also, during colonial times, specifically during Alexander Hamilton's era, the only legal tender generally accepted after three years was Spanish silver; in fact, you could hardly buy a loaf of bread or a bottle of milk at the time without paying in Spanish silver. That was in effect between 1792 and 1834, and after that, Spanish gold was the standard until 1857. By the way, all of that silver and gold came from the mines of Bolivia, Peru, and Mexico. What this means is that, although indirectly, we owe much to all three countries, as well as to their people for mining that silver and gold.

BRAIN TICKLERS
Set # 30

Ejercicio

Translate these four sentences into Spanish:
1. Today I am happy because it is Friday.
2. Generally I am an optimist (*optimista*), but today I am sad (*triste*).
3. He is very busy (*ocupado*) with his work.
4. Last week I visited my aunt.

Answers are on page 154.

BIEN VALE LA PENA
IT'S WELL WORTH IT

The curriculum vitae.

You may be wondering what this means—it means *résumé*. In Spanish you could also use *la hoja de vida*, or *historial de vida*, although it would be applicable only in the United States. Of course, we recommend you use *el currículum vitae* (abbreviated *CV*), or simply *vitae*, especially in the academic community.

How do you prepare your CV in Spanish?

Everybody has a different way of doing it; in other words, there is no set style in terms of contents, order, language, how long, or how short. It must include, however, certain basic information, such as personal data, education, and experience. We will give a model in Spanish, although we are mainly concerned with the information given rather than with the style used. You can change it around in any way you please.

Datos personales.

Nombre:	Federico López Suárez
Domicilio:	Avenida Los Olmos 44, 5o. dcha.
	00485 Salamanca, España
Teléf:	469 612 995
Fax:	469 612 996
Correo electrónico:	Lópezs@att.net.es

Competencia principal y preferencia:

Gerencia de ventas de todo tipo a nivel nacional o internacional. Dispuesto a trasladarse a cualquier lugar de España o del extranjero.

Estudios.

Bachiller en Letras, Colegio La Asunción, Salamanca. Graduado en 1995.
Administración de Empresas, Universidad Alcalá de Henares. Graduado en 2000.
Parte de estos estudios fueron sufragados por dos becas concedidas en 1998.

Experiencia profesional.

Exportaciones Ibéricas, S.A. Miguel de Unamuno 92, Segovia. Sub-gerente de ventas, 2000–2003. A cargo de un departamento de cinco empleados. Supervisión total de toda actividad de ventas dentro y fuera de España.

Telecomunicaciones Nacionales, S.A. Avenida América 155, Valladolid.

Gerente de ventas de 2003 hasta la fecha. Asumió el puesto para montar, organizar y dirigir el departamento de ventas de esta nueva empresa. En menos de dos años se lograron ventas que sobrepasaron los diez millones de pesetas, muchas de ellas en distintos países europeos, como Alemania e Inglaterra. La empresa recientemente fue adquirida por una poderosa empresa francesa donde se transladarán todas las operaciones. Preferiría no vivir en Francia.

Otros datos.

Ha viajado por toda España y Europa. Siendo niño residió por cuatro años en Alemania donde su padre trabajaba. Dominio del español y buen dominio del inglés, con conocimientos básicos del alemán.

Referencias por solicitud.

BRAIN TICKLERS
Set # 31

Ejercicio

Contesta esta preguntas en oraciones completas:

1. ¿Cómo te llamas? Incluye nombre y apellido.
2. ¿Cuál es tu domicilio o dónde vives? Incluye el código postal.
3. ¿Cuál es tu número de teléfono? Incluye el código de la zona.
4. ¿Cuál es tu correo electrónico?

Answers are on page 154.

¡Ojo!—Watch Out!

Llamarse in Spanish means literally *to be called*. It is a reflexive verb that means that it must be used with the reflexive pronouns, as in:

Me llamo Raimundo.	My name is Raimundo.
Ella se llama Maruja.	Her name is Maruja.

Nombre is name, especially referring to your first name, unless you are asked *¿Cuál es tu nombre completo?* (What is your full name?), in which case you would give your first and last names. You could also be asked *¿Cuál es tu nombre y apellido?* (What is your first and last name?). The question *What is your name?* in Spanish can be asked two ways:

¿Cómo te llamas?
¿Cuál es tu nombre?

Notice the use of *cómo* with *llamarse* and of *cuál* with *nombre*. Both questions ask mainly for your first name, although *¿Cómo te llamas?* can also be asking for your full name.

DILO COMO YO
SAY IT LIKE I DO

Pronunciation of the *h*

Never, never, never pronounce the *h* in Spanish. It is totally, absolutely mute, silent, as if it weren't there. It is purely an etymological letter, with no phonetic value; however, you can't leave it out in writing. It must be included always. So, these words, although written with *h*, are pronounced:

humo>	umo
hambre>	ambre
ahora>	aora
hay>	ay

Write it always, but never pronounce it.

Pronunciation Practice

Say these words out loud:

honor	historia	alcahuete	ahí
vehículo	búho	hermoso	hispano

> **¿Sabías que?** In 1735, Spanish was taught for the first time in the New York public schools, and in 1751, the first Spanish textbook was published with the title *A Short Introduction to the Spanish Language.*

ALMA HISPÁNICA
HISPANIC SOUL

Rómulo Gallegos

He is considered a master of modern Hispanic American literature and among its finest novelists. He was born in Caracas in 1884 and died there in 1969. He was married to Teotiste Arocha Egui, who died in Mexico City, where Gallegos had gone into exile. Educator, writer, and politician, he was named secretary of education in 1937 and proclaimed president of the republic in 1947, but he was overthrown by a military coup the following year. He wrote several novels—*Pobre Negro, El Último Solar, Canaima, Cantaclaro,* but his most celebrated work was *Doña Bárbara* (1929), which was translated into several languages and a movie was made by the same name, starring the famous Mexican movie star María Félix. In all of his works, but especially in *Doña Bárbara,* civilization and barbarism clashed in a struggle only too common in most Hispanic American countries. Gallegos is a true master in the description of typical landscapes and in the creation and development of his characters.

The writings of Rómulo Gallegos:

Doña Bárbara (Excerpt)

Esta mujer se entretenía enamorando hombres que después *despojaba de* sus tierras y riquezas, o simplemente los mataba. Doña Bárbara comenzó a *comportarse* así *debido a* que cuando era joven había tenido un gran amor, Asdrúbal, al cual asesinaron, comenzando así los problemas de venganza contra los hombres. En uno de sus *enamoramientos* misteriosos, Doña Bárbara estuvo con Lorenzo Barquero con el que tuvo una hija, Marisela. Luego expulsó a su hija y *amante quedándose* con las tierras de él.

To help you better understand this passage, here is the meaning of some key words.

despojaba de	stripped of
comportarse	to behave
debido a	owing to/because of
enamoramientos	infatuations
amante	lover
quedándose	taking over/keeping for herself

BRAIN TICKLERS
Set # 32

Ejercicio

Contesta estas preguntas en oraciones completas:
1. ¿Qué clase de mujer era Doña Bárbara?
2. ¿Por que se sentía así hacia (toward) los hombres?
3. ¿Con quién tuvo una hija?
4. ¿Qué le quitó a Lorenzo Barquero?
5. ¿Cómo se llamaba su hija?

Answers are on page 154.

PLUMA EN MANO
PEN IN HAND

Mi primera carta en español/
My first Spanish letter

Key words to learn:

la carta	letter
la carta personal	personal letter
la carta de negocios	business letter
la fecha	date
la firma	signature
Estimado/a	Dear (formal)
Querido/a	Dear (intimate)

Other related words:

a	to
de	from
el remitente	sender
el sello/la estampilla	postage
el correos	post office
el cartero	mailman/woman
la entrega	delivery
el correo regular	regular mail
la entrega especial	special delivery
el correo certificado	certified mail
el comprobante de entrega	proof of delivery
el papel	paper
el sobre	envelope
el paquete	package
PD	P.S.
ir a correos	to go to the post office
enviar una carta	to send a letter
recibir una carta	to receive a letter
envolver	to wrap
atar	to tie
pegar	to glue
el correo nacional	domestic mail
el correo extranjero	foreign mail

el código postal	zip code
por aéreo	air mail
por barco	by boat

Modelo de una carta sencilla en español, dirigida a una persona amiga:

La Paz, 5 de julio de 2011

Querida Paulina:

Antes que nada quiero saludarte a ti y a tu familia. Espero que todos estén bien y gozando del buen clima de Puerto Rico.

La última vez que supe (knew) de ti te preparabas para hacer un viaje a Buenos Aires, donde tienes a tus tíos. ¿Hiciste por fin (finally) el viaje? ¿Cómo están tus tíos y primos? Me dicen (they tell me) que Buenos Aires es una gran ciudad, con excelentes avenidas y restaurantes. Me gustaría visitarlo un día (one of these days).

Por aquí todo marcha (goes) como de costumbre. La Paz creciendo y empeorando (getting worse) de contaminación con más carros y más gente. Parece (it seems) que todo el país ha venido a parar (has come) a la ciudad y ya no se puede (and one cannot even) andar por las calles, aunque sigue siendo (continues to be) una ciudad encantadora y con mucha historia. ¡No la cambiaría por nada! (I wouldn't change it for anything!) Mi familia muy bien, unos trabajando y otros estudiando, como siempre (as always). Mi hermano José Alberto se gradúa pronto, y mi hermana Rosario pronto se casará, dentro de (within) unos seis meses. ¿Vienes a la boda (wedding)? Espero que sí porque tengo muchas ganas de verte.

Te dejo (I leave you) porque tengo que acompañar a mi madre al mercado.

Que estés muy bien y muchos abrazos y besos a todos de tu amiga que no te olvida (forgets you).

Marisol

PD - Espero que me escribas pronto.

¿Cuánto sabes? If I sign off a letter to a friend saying *¡Recuerdos!*, what am I saying?
If you can't come up with the answer, it means: *Regards!*

BRAIN TICKLERS
Set # 33

Ejercicios

A. Answer these questions:

1. How would you address a letter in Spanish to your cousin Bernardo?
2. And to your friend Leticia?
3. What about to a dean of a college?
4. And to your Spanish teacher?

B. Write a letter in Spanish to a good friend, telling her:

a. that you miss her (echar de menos)
b. that you are studying very hard and that you have an exam tomorrow
c. that you are planning to go on vacation to Acapulco in the summer
d. that your family is fine
e. that you have a new dog
f. that you are hoping she can visit soon and spend some time with you.

Answers are on page 154.

ASÍ SOMOS
THIS IS WHO WE ARE

The treasures of Spain

When it comes to talking about the treasures of Spain, it is very hard to decide what treasures to include, since there are just too many of them.

Spain is very old and has seen many cultures cross over from the Mediterranean to settle there. Each one left many indelible marks that have survived the passing of centuries: the Phoenicians, Greeks, Romans, and Arabs, among others. They settled in Spain at the peak of their glory with some of the greatest minds in the arts, architecture, science, and warfare. Of a long list of treasures, we have chosen the following five:

1. The Aqueduct of Segovia
2. The Alcazar of Segovia
3. The Alhambra
4. The Prado Museum
5. The Escorial

1. The Aqueduct of Segovia. El acueducto de Segovia

Segovia, Spain

Located in the city of Segovia, about one hour north of Madrid. Built by the Romans during the time of Emperor Trojan between the second half of the first century and the first half of the second, making it about 2,000 years old. It consists of 320 arches and 20,400 solid granite stone blocks, and has a length of 1,615 feet (4922 m). To build it, the Romans did not use mortar or concrete, but laid the blocks one on top of the other in perfect balance. The three central arches rise to a height of 102 feet (31 m). The fact that it was built without any mortar is most amazing and a grand testimony to the Romans' architectural genius. The aqueduct still functions today, bringing water from a distance of about 6 or 7 miles (10–12 km), starting at Fuenfría through the Río Frío.

2. The Alcazar of Segovia. El alcázar de Segovia

Segovia, Spain

This is one of the great castles of Spain and Europe. It is said that Walt Disney was so impressed with it that he used it as a model for the one he built in Walt Disney World in Florida. Indeed, it is quite similar. The castle was built in the eleventh century as a palace and later served as a military fortress. A fire nearly destroyed it in 1862, and it was extensively renovated. The Catholic monarchs of Spain, Queen Isabella of Castile and King Ferdinand of Aragón, were married there in 1469. Most of the kings of Spain, but especially those of the Trastámara dynasty, lived there at one time or another; so did Ferdinand III and Alfonso X the Wise. King Philip II took very good care of the castle and carried out major alterations. The castle sits on a high hill overlooking the Eresma and Clamores rivers. The keep, the most prominent part of the castle, was begun by John II and completed by his successor Henry IV, or perhaps even by Queen Isabella herself. The walls and ceilings are in the Mudéjar style.

3. The Alhambra of Granada. La Alhambra de Granada

Granada, Spain

This is one of the most revered and admired places in the world, a true marvel of Spain's Moorish or Islamic influence. The name *Alhambra*, from *Al Hamra*, means *The Red One* in Arabic. Washington Irving was so struck by it that he wrote his celebrated *Tales of the Alhambra* (1832) after residing in Spain between 1826 and 1829. And the Catholic monarchs of Spain, Queen Isabella and King Ferdinand, spent their honeymoon there. Not a bad choice at all; in fact, they so admired it that Queen Isabella expanded it, building a palace adjacent to the Palace of the Lions, and so did Emperor Charles V who built his own palace in the sixteenth century designed by the renowned Pedro Machuca. Most of the original construction of the Alhambra, for example, the Royal Palace and the Alcazaba, was done in the thirteenth century by Mohammed V, together with his father Yusuf I. Its two huge square towers, the Torre del Homenaje (the Keep) and Torre de la Vela (Watchtower) are visible from far away. The Alhambra stands on hilly ground overlooking the city of Granada with the Sierra Nevada in the background. Inside, one stands in wonder, admiring, among many other intricate designs and decorations, the walls clad half in tiles and stucco. The gardens and courtyards, especially the Generalife, mostly built after the Reconquest, and Patio de los Leones add to the striking beauty of the complex. In the Sala de Embajadores it is believed that King Boaddil surrendered Granada to the Catholic monarchs in 1492.

4. The Prado Museum. El museo del Prado

Madrid, Spain

Unquestionably one of the world's  finest museums, it houses the master-pieces of such classic greats as Velázquez, Goya, El Greco, Murillo, Zurbarán, Rembrandt, Rubens, Titian, and Botticelli, among many others. Part of the great Italian paintings collection was brought in by Velázquez himself from Rome and Venice, as he had pledged King Philip IV he would do. In all, eleven Spanish kings in a period of three centuries were instrumental in the acquisition of most of the collection, including Philip II. Despite Spain's great power all over the world, none of the paintings was looted or taken by force (as was the case in many other European museums), but each one was purchased or acquired as gifts or through inheritance. The gallery alone holds 8,600 paintings from all over the world, as well as thousands of sculptures, furniture, jewelry, and coins, from the sixth to the nineteenth centuries. The museum was begun under the reign of King Charles III, who was responsible for embellishing most of Madrid, and was inaugurated on November 19, 1819. It is located on one of Madrid's finest boulevards, El Paseo del Prado, from which the name of the museum was taken. Behind the museum is the Monastery of San Jerónimo el Real. Here at the Prado you can admire, for hours on end, the great works of Velázquez (widely considered one of the greatest painters of all time), such as *Las Meninas* (The Maids of Honor), *Las Lanzas o La Rendición de Breda* (The Surrender of Breda), *Las Hilanderas* (The Fable of Arachne), the magnificent portraits of Prince Baltasar Carlos and the Infanta Margarita, and Goya, especially, his two Majas.

5. The Escorial. El Escorial

El Escorial, Spain

Often called the Eighth Wonder of the World, the Escorial is primarily a palace, church, monastery, mausoleum, college, library, and art gallery. It is located in the Sierra de Guadarrama, about 27 miles (45 km) northwest of Madrid. Its proper name is Real Monasterio de San Lorenzo del Escorial, taking the name, Escorial from the small town in the vicinity. It was built by King Philip II to commemorate the Spanish victory over the French at the Battle of San Quintín in 1557. The original architect was Juan Bautista de Toledo, who was succeeded by Juan de Herrera when he died in 1567. King Charles III built an addition to it. The structure was devastated by two fires and looted by French troops in 1807. It occupies an area of about 500,000 square feet with four main facades. The principal front is 744 feet long and 72 feet high (227×22 m), and each of the four towers rises about 200 feet (61 m). Adjacent to it is the Monastery of Saint Laurence, served since 1885 by the Augustinians. Philip II, whose quarters were very small, died there. Through an opening in the wall he could see the celebration of mass when he was ill. In the mausoleum, or Crypt of Kings, are entombed every Spanish king since Charles V, as well as the only Queen, Queen Isabella II. Other members of the royal family are entombed in crypt rooms nearby. One of the greatest jewels of the Escorial is its library, housing some 7,000 engravings, 35,000 books, including 4,627 Greek, Latin, Arabic, and Hebrew manuscripts, among them an illuminated copy of the Gospels and the Apocalypse of Saint John. Many of the tapestries were designed by Goya, and its gallery holds masterpieces by such greats as Velázquez, Tintoretto, Pantoja, Zurbarán, and Titian.

BRAIN TICKLERS—THE ANSWERS

Set # 28, page 132

A.
1. politician
2. aqueducts
3. transportation
4. Europeans
5. operations
6. relatively
7. common
8. innumerable

B.
1. extranjero
2. Nunca he visto antes carreteras
3. están hechos
4. echa mano
5. mejorarme
6. dispuesto
7. trabajadores
8. El acueducto
9. sistemas políticos
10. La economía

C.
1. V   2. V   3. F   4. V   5. F

Set # 29, page 137

Piénsalo bien
A. Answers will vary.
B.
1. La mujer rubia llegó a la fiesta con vestido y zapatos negros.
2. El hombre alto llevaba unas botas negras.
3. Correct.
C. Answers will vary.
D. Answers will vary.

E.
1. más bonita que
2. más cara que
3. el más alto de
4. los peores
5. más joven que

Set # 30, page 141

Habla popular
1. Hoy estoy contento porque es viernes.
2. Por lo general soy optimista, pero hoy estoy triste.
3. Está muy ocupado con su trabajo.
4. La semana pasada visité a mi tía.

Set # 31, page 143

Bien vale la pena
Answers will vary.

Set # 32, page 146

Alma hispánica
1. Answers will vary.
2. Answers will vary.
3. Lorenso Barquero
4. sus tierras
6. Marisela

Set # 33, page 149

Pluma en mano
A. Answers will vary.
B. Answers will vary.

Cuatro ruedas para todo

Four wheels for everything

Desde que se inventó *la rueda*, hace miles de años, *el ser humano* ha preferido *montar* en ella que caminar. Claro que *no fue* hasta entrado el siglo XIX que realmente *se valió de ella como medio de* transporte. Anteriormente era el camello, el caballo, hasta el burro y la llama; hoy lo es el automóvil, el autobús, el tren, el camión, hasta el avión con las que *despega y aterriza*. Se depende tanto de ellas que para *hasta ir* a la esquina a comprar comida, o a la farmacia, a comprar algún medicamento, preferimos hacerlo en cuatro ruedas.

Realmente, en los últimos cincuenta años la explosión del uso del automóvil ha sido extraordinaria. Hoy conduce todo el mundo, desde el más joven hasta el más anciano *y se hace*, mayormente, por la enorme *ventaja* de que el automóvil *nos libera*, nos da *alas* para transladarnos *de un lugar a otro* nosotros mismos, sin *contar* con nadie. Todo lo que tenemos que hacer es darle a la llave *y allá vamos* a donde *nos parezca* y tomándonos el tiempo que más *nos convenga*. Claro que el *conducir* requiere una gran responsabilidad, pues no sólo tenemos que *tener cuidado* de nosotros mismos, sino que *hay que* estar pendiente del otro *conductor*, del otro automóvil. Tenemos, además, que observar todas *las señales* de tráfico, conducir sensatamente, no marchar a alta velocidad y nunca, nunca, conducir si estamos cansados, con sueño, o si nos hemos tomado licor. De hacerlo, arriesgamos tener un accidente que puede ser fatal para nosotros y para otros. Conducir, también, *conlleva* un alto costo que nos *chupa* gran parte del dinero que ganamos, como son los pagos del automóvil que hay que hacer, sobre todo si es nuevo, seguro, gasolina, y mantenimiento. Todo esto resulta carísimo y cada día aumentan más todos los costos, obligando a la persona a trabajar más, a ganar más dinero, pues *las cuentas* vienen todos los meses y hay que pagarlas. Todos queremos un coche nuevo, *de paquete, como se dice*, y en el que se pueda *confiar*. A nadie le gusta un *cacharro* que nos dé problemas y *nos humille* cuando nos vean por ahí. Mientras más caro y más lujoso, mejor, aun si nos da cinco millas por galón, como los SUVs, verdaderos *tragagasolina*, o los carros *de marca* importados, como el Mercedes o BMW. A todos nos gusta *presumir*, que piense la gente que somos gente solvente y de grandes recursos, millonarios, aunque la verdad sea otra. Como dice el refrán, *las apariencias engañan. Vamos a ver* en *qué parará todo esto* en la próxima década, con más coches en la carretera, con más *tapones o tranques*, y con más *humo viciado* que tendremos que respirar. *No extrañe que*, como en la China, volvamos a la bicicleta o aún quizá al burro.

Vocabulario básico

la rueda	wheel
el ser humano	human being
montar	to ride
no fue	it wasn't
se valió de ella	used it
como medio de	as a means of
despega y aterriza	takes off and lands
hasta ir	even to go
y se hace	and it is done
ventaja	advantage
nos libera	frees us
alas	wings
de un lugar a otro	from one place to another
contar	to rely
y allá vamos	there we go
nos parezca	pleases us
nos convenga	that is more convenient for us
conducir	to drive
tener cuidado	to be careful
hay que	one must
conductor	driver
las señales	signs
conlleva	to entail
chupa	takes away
las cuentas	bills
de paquete	brand new
como se dice	as they say
confiar	to trust
cacharro	clunker
nos humille	humiliates us
tragagasolina	gas guzzlers
de marca	make/well-known make
presumir	to show off
las apariencias engañan	appearances can be deceiving
Vamos a ver	Let's see
en qué parará	how this will end
tapones	bottlenecks
tranques	traffic jams
humo viciado	foul smoke
No extrañe que	Don't be surprised

¡Ojo!—Watch Out!

There are two verbs in Spanish for drive: *conducir* and *manejar*. In the present indicative, *conducir* is conjugated like *conocer* (to know someone), irregular in the first person singular: *conduzco* (I drive). For driver, you can use *conductor* o *chofer*.

BRAIN TICKLERS
Set # 34

Ejercicios

A. By looking at these words, you should know what they mean. Write the meaning of each one:

1. inventó
2. transporte
3. camello
4. corporación
5. accidente
6. mantenimiento
7. lujoso
8. millonarios
9. década
10. bicicleta

B. Traduce la palabra o las palabras entre paréntesis:
1. Yo también tengo (four wheels) sin las que no puedo vivir.
2. En los aeropuertos se ven muchos aviones (take off and land).
3. A mí no me gusta (to drive) en la ciudad.
4. El carro de mis padres es (brand new), pero el de mi hermano es (a clunker).
5. Hoy en día (one must work more) (to make more money).

C. Basado en el pasaje, dinos si cada una de estas afirmaciones es *verdadera o falsa*:

1. El automóvil nos da mucha libertad de desplazamiento.   V   F
2. Hoy hay muchos más automóviles que hace un siglo (century).   V   F
3. En las carreteras se ven hoy pocos camiones.   V   F
4. Un coche de lujo cuesta poco dinero.   V   F
5. Nos gusta que la gente piense que somos millonarios.   V   F

Answers are on page 173.

¿Sabías que? How much is Florida worth? The United States paid $15 million for Louisiana, $7 million for Alaska, and nothing for Florida, which was ceded by Spain in 1819. Although a treaty was signed to cede Florida for $5 million, Spain was never paid. But even if the $5 million had been paid, think of what $27 million bought—about one third of the continental United States! This is what a CEO of a large corporation makes in one year, or what a leading Hollywood star makes for one movie. And if you add to all this the big chunk of land ceded by Mexico to the United States, it becomes the biggest real estate deal in history!

PIÉNSALO BIEN
THINK IT THROUGH

The adverb. El adverbio

What the adverb does is simply to modify the verb, just like an adjective modifies the noun, as in:

Él camina despacio.	He walks slowly.
Él no actúa bien.	He doesn't act properly.

That is their main function. However, they can also modify an adjective or another adverb, as in:

Él es muy alto.   He is very tall.

Here *muy* (very) is an adverb modifying an adjective, *alto* (tall) but in:

Él camina muy despacio.   He walks very slowly.

Muy (very), an adverb, modifies another adverb, *despacio* (slowly).

But again, as we said, the main function of an adverb is to modify a verb, and this is what you should really know and remember well.

Many phrases also function as adverbs and are called adverbial phrases or clauses, as:

al amanacer	at dawn
en fin	well
por último	at last
tal vez	perhaps

There are several kinds of adverbs. Here are the most common:

Of place:

aquí	here	*lejos*	far
allí	there	*dentro*	inside
allá	over there	*fuera*	outside
cerca	close		

Of time:

hoy	today	*antes*	before
ayer	yesterday	*después*	after
mañana	tomorrow		

Of manner:

bien	well	*fácilmente*	easily
mal	bad	*así*	thus
despacio	slowly		

Of quantity:

más	more	*poco*	little
mucho	a lot/much	*tanto*	so/so much
bastante	enough		

Of order:

sucesivamente	successively
primeramente	first of all
últimamente	recently/lately

Of affirmation:

sí	yes
también	also
ciertamente	certainly

Of negation:

no	no	*jamás*	never
nunca	never	*tampoco*	either

Of doubt:

quizá/quizás   maybe/perhaps

Many adverbs in Spanish are formed by adding *-mente* to the adjective, as in

claramente	clearly
fácilmente	easily
normalmente	normally/usually

Thus *-mente* generally equals the English *-ly*. If the adjective is masculine, ending in *-o*, you must change the *o* to *a* as in *lento> lentamente* (slow/slowly).

BRAIN TICKLERS
Set # 35

Ejercicios

A. Give the adverbs for the following adjectives:

1. apurado	4. igual
2. difícil	5. misteriosa
3. duro	

B. Using any of the adverbs given above (of place, time, etc.), make five sentences with each.

C. Tell how many adverbs are in this sentence and write them below:

Salimos al amanecer para llegar muy temprano.
A total of _____ adverbs.

Answers are on page 173.

MÁS ES MEJOR
MORE IS BETTER

Nouns

el volante/timón	steering wheel
el freno	brake
el freno de mano	hand brake
el acelador	gas pedal
el cambio	shift
el asiento	seat
el cinturón de seguridad	seat belt
la bolsa de aire	air bag
el baúl/maletero	trunk
el parabrisas	windshield
la licencia de conducir	driver's license
la placa	plate
la matrícula/registración	registration
el semáforo	traffic light
la multa	fine/ticket
el peatón	pedestrian
el cruce	crossing
a la derecha	to the right
a la izquierda	to the left
la señal de alto	stop sign
la velocidad	speed
el peaje	toll
el choque	crash
el espejo retrovisor	rearview mirror
las luces	lights
el tablero	dashboard
la autopista	freeway
el parqueo/estacionamiento	parking
el garage	garage
la gasolinera	gas station
el asiento	seat
el baúl	trunk
el mecánico	mechanic

Verbs

acelerar	to accelerate/speed up
frenar	to brake
parar	to stop
retroceder	to back up/go backward
doblar/virar	to turn
seguir	to continue (ahead)
ceder	to yield
ceder el paso	to yield the right of way
aparcar/parquear/estacionarse	to park

¡Ojo!—Watch Out!

The word *parking* is commonly used in Spain's larger cities, just like *patio* and *plaza* are commonly used in the United States. Of the three Spanish words, *aparcar, parquear,* and *estacionarse,* the latter is the most commonly used. The same occurs with *car> carro, auto, automóvil, coche, máquina.* When in doubt, use *automóvil.* Another tricky word is *computer> computadora, computador, ordenador.* The first one is your best choice. *Carretera* in Spanish is any kind of a road, which in the United States is far from true—*road, roadway, freeway, speedway, highway, turnpike,* etc. *Autopista* is also used for what is in the United States a four-lane highway.

HABLA POPULAR EVERYDAY SPEECH

Here are more idioms, expressions, and sayings:

no sea que	or else
ni siquiera	not even
luego que	as soon as
junto con	together with
en realidad	as a matter of fact
el caso es	the fact is

en particular	especially
dado que	supposing/given that
por poco	almost
de segunda mano	secondhand
quedar en	to agree on
al rato	shortly
pagar a plazos	to pay in installments
no hay remedio	there's nothing we can do
tener agallas	to have guts
tener en cuenta	to take into account
andar por las nubes	to be on cloud nine
¡socorro!/¡auxilio!	help!
Nunca es tarde si la dicha es buena.	Better late than never.

¿Sabías que? Who discovered Hawaii? To the English it was James Cook in 1778. To the Spaniards, it was Juan de Gaitán in 1555, based on a map by Ortelius and Mercator where Hawaii is called *Desgraciada* (Unfortunate), and on a Spanish map (now at the Naval Museum in Madrid), noting that Hawaii was discovered by Juan de Gaitán. Also, when he got there, Cook found a piece of Spanish armor now preserved at the British Museum.

BIEN VALE LA PENA
IT'S WELL WORTH IT

The job interview. La entrevista de trabajo

E> entrevistador (interviewer)
T> Tú (you)

T: Buenos días.
E: Buenos días.
T: ¿Cómo está usted?
E: Bien, ¿y usted?
T: Muy bien, gracias.
E: Usted es el Sr. Hernán Fernández, ¿no?
T: Así es.

E: ¿Y la posición que le interesa es la de gerente de ventas?

T: Sí, señor.

E: ¿Trajo su currículum vitae?

T: Sí, señor. Aquí lo tiene.

E: ¿Se graduó de la universidad?

T: Sí, hace cuatro años.

E: ¿Qué estudió?

T: Administración de empresas.

E: Veo que ha tenido bastante experiencia en este campo.

T: Más de diez años en total.

E: ¿Por qué dejó su último empleo?

T: La empresa se trasladó a Francia.

E: ¿Qué sueldo tiene pensado ganar?

T: ¿Cuánto paga esta posición?

E: $45,000 al año, más beneficios. ¿Qué le parece?

T: Más o menos lo que yo pensaba.

E: Déjeme darle algunos datos de esta empresa. La empresa se especializa en la manufactura, venta y distribución de artículos del hogar y lleva de fundada treinta años. Es una empresa de propiedad familiar, dirigida por el hijo del fundador, el Sr. Gutiérrez, que es el presidente de la Junta Directiva. La ventas anuales sobrepasan los diez millones de dólares y sus productos se venden por todo el mundo, principalmente en Sur América. Contamos sucursales en México, Puerto Rico, y Argentina. Ahora, en cuanto a su responsabilidad, dado que se le ofreciera este trabajo, sería la de administrar todo lo relacionado con las ventas, para lo cual tendría que viajar a menudo. ¿Tiene usted alguna objeción a esto?

T: No, señor, me encanta viajar y conozco muy bien esos países que ha mencionado más otros muchos. Durante un tiempo me pasé casi tres meses viajando por el continente.

E: Eso es algo a su favor. ¿Qué idiomas habla además del español?

T: Bien bien, el inglés, con algunos conocimientos de italiano.

E: ¿No habla portugués?

T: Algo, pero no mucho. También estuve en Brasil.

E: Me parece que es usted un buen candidato para esta posición, aunque no le puedo garantizar nada. Aún tenemos que entrevistar a otros candidatos.

T: Lo comprendo perfectamente. ¿Cuándo me avisarían?

E: Calcule en dos o tres semanas; se le llamaría por teléfono en caso de que la empresa estuviera interesada en sus servicios. ¡Ah, antes de que se me olvide! ¿Nos puede proporcionar algunas referencias?

T: Sí, señor. Aquí tiene los nombres.

E: Pues bien, Sr. Fernández, ha sido un placer en conocerle y ojalá que todo salga bien para usted. Le agradezco su interés en nuestra empresa y le deseo mucha suerte. Nos vemos pronto, espero…

T: El gusto ha sido mío. Quedo pendiente de sus noticias. Hasta luego.

BRAIN TICKLERS
Set # 36

Ejercicios

A. Conteste estas preguntas en oraciones completas:
1. ¿Cómo se llama el solicitante (applicant)?
2. ¿Qué tiempo hace que se graduó el solicitante de la universidad?
3. ¿Por qué dejó su último empleo?
4. ¿A qué se dedica la empresa?
5. ¿Dónde tiene sucursales (branches)?
6. ¿Cree usted que el entrevistador está interesado en darle la posición al solicitante? ¿Por qué sí o por qué no?
7. ¿Cómo se le avisa al solicitante si se le va a ofrecer el puesto?

B. Give the meaning of these words/phrases:

1. Aquí lo tiene	6. me pasé
2. Veo que	7. Algo
3. Más o menos	8. en caso de que
4. Junta Directiva	9. perfectamente
5. dado que	10. semana

Answers are on page 173.

¡Ojo!—Watch Out!

Even though many Hispanic countries have their own units of currency, others, such as Colombia, Chile, Argentina, Mexico, Cuba, the Dominican Republic, and Uruguay, use *peso* as their standard unit of currency. *Peso* means weight in Spanish, and during colonial times it consisted of a piece worth eight reales, which later became the *peso*. Some of the units of currency of the other countries are: *sol* (Peru), *bolívar* (Venezuela), *balboa* (Panamá), *córdoba* (Nicaragua), *boliviano* (Bolivia), *colón* (El Salvador, Costa Rica), *lempira* (Honduras), *euro* (Spain). In Ecuador it used to be *sucre*, but it is now the dollar. Keep in mind, however, that according to the Associated Press, South America is heading for the establishment of a single unit of currency, just as happened in Europe.

DILO COMO YO
SAY IT LIKE I DO

Pronunciation of the x, y, z

The *x* in Spanish is pronounced as in English between vowels (ks), and as *s* before a consonant, as in: *examen, expreso*.

The *y*, before a vowel, is pronounced similarly to the English *y* in *yes*. The conjunction *y* (and), and the *y* at the end of a syllable are pronounced like *i*, as in: *Juana y Pedro, mamey*.

The *z* is always pronounced *s* in Hispanic America, while in most of Spain it is pronounced like the English *th* in *three, think*: *cruzar, zapato*.

Pronunciation Practice

Say these words out loud:

yodo	yuca	yunque	yegua	yarda
yo y tú	yema y yeso	yerno y yerna	yogurt y yerba	
caray	soy	batey	Camagüey	estoy

ALMA HISPÁNICA
HISPANIC SOUL

Antonio Machado

Here is a man who shines in Spanish letters, a poet with so much sensitiviy that it sends shivers down your spine when you read his work. The purest of pure lyricism, the language of the soul at its finest. If you appreciate poetry, Machado will forever be one of your favorites.

He was born in Seville in 1875 and died in a small town in France, Colliure, in 1939, near the end of the Spanish Civil War. In fact, he left Spain with his mother and other relatives (as well as many other Spanish refugees) that year, and died a few days before his mother. He lived in Paris where he worked at the Garnier House. He then returned to Spain, to Soria, where he married his beloved Leonor in 1909, when she was 16. In 1911, they traveled to Paris where Leonor fell ill and returned to Soria where she died in 1912. From that moment on, Machado was a different man. His life has been shattered by his wife's unexpected death. He longed for the years past and the love they both shared.

The writings of Antonio Machado

Señor, ya me arrancaste lo que más quería
oye otra vez, Dios mío, mi corazón clamar
tu voluntad se hizo, Señor, contra la mía,
Señor ya estamos solos mi corazón y el mar.

Ayer soñé que veía
a Dios y que a Dios hablaba;
y soñé que Dios me oía...
Después soñé que soñaba.

Anoche soñé que oía
a Dios, gritándome: ¡Alerta!
Luego era Dios quien dormía
y yo gritaba: ¡despierta!

To help you better understand the poems, here is the meaning of some key words:

oye	listen	*soñé*	dreamed
clamar	clamor	*oía*	heard
voluntad	wish	*gritándome*	yelling (to me)
solos	alone	*Luego*	later
mar	sea	*dormía*	slept

Review

A. Review the three poems. In the first poem, what is Machado inferring?

B. What about in the other two?

PLUMA EN MANO
PEN IN HAND

La contaminación ambiental/Air pollution

Si nos ponemos a pensar, respiramos veneno (poison) en todo momento de nuestras vidas. A pesar de (despite) todo lo que digan, de todas las leyes y regulaciones (laws and regulations) de las que se habla (what they say), de todos los grupos que protestan, cada día la contaminación ambiental o polución se agrava. Nadie la puede contener (It can't be contained) y en poco la pueden mejorar (improve) por la sencilla razón (simply) del progreso que se nos viene encima (that overwhelms us). El hollín (soot) de las grandes fábricas, los gases que despiden (emit) los automóviles y otros vehículos de motor, la niebla tóxica (smog) que nos envuelve y poco a poco nos van acabando (doing us harm), contribuyendo enormemente a infinitas enfermedades y trastornos que nos aquejan (afflict us). Y no solamente debemos preocuparnos por lo que respiramos, sino de igual forma por lo que comemos, por lo que metemos en la boca (what we put in our mouth) y todo producto que compramos para limpiar, para desinfectar, para embellecernos, y no dejemos fuera (leave out) los materiales para la construcción, como pinturas, barnices, pegamentos (glues), etc. Nadie quiere volver a los tiempos de las cavernas (cave times), ni vivir en la selva (jungle) a lo (like) Tarzán, pero sí pedimos y esperamos que se nos considere y se nos cuide, que se nos proteja, y que no se ande con tanta mentira (lie) para embaucarnos (trick us). Esperamos que todo esto no se haga a propósito (on purpose) para que nos sigamos enfermando y salgan ganando aún más (gaining even more) las grandes corporaciones farmacéuticas y todo el sistema de cuidado médico del país.

BRAIN TICKLERS
Set # 37

Ejercicios

A. Choose five words/idioms from the list below and write a Spanish sentence with each:

pensar   en todo momento
contaminación ambiental   nadie
mentira   preocuparse   a propósito

B. Give the infinitive forms of the following verbs from the passage:
1. ponemos   4. pedimos
2. protestan   5. haga
3. pueden

C. Of the verbs from **Ejercicio B** above, give the *I* form (1st person singular) of the indicative for each.

D. Write three sentences in Spanish about the dangers of today's air pollution.

Answers are on page 173.

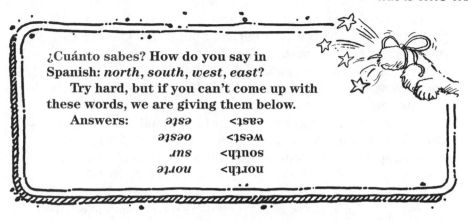

¿Cuánto sabes? How do you say in Spanish: *north, south, west, east*?

Try hard, but if you can't come up with these words, we are giving them below.

Answers:

east>	*este*
west>	*oeste*
south>	*sur*
north>	*norte*

ASÍ SOMOS
THIS IS WHO WE ARE

The treasures of Mexico

Mexico is a unique country, so unique that it stands alone in the community of nations, a rose in a garden, the sun in the sky. And it is all because of its history, for what it was and for what it could one day be again.

Mexico's real treasure is its people, a mix of the finest of two civilizations fused together by destiny—the Aztecs and the Spanish, each giving to the other the very essence of their existence, sometimes by force, mostly at the beginning, sometimes willingly once they gained a better knowledge and understanding of their fateful encounter. Every city, every town, every corner in Mexico exudes its glorious past and attests to its greatness in the human pursuit of perfection. An imposing cathedral is in the heart of Mexico City in what is known as the *Zócalo*, the largest square in all of Hispanic America. The Zócalo was built by the Spaniards on what used to be the Aztec seat of government, religion, and life of more than 80 magnificent structures such as temples, buildings, and palaces, all built by the Aztecs when they settled there in the beginning of the fourteenth century. The cathedral was begun in 1572, and it took an amazing 250 years

to complete, being one of the largest in the world. Adjoining the cathedral is the National Palace, built in 1693, where the president of Mexico resides. The National Palace occupies the same site as the former palace of the emperor Moctezuma. The frescoes of Mexico's greatest painter, Diego Rivera, which took him six years to complete, can be seen everywhere within the palace's walls. Also adjoining the cathedral and palace is the church of *El Sagrario*, built in 1749, in a perfect Baroque style, or more specifically, Churrigueresque style, typical of many Hispanic American structures. It's in Mexico City, but if you go to some of the other cities, such as Guadalajara, Taxco, Cuernavaca, Jalisco, Oaxaca, you will also be transported in time and be totally convinced of Mexico's greatness; that includes also the food, and the customs and, most definitely, as we said, the people and their unique way of life. And then there are the pyramids of Teotihuacán and Tula, the ancient Toltec city, where the glory of pre-Columbus Mexico can be seen at its highest, and the Aztec calendar, one of the many calendars of Mesoamerica, consisting of a 365-day cycle and a 260-day ritual cycle, which combined formed a 52-year century. The solar calendar of 365 days consisted of 18 months of 20 days each, with an additional period of 5 to 6 days added at the end. It was discovered in 1790 near the Great Aztec Temple in the Mexican capital.

BRAIN TICKLERS—THE ANSWERS

Set # 34, page 158

A.
1. invented
2. transportation
3. camel
4. corporation
5. accident
6. maintenance
7. luxurious
8. millionaires
9. decade
10. bicycle

B.
1. cuatro ruedas
2. despegar y aterrizar
3. conducir/manejar
4. de paquete–un cacharro
5. hay que trabajar más – para ganar más dinero.

C.
1. V   2. V   3. F   4. F   5. V

Set # 35, page 161

Piénsalo bien
A.
1. apuradamente
2. difícilmente
3. duramente
4. igualmente
5. misteriosamente

B. Answers will vary.

C.
3—al amanecer—muy—temprano

Set # 36, page 166

Bien vale la pena
A.
1. El solicitante se llama Hernán Fernández.
2. Hace cuatro años que se graduó.
3. Dejó su último empleo porque la empresa se trasladó a Francia.
4. La empresa se dedica a la manufactura, venta y distribución de artículos del hogar.
5. Tiene sucursales en México, Puerto Rico y Argentina.
6. Answer will vary.
7. llamándole por teléfono.

B.
1. Here it is
2. I see that
3. More or less
4. Board of Directors
5. supposing/given that
6. I spent
7. Something
8. in case
9. perfectly
10. week

Set # 37, page 170

Pluma en mano
A. Answers will vary.

B.
1. poner   4. pedir
2. protestar   5. hacer
3. poder

C.
1. pongo   4. pido
2. protesto   5. hago
3. puedo

D. Answers will vary.

No hay mejor educación que el viajar

Traveling is the best education

El mundo es amplio, maravilloso, *sorprendente*. Hay tanto que ver, tanto que aprender, que nadie puede permanecer entre las cuatro paredes de su pueblo o ciudad, *sin echar al menos un vistazo* a lo que está fuera de nuestra frontera. Pero, como todo en la vida, hay que saber viajar, saber *lo que se va a ver* y el porqué. Como primer paso, hay que apartarse de las grandes zonas metropolitanas y seguir una *pauta* distinta a la del turista común. *Nada de* hoteles de lujo o caravanas a los *lugares de interés* en los que *se ve y no se ve*, en los que se aprende y no se aprende. Tampoco hay que viajar como un *vagabundo*, con una maleta *a cuestas* y *deambular* de un lado para otro. No. Todo país, todo rincón de la tierra tiene su *encanto* y algo único que *mostrar*, y mejor es hacerlo con alguien querido al lado, *se quiere decir*, *mezclándose* con la gente y aprendiendo de ella *de viva voz* y no de un guía turístico, y contando con tiempo, el que sea, para poder absorber y apreciar lo que *se tiene delante* sin que nadie *nos lo empañe*. A Europa, por ejemplo, no se va buscando hamburguesas y papas fritas, *como no* se viene a Estados Unidos buscando un *cocido* o una *sopa de lentejas*. Cada país es que como es, y *da lo que da* y no hay que ir buscando otras cosas que, si bien existen donde vivimos regularmente, no tiene por qué haberlas en otras partes. *Ya sabemos* de la globalización, y que en Roma, Madrid, o Viena, hay McDonald's y puede tomarse Coca-Cola. ¿Pero *a quién se le ocurre* ir a París y comerse un Big Mac, o a Lisboa y tomar leche con la comida? Una señora viajó una vez a París y vino *quejándose* de que no había podido comer frijoles negros ni *platanitos maduros*, razón por la cual *juró* nunca más volver allí. O el turista norteamericano que va a Barcelona y se queja de que en el hotel no había jacuzzi, o que servían el almuerzo a las 3 en vez de a las 12, o que *había ternera* y no *carne de res*. Cada país tiene sus costumbres y reglas, y al que no le guste *con quedarse en casa tiene*.

Con el viajar se nos amplía nuestra perspectiva del mundo y de la vida, quizá *en mayor grado* que en la escuela, pues lo que aprendemos no es teoría ni *a través* de fotos o películas, sino que es el verdadero *aprendizaje* que nos entra por nuestros *propios* ojos y oídos. No es igual que se nos hable de México, que ver a México, como no es igual que se nos hable del Cañón del Colorado, que verlo. Y si lo que realmente nos interesa es aprender un nuevo idioma, el que sea, estando en el país que se habla por cierto tiempo, lo aprenderemos más rápido y mejor que en 100 horas en el laboratorio de lenguas. Adónde viajar? No hay país feo *ni en el que no* se aprenda algo distinto, algo que nos instruya. Claro que hay algunos más interesantes que otros, pero todo dependerá de lo que cada cual *busque* y le interese. El itinerario de un viaje interesante *para los* que viven en Estados Unidos, sería comenzar en Egipto, después Grecia, Italia, España, Inglaterra y, *de regreso* a América, parar unos días en Lima y después en México. Se necesitarían dos meses y algo de dinero, pero la experiencia sería *inolvidable*.

Vocabulario básico

sorprendente	surprising
sin echar al menos un vistazo	without at least taking a look
lo que se va a ver	what one will see
pauta	norm
Nada de	No
lugares de interés	places of interest
se ve y no se ve	one can see and not see
vagabundo	vagabond
a cuestas	on one's shoulders
deambular	to wander
encanto	charm
mostrar	to show
se quiere decir	that's to say
mezclándose	mingling
de viva voz	personally
se tiene delante	one has in front/one can see
nos lo empañe	fogs it over for us
como no	like one doesn't
cocido	Spanish stew with meat and chick-peas
sopa de lentejas	lentil soup
da lo que da	and offers what it can
Ya sabemos	We already know
a quién se le ocurre	who in his/her right mind
quejándose	complaining
platanitos maduros	fried plantains
juró	swore

había ternera	there was veal
carne de res	beef
con quedarse en casa tiene	can stay home
en mayor grado	to a greater degree
a través	through
aprendizaje	learning
propios	own
ni en el que no	neither one in which
busque	looks for
para los	for those
de regreso	on the way back
inolvidable	unforgettable

¿Sabías que? About 30 percent of U.S. geographical names are Spanish or were designated Spanish names when they were first discovered. And no less than 2,000 U.S. cities also have Spanish names.

BRAIN TICKLERS
Set # 38

Ejercicios

A. By looking at these words you should know what they mean. Write the meaning of each one.

1. frontera
2. zonas
3. turista
4. único
5. guía
6. hamburguesas
7. regularmente
8. partes
9. frijoles
10. teoría

B. Traduce la palabra o las palabras entre paréntesis.
1. (There is so much to see) en México.
2. De vez en cuando hay que salir. No se puede estar siempre entre (four walls).
3. A mí no me gustan los (tourist guides).
4. (Where we live) hay muchos parques.

5. Para apreciar bien el Cañón de Colorado hay que (see it) en persona.
6. Yo siempre tomo (milk) con las comidas.
7. Una (custom) típica de España es dormir la siesta.
8. Al viajar se debe tener un buen (itinerary).
9. A mis padres les gustaría mucho visitar (Italy).
10. Y a mis tíos les gustaría mucho visitar (England).

C. Basado en el pasaje anterior, dinos si cada una de estas afirmacioanes es *verdadera o falsa*:

1. Al viajar debe uno apartarse de las zonas metropolitanas.   V   F
2. Es mejor visitar los lugares de interés solo.   V   F
3. A los norteamericanos no les gustan las papas fritas.   V   F
4. En Barcelona se sirve el almuerzo a las doce.   V   F
5. Ningún país es feo.   V   F

D. Give the Spanish for the following:

1. to travel   4. to serve
2. to see   5. to depend
3. to drink/take

Answers are on page 193.

¡Ojo!—Watch Out!

Ir de paseo is a very common Spanish idiom meaning to go out for a walk, a stroll, a ride, anything that is fun and enjoyable. *Paseo*, a noun, can mean an avenue, as in *el Paseo del Prado*, a famous avenue in Havana, or *el Paseo de la Castellana*, a well-known avenue in Madrid.

PIÉNSALO BIEN
THINK IT THROUGH

The article. El artículo

There are four articles in Spanish with their usual plural forms:

Definite articles:

So called because they determine the extension of the noun they precede. It is not the same to say *el libro* (the book) as *un libro* (a book). When we say *el libro*, we are referring to a particular book, but when we say *un libro*, we make no reference to a particular book, but to any book. Compare these two sentences:

Ayer compré el libro que querías./ Yesterday I bought the book you wanted—meaning that both you and the other person know what the book is, and

Ayer compré un libro para entretenerme./ Yesterday I bought a book to entertain myself.

DEFINITE ARTICLES:

singular	plural
masculine: *el*	*los*
feminine: *la*	*las*

These four articles in English equal one single article: *the*, with no reference whatsover to gender or number:

el libro	the book
la casa	the house
los libros	the books
las casas	the houses

INDEFINITE ARTICLES:

singular	plural
masculine: un	unos
feminine: una	unas

These four articles in English equal either *a*, *an*, or *some* in the plural:

un libro	a book
una casa	a house
unos libros	some books
unas casas	some houses

The neuter article *lo* (it) is mainly used to make an adjective a noun, to express an abstract idea, as explained earlier: *lo bello* (the beautiful*)*, *lo fantástico* (the fantastic). It should not be confused with the direct object *lo*, which we will cover later; for example, as in: *lo hice* (I did it). This article *lo* is also used in many idiomatic phrases, such as: *lo dicho/*what has been said, or with an adjective or adverb, as in: *comprendo lo fácil que es/*I know how easy it is. Some common English expressions referring to persons, things, or events are totally left out in Spanish, as in *who is it* (¿quién es), *what is it* (¿qué es), *when is it* (¿cuándo es), and in impersonal expressions, such as *it is nice to see you/*me alegro de verte, and when referring to the weather or time, as in *it is raining/*está lloviendo, *it is nine o'clock/*son las nueve en punto. It also expresses the relative pronoun in English, as in *no sé de lo que hablas/*I don't know what you're talking about.

Important: Combined with the prepositions *a* or *de*, the masculine singular definite article *el* fuses together with both: *a+el > al*, *de+el > del*, but NOT with the masculine singular pronoun *él*. This happens all the time, no exceptions. Examples:

Fui al cine.	I went to the movies.
el motor del carro	the engine of the car

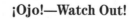

¡Ojo!—Watch Out!

With feminine nouns beginning with a stressed *a* or *ha*, the masculine article is used, as in: *el agua* (the water), *el hambre* (hunger), to avoid cacophony (combination of discordant sounds).

BRAIN TICKLERS
Set # 39

Ejercicios

A. Completa los espacios en blanco con el artículo definido apropiado:
1. Tenemos que escribir _____ ejercicio para mañana.
2. Rogelio y Encarnación van a _____ playa el sábado.
3. No me comí _____ frijoles porque me hacen daño.
4. Todas _____ banderas del mundo son bonitas.
5. _____ platos y _____ servilletas (napkins) están ya en la mesa.

B. Completa los espacios en blanco con el artículo definido o indefinido según corresponda:
1. _____ herramientas (tools) que te presté ayer son muy caras.
2. En esa librería venden _____ libros muy raros.
3. _____ edificio que está en la esquina no me gusta.
4. Mis padres salen siempre con _____ tíos de mi amiga.
5. Cuando pueda me voy a comprar _____ zapatos negros.

C. Completa los espacios en blanco con *al* o *del*, según corresponda:
1. Llegaremos allí _____ mediodía.
2. Mañana pensamos ir _____ zoológico (zoo).
3. Regresarán _____ teatro a medianoche.
4. Salen _____ colegio por la tarde.
5. No vamos _____ restaurante porque está cerrado.

D. Give the definite article for the following:
1. _____ hambre
2. _____ alma
3. _____ ángel
4. _____ hábito
5. _____ hamaca

Answers are on page 193.

MÁS ES MEJOR
MORE IS BETTER

Nouns

el metro	subway
la agencia de viajes/pasajes	travel agency
el cheque de viajeros	traveler's check
la tasa de cambio	exchange rate
la moneda nacional	national currency
el boleto/pasaje	ticket
el viaje de ida/el viaje de vuelta	one-way trip
el viaje de ida y vuelta	round trip
la aduana	customs
inmigración	immigration
a bordo	on board
la llegada	arrival
la salida	departure
el equipaje	luggage
la maleta	suitcase
el bolso de mano	handbag
al registro	search
el detector de metales	metal detector
el abordaje	boarding
la sala de espera	waiting room
el aeropuerto	airport
la visa	visa
el boleto	ticket
el viaje	trip
el vuelo	flight

Verbs

volar	to fly
llegar	to arrive
partir	to depart
cargar	to carry
llevar	to take
abordar	to board
inspeccionar	to inspect
montar	to get on/ride
subir	to go up
bajar	to go down

esperar	to wait
apurarse	to hurry up
pesar	to weigh

HABLA POPULAR
EVERYDAY SPEECH

Here are more idioms, expressions, and sayings.

de ahí	hence
por aquí/por acá	around here
de aquí en adelante	from now on
por el/la presente	for now
siempre que	whenever
mientras que/en tanto que	whereas
por el/la/los/las que	whereby
en el/la/los/las	wherein
en cualquier parte/lado	wherever
a propósito	by the way
más bien	rather
tanto mejor	so much the better
mojarse los labios	to take a sip
tomar el pelo	to tease
sacar los trapos sucios	to air the dirty linen
Los ojos son el espejo del alma.	The eyes are the mirror of the soul.

¿Sabías que? A relative of Emily Da Silva Nathan, Emma Lazarus, a Sephardic Jew, was the author of the poem now inscribed on the Statue of Liberty: *Give me your tired, your poor, Your huddled masses yearning to be free.* Another Nathan, Annie Nathan Meyer, was the founder of New York's prestigious Barnard College. And another Sephardic family, the Seixas (later Saks), were the founders of the world-famous department store, Saks Fifth Avenue in New York. Sephardic Jews lived for centuries in Spain and were expelled in the fifteenth century. They contributed greatly to Spain and are an intrinsic part of Spanish culture. Today, many of them still speak Spanish and follow many of the Spanish customs.

BIEN VALE LA PENA
IT'S WELL WORTH IT

Holidays. Días de fiesta

Here we will give only some of the national holidays of the United States with their Spanish counterparts.

La Navidad	Christmas
El Fin de Año	New Year's Eve
El Día de Fin de Año	New Year's Day
El Día de Martin Luther King, Jr	Martin Luther King, Jr's Day
El Día de San Valentín	Valentine's Day
El Día de los Presidentes	Presidents' Day
El Día de San Patricio	St. Patrick's Day
El Domingo de Ramos	Palm Sunday
El Viernes Santo	Good Friday
El Domingo de Pascua	Easter Sunday
El Día de los Inocentes	April Fools Day
El Día de las Madres	Mother's Day
Día en que se celebra a los caídos en las guerras	Memorial Day
El Día de los Padres	Father's Day
El Día de la Independencia	Independence Day
El Día del Trabajo	Labor Day
El Día de la Raza	Columbus Day
El Día de las Brujas	Halloween
El Día de todos los Santos	All Saints Day
El Día de las Elecciones	Election Day
El Día de los Veteranos	Veterans' Day
El Día de Acción de Gracias	Thanksgiving Day

¿Sabías que? In addition to many other holidays, big celebration days for Hispanics are *La Nochebuena* (Christmas Eve) and *El Día de Reyes* (The Three Wise Men's Day) on January 6th. *El Día de la Raza* is Columbus Day, and it means, literally, the *Day of the Race*, honoring the great mosaic of Hispanic races and cultures.

DILO COMO YO
SAY IT LIKE I DO

Pronunciation of the vowels

Generally speaking, Spanish has five vowels and five sounds. This works greatly to your advantage, as the student, especially when you are used to the same five vowels in English with multiple different sounds, some 27 in total. No matter what their position is within a word—whether they are stressed or not, whether they precede or follow a consonant, are used beginning or ending a syllable, or one same vowel following another—you can safely assume that each one of the five Spanish vowels are always pronounced the same. Nothing like the *oo* or *ee* in English at all, ever. We are giving you, below, the approximate sound of each one of the vowels:

a	close to the *a* in *father*, as in: *casa, calabaza, cama*
e	close to the *e* in *pen*, as in: *Pepe, pelele, bebé*
i	close to the *ee* in *seen*, as in: *sí, siglo, silla*
o	close to the *o* in *robe*, as in: *oro, ola, cosa*
u	close to the *oo* in *boot*, as in: *uno, luna, mucho*

Pronunciation Practice

A. Say these words out loud:

mamá	mañana	barbacoa	camaleón	salga
enero	mes	este	mesero	nené
abril	minoría	silbido	asimismo	risa
lobo	como	solo	bobo	noto
pulso	susurro	puma	púrpura	tuba

B. And now, say these words out loud:

papanatismo	pupilaje	abracadabra
cantaclaro	horrorosidad	cosmopolita
alibabá	cucurrucú	locomotora
fantasmagórico		

¿Cuánto sabes? How is your sense of geography? See if you can do this: From New York City, match the Hispanic countries in column A with their correct direction in column B:

Column A   Column B
1. México   a. sudeste
2. España   b. sudoeste
3. Puerto Rico c. este
4. Colombia   d. sur

Answers: 1-b, 2-c, 3-a, 4-d

And what about *el Mar Mediterráneo*? Circle the right location from New York City:

norte   este   oeste   sur

Answer: *este*

ALMA HISPÁNICA
HISPANIC SOUL

Ricardo Palma

Ricardo Palma was one of the masters, perhaps the greatest one, of the *costumbrismo* (literary genre about local customs) in Peru, especially during colonial Lima in the eighteenth century (then the Americas' most majestic city). Many of the things we know today about that period are because of his *Tradiciones peruanas* (Peruvian Traditions). In an amusing picaresque style, he vividly portrays general life in Lima from the Incas to contemporary times. As writer Raúl Porras Barrenechea once wrote: He (Palma) "opened the eyes of colonial Lima during the period of the Viceroys." He was the consummate narrator, the storyteller who animated customs, folklore, and people alike, from viceroys to beggers, from ladies of high society to the typical women of the streets. About his *Tradiciones* he once confessed to a friend that "he was not the writer, the historian, but rather those we call the people." He began his *Tradiciones* in 1852 and completed six series from 1872 to 1883, followed by several others. One of the things that stands out about Palma is his belief that language must reflect evolution, that it is not up to scholars behind a desk, as he called members of the Spanish Royal Academy of Language, to dictate or at least limit the natural growth and development of a language. He was, thus, deeply concerned with linguistics and the use of his own language and style, which has been categorized as eminently popular and American. Palma is also revered for his total dedication to the National Library of Peru where he was the director from 1883 to 1912. He replenished some 4,000 volumes that were looted during the War of the Pacific, many of which he had himself donated, and many through donations from friends around the world.

The writings of Ricardo Palma

Tradiciones peruanas

Mujer Hombre

No fue en América Doña Catalina de Erauzo, bautizada en la historia colonial con el *sobrenombre* de la "Monja alférez", la única hija de Eva, ni la sola *monja* que cambiara las faldas de su sexo por el traje y costumbres *varoniles*.

El 25 de octubre de 1803 se comunicó de Cochabamba a la *Real Audiencia de Lima* el descubrimiento de que un caballero, conocido en Buenos Aires y en Potosí con el nombre de Antonio Ita, no era tal varón con derecho de varonía, sino doña María Leocadia Álvarez, monja *clarisa* del monasterio de la villa de Agreda, en España... terminó por espontanearse declarando su verdadero nombre de María Leocadia Álvarez y su condición de monja escapada, no por *amoríos carnales*, sino por espíritu aventurero, como doña Catalina de Erauzo.

To help you better understand this passage, here is the meaning of some key words:

sobrenombre	nickname
monja	nun
varoniles	manly, masculine
Real Audiencia de Lima	High Court of Lima
clarisa	Order of Saint Claire
amoríos carnales	love affairs

BRAIN TICKLERS
Set # 40

Ejercicios

Answer these questions in English:

1. According to the story, how many women disguised themselves as men and what were their names?

2. What do you think was the reason for their behavior?

3. What is *Cochabamba*?

4. Where is the *Monasterio de Agreda*?

5. How would you translate *hija de Eva*?

Answers are on page 193.

¿Sabías que? During the Spanish colonial period in South America, a total of 12,412 books were published as compared to only 500 in the U.S. colonial period.

PLUMA EN MANO
PEN IN HAND

Mis vacaciones pasadas/My last vacation

He viajado mucho, visto muchos lugares y todos me han gustado. Pero hasta ahora (until now) no ha habido nada (nothing) comparable a mi viaje a Puerto Rico, mi primero y desde luego (of course) no el último (the last one). Le di la vuelta a la isla (around the island) y me quedé varios días en San Juan, la capital, en la playa de Luquillo. Me hospedé (I stayed) en el hotel Conquistador que ya no sé si sigue allí (if it is still there). De ahí,

por carretera (by road) me fui a Ponce, en el extremo sur de la
isla, y al regreso me quedé en Mayagüez el resto del tiempo, en
casa de unos amigos que vivían cerca del ingenio (sugar mill)
Igualdad, en un caserón viejo pero encantador (enchanting).
Todas las mañanas, bien tempranito (very early), me levantaba y
a pie (walking) me iba a la playa de Añasco. Allí, me tiraba en
la arena (sand) debajo (under) una palma a disfrutar del paisaje
y de la brisa (breeze) tropical y de un cielo tan claro y un sol
(sun) tan intenso que me cegaba (blinded me). Al rato (in a little
while) me levantaba y corriendo me tiraba (threw myself) en
el mar respirando el olor (smell) incomparable de las aguas
caribeñas.Olor a mar, olor a limpio, olor a historia. Allí me
estaba hasta el atardecer (dusk). Luego me iba (went) al hotel
de Mayagüez que estaba cerquita (very close) y allí charlando y
comiendo se me iban las horas volando (hours went flying by).
Antes de regresar a casa, me daba otra vuelta (another walk)
por la playa, ya de noche (already night) a ver las estrellas. El
espectáculo ante (before) mis ojos me sobrecogía (overwhelmed
me) sin poder creer que pudiera haber (that there could be) en
el mundo tal (such) maravilla.¡Ay Dios mío! Luego a casa al
banquetazo (great feast) que me esperaba, a la cama (to bed)
a descansar y soñar…

BRAIN TICKLERS
Set # 41

Ejercicios

A. Choose five words/idioms from
   the list below and write a Spanish
   sentence using each:

   hasta ahora   hospedarse
   temprano   olor
   maravilla   isla
   carretera   estrella

B. Taken from the passage on the previous pages, give the infinitive forms of the following verbs:
1. di _____   4. me tiraba _____
2. me quedé _____   5. charlando _____
3. fui _____

C. Match the definitions in column A with the words in column B:

Column A	Column B
1. es la capital de Puerto Rico	a. Mayagüez
2. nombre de la playa donde está/ estaba el hotel Conquistador	b. Ponce
3. ciudad de Puerto Rico que está al extremo sur de la isla	c. Añasco
4. ciudad donde me quedé el resto del tiempo	d. San Juan
5. ombre de la playa donde me gustaba ir	e. Luquillo

D. All of the verbs below are regular. Give the imperfect indicative of each according to the person given in parentheses:
1. disfrutar (yo):
2. ver (ellos):
3. charlar (tú):
4. correr (ella)
5. descansar (nosotros):
6. vivir (usted):
7. volar (él):
8. soñar (ustedes):
9. hospedarse (yo):
10. dar (vosotros):

Answers are on page 193.

ASÍ SOMOS
THIS IS WHO WE ARE

The treasures of Peru

Sometimes we think that we must travel to Europe or Asia to see some of the great historical wonders of the world. Seldom do we think that right here, in America, especially in the countries to our south, there are as many such wonders as any other place on earth. Take Peru, for instance: Step back in time and put yourself in the first half of the sixteenth century. Do you know what actually transpired there during that period? Think of the Incas and the Spaniards, of one of the most advanced civilizations that ever existed, the Incas, and a country at the peak of its glory, Spain, and how they came together in an epic of Homeric proportions. Think of Lima today, rightly called in the past *la Ciudad de los Reyes*, the City of Kings, founded on January 18, 1535, a great city indeed, and the Lima of the sixteenth and seventeenth centuries. It rivaled the greatest cities in Europe, and was one of the centers of the universe at the time, the absolute pride of the Spanish empire in America for more than two centuries. There is so much to see in Peru that you would be hard-pressed to decide where to begin. But let's concentrate on two places: Lima and Machu Picchu.

In Lima, the Plaza de Armas, or Plaza Mayor, is stunning, with the following major attraction: the cathedral, for which Francisco Pizarro himself placed the first stone on January 18, 1535; he also inaugurated the first church on March 11, 1540. The first mass was celebrated on August 15, 1622. The archbishop Jerónimo de Loayza wanted to make it like the cathedral of Seville, if not better. Other attractions in the Plaza are the Archbishop's Palace, the Government Palace, and Town Hall. Machu Picchu, or as it is commonly called, the Lost City of the Incas, is one of the greatest marvels of the world in terms of its location and architecture. It is not really a city, but a country retreat for the Incas. It is located on a mountain above the Urubamba Valley at an elevation of 6,750 feet (2057 m). Machu Picchu was discovered, or perhaps rediscovered, in 1911 by Yale professor Hiram Bingham III. It is believed that the city was built by Sapa Inca in 1440; it mainly consists of a large palace, numerous temples, and other buildings for the staff. Some of the stone structures did not use mortar but precise cutting blocks aligned in unique shapes. People from around the world have been flocking into Machu Picchu ever since the magazine *National Geographic* devoted an entire issue (April 1913) to it. Besides Lima and Machu Picchu, the Amazonian basin that occupies almost half of Peru and the Peruvian Andes are sights to behold. We can't fail to mention also the city of Cuzco, the ancient Inca capital.

BRAIN TICKLERS—THE ANSWERS

Set # 38, page 178

A.
1. frontier
2. zones
3. tourist
4. unique
5. guide
6. hamburgers
7. regularly
8. parts
9. beans
10. theory

B.
1. Hay tanto que ver
2. cuatro paredes
3. guías turísticos
4. Donde vivimos
5. verlo
6. leche
7. costumbre
8. itinerario
9. Italia
10. Inglaterra

C.
1. V   2. V   3. F   4. F   5. V

D.
1. viajar
2. ver
3. tomar
4. servir
5. depender

Set # 39, page 182

Piénsalo bien
A.
1. el   3. los   5. Los – las
2. la   4. las

B.
1. Las   3. El   5. unos
2. unos   4. los

C.
1. a   3. del   5. al
2. al   4. del

D.
1. el   3. el   5. la
2. el   4. el

Set # 40, page 189

Alma hispánica
1. 2; Catalina de Erauzo and María Leocadia Álvarez
2. Answers will vary.
3. a city in Bolivia
4. España
5. daughter of Eve

Set # 41, page 190

Pluma en mano
A. Answers will vary
B.
1. dar
2. quedarse
3. ir
4. tirarse
5. charlar

C.
1. d   3. b   5. c
2. e   4. a

D.
1. disfrutaba
2. veían
3. charlabas
4. corría
5. descansábamos
6. vivía
7. volaba
8. soñaban
9. me hospedaba
10. dabais

Con buen gobierno avanzan los pueblos

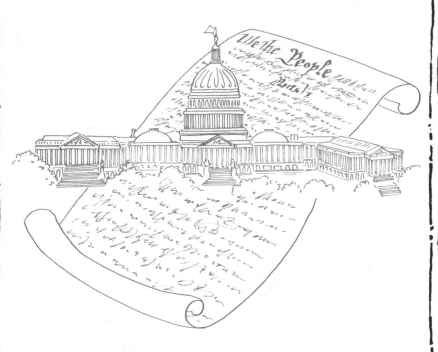

Nations advance with good government

Los gobiernos *promulgan* leyes que el pueblo *acata* u obedece. Si no fuera por ellas, caeríamos todos en *la barbarie*, en la anarquía, en nuestra propia destrucción. Pero hay gobiernos con muchas leyes que por lo general se ignoran, mientras que hay otros, *los menos*, en los que la ley *reina* victoriosa. Uno de estos países son los Estados Unidos, nación basada totalmente en un sistema de leyes inquebrantables que se *han mantenido* sin interrupción *por más de* doscientos años. A este sistema de leyes se le llama la Constitución de los Estados Unidos de América, ratificada en 1787. Un grupo de patriotas, un sueño y una feliz realidad que *nos ha llevado* por un largo camino hasta nuestros días, unas veces dando *vueltas y tumbos*, y otras muy derechito con un *rumbo* muy preciso.

Esta Constitución, la más antigua aún *en vigencia*, es el *amparo y refugio* de todo ciudadano estadounidense. En 7 artículos y 27 enmiendas, *se abarca* todo cuanto se necesita para dirigir un país por el camino de la democracia, por el camino del triunfo. En ella se establecen tres *poderes* federales: Legislativo, Judicial, y Ejecutivo, que representan *la balanza del poder*, es decir, que el poder no reside en *ninguno de ellos en particular*, sino en todos, uno pendiente y vigilante del otro y siempre *dispuestos* los tres a mantener el equilibrio. El Legislativo *lo compone* el Congreso, formado por el Senado y la Cámara de Representantes, legisladores, o diputados; el Judicial lo componen los nueve *jueces* del Tribunal Supremo; y el Ejecutivo un Presidente y Vicepresidente. A los componentes del Poder Legislativo *los elige* el pueblo, al igual que al Presidente y Vicepresidente del Poder Ejecutivo. A los nueves jueces del Tribunal Supremo los nombra el Presidente de la nación. O sea que los legisladores promulgan las leyes, el Presidente las ejecuta, y cuando hay *divergencias* o disputas decide el Tribunal Supremo. Este sistema de gobierno federal es el que siguen los estados de la Unión, así como las ciudades y pueblos aunque con nombres distintos. Por ejemplo, en ellos, el que dirige será un *alcalde*, y el legislador un comisionado, pero sus funciones son equivalentes aunque en muchísimo *menor grado*. Cada cuatro años se elige al Presidente, cada seis años a los senadores, y cada dos años a los representantes. Al Presidente sólo *se le puede elegir* dos veces pero *en cuanto a* los otros no hay límites. Al Presidente de la nación no lo elige el pueblo *sino* los electores que asignan los distintos estados. Es decir, que un candidato que obtenga la mayoría del voto popular puede *perder* las elecciones si no lo han elegido por mayoría los electores.

La estabilidad política logra la paz, bienestar y progreso de los pueblos, *a diferencia de* los sistemas de gobierno dictatoriales *en los que* el poder descansa en un individuo y en los que el pueblo, el verdadero *soberano*, poco influye. En otros gobiernos el poder descansa, por tradición mayormente, en una monarquía, aunque modernamente son *monarquías parlamentarias* y en los que el monarca o rey, o en algunos casos la reina, como en Inglaterra, son simplemente figuras a las que se venera y honra pero *carentes* de poder alguno. Así es el sistema español actual, aunque *hubo un tiempo* en que España estaba *regida* por un dictador, *como lo estaban* Italia y Alemania. La América hispana tuvo sus épocas de dictaduras, *golpes de estado* y revoluciones, pero *paulatinamente* se va imponiendo un sistema democrático que *augura* un futuro más seguro y progresivo.

Vocabulario básico

promulgan	promulgate/enact
acata	obeys
la barbarie	barbarism
los menos	the lesser number
reina	reigns
han mantenido	have maintained
por más de	for more than
nos ha llevado	has taken us
vueltas y tumbos	turns and jolts
rumbo	course/direction
en vigencia	in force
amparo	protection
se abarca	is covered
poderes	powers
la balanza del poder	balance of power
ninguno de ellos en particular	none of them in particular
dispuestos	ready
lo compone	is composed
jueces	judges
los elige	are elected
divergencias	differences

alcalde	mayor
menor grado	lesser degree
se le puede	can be
sino	but
perder	to lose
a diferencia de	in contrast to
en los que	in which
soberano	sovereign
monarquías parlamentarias	parliamentary monarchies
el rey	king
la reina	queen
carentes	lacking
hubo un tiempo	there was a time
regida	ruled
como lo estaban	as were
golpes de estado	coups
paulatinamente	gradually
augura	foretells/predicts

PIÉNSALO BIEN
THINK IT THROUGH

The pronoun. El pronombre, Part 1

Pronouns are very confusing as there are many of them with different functions. For example, *se* can be a reflexive pronoun or an indirect object pronoun, as in *él se baña* (he takes a bath), reflexive pronoun, *se lo di* (I gave it to him), indirect object pronoun. They are also confusing because of their placement within a sentence, sometimes preceding the verb, while others are attached to it, as in: **lo** *hago* (I do it), *¡hágalo!* (do it!), **lo** *voy a hacer/voy a hacerlo* (I am going to do it), **lo** *estoy haciendo/estoy haciéndolo* (I am doing it). As you can see, in those sentences, the *lo* (it) is all over the place. And the same pronoun *me* can have different functions, as in *me visto* (I get dressed), reflexive; *me llamó* (he/she called me), direct object; *me lo compró* (he/she bought it for me), indirect object. Notice that with the exception of the reflexive pronoun, in English it is not that different: *me* used as both a direct and indirect object pronoun. Confused? Yes, we know and must ask you to pay attention to what comes next.

First of all, a pronoun is used as a substitute for a noun. For example:

María estudia italiano.	Mary studies Italian.
Ella estudia italiano.	She studies Italian.

The *Ella* (She) pronoun replaces *María* (Mary), a noun/subject. In Spanish, there are five kinds of pronouns:

Personal pronouns
Possessive pronouns
Demonstrative pronouns
Relative pronouns
Indefinite pronouns

In this lesson we will first discuss the personal pronouns and possessive pronouns, and then the demonstrative pronouns, relative pronouns, and indefinite pronouns.

Personal Pronouns

We have already seen the personal pronouns:

yo	I
tú	you
él, ella, usted	he/she/you
nosotros	we
vosotros	you
ellos, ellas, ustedes	they

Possessive Pronouns

The possessive pronouns are

mío/mía	mine
tuyo/tuya	yours (familiar singular)
suyo/suya/de usted	his/hers/yours (*de usted*>polite singular)
nuestro/nuestra	ours
vuestro/vuestra	yours (familiar plural)
suyo/suya/de ustedes	theirs (*de ustedes*>polite plural)

All of them have plural forms.

When they are placed before the noun, the forms: *mío/mía, tuyo/tuya, suyo/suya* change to *mi, tu, su*, respectively, for example:

la casa es mía	the house is mine
mi casa	my house
la casa es tuya	the house is yours (familiar)
tu casa	your house (familiar)

la casa es suya	the house is his/hers/yours (polite)
su casa	his/her/your house (polite)

All three have plural forms: *mi> mis, tu> tus, su> sus*. For example:

Singular	Plural
mi casa	*mis casas*
tu casa	*tus casas*
su casa	*sus casas*

Personal object pronouns can be used with or without a preposition.

Without a preposition		With a preposition
me	me	*mí* (when combined with *con> conmigo*)
te	you	*ti* (when combined with *con> contigo*)
lo/la/le/se	him/her/it/you	*él/ella/a usted*
nos	us	*nosotros*
os	you	*vosotros*
los/las/les/se	them	*ellos/ellas/a ustedes*

To these we would have to add the reflexive pronoun *se* as an object without a preposition (himself/herself/itself), and *sí* when used with a preposition> *para sí* (for himself/herself/itself). Also, when combined with the preposition *con*, *sí* changes to *consigo*.

When the pronouns are used without a preposition, they are attached to the verb if it is a present participle, infinitive, or command. When the pronouns are used with a preposition, they generally follow the verb.

Before we go any further, let's have some examples of the object pronouns used without and with a preposition.

Without a preposition:

Me dijo que vendría.	He told me he would come.
Él está escribiéndonos una carta.	He is writing us a letter.

With a preposition:

Eso es para él.	That is for him.
Ellos vienen conmigo.	They come with us.
No quieren hablar contigo.	They don't want to talk with you.

BRAIN TICKLERS
Set # 42

Ejercicios

A. First, answer these two questions:
   1. What does a pronoun do? Give an example in Spanish with the English equivalent.
   2. How many kinds of pronouns are there in Spanish? List them.

B. Traduce el pronombre entre paréntesis:
   1. (We) trabajamos en una fábrica de metales.
   2. No está bien que (them, masc.) lo hagan.
   3. ¿Dónde vas (you, sing., familiar)?
   4. ¿Hablan (you, plural pol.) ruso?
   5. (I) me despierto a las 7am.
   6. Nos gusta mucho (your, sing. pol) automóvil.
   7. Esa lámpara es (mine), no (yours, pl. pol.).
   8. (Our) abuelo se llama Miguel.
   9. (My) sillas son muy antiguas.
   10. ¿Quieres venir (with me) al teatro?
   11. Primero vamos a casa de (my) tía Consuelo.
   12. Sí, me gustaría ir (with you) a la playa.
   13. Esa carta es para (me).
   14. ¿A qué hora (do I call you, sing. fam.)?
   15. (He) me dijo que hablara con (her).

C. Translate these sentences into Spanish:
   1. She is the mother of Leticia.
   2. I love my job.
   3. It is our duty to do it.
   4. We are happy to go with you.
   5. I don't want to go with them.

Answers are on page 226.

The pronoun. El pronombre, Part 2

Here we will discuss:
- Demonstrative pronouns
- Relative pronouns
- Indefinite pronouns

Demonstrative pronouns

In Spanish, the demonstrative pronouns are:

mas. sing.	fem. sing.	masc. pl.	fem. pl.
éste (this one)	ésta (this one)	éstos (these ones)	éstas (these ones)
ése (that one)	ésa (that one)	ésos (those ones)	ésas (those ones)
aquél (that one over there)	aquélla (that one over there)	aquéllos (those over there)	aquéllas (those over there)

For the neuter:

esto (this one)	eso (that one)	aquello (that one over there)	no fem. form

Notice that the neuter forms have no written accent.
How they are used:

éste/ésta/éstos/éstas:	when the person/s or thing/s is/are near the person doing the speaking, as in *éste es mío* (this one is mine, referring to a book)
ése/ésa/ésos/ésas:	when the person/s or thing/s is/are near the person who is listening, as in *ése es mío* (that one is mine, referring to a book)
aquél/aquélla/ aquéllos/aquéllas:	when the person/s or thing/s is/are far from the person talking and the person listening, as in *aquél es mío* (that one over there is mine)

When the demonstrative pronouns are placed before the noun they become adjectives, since they help describe the noun, in which case they do not have a written accent mark, as in *este libro* (this book), *esos libros* (those books), *aquellos libros* (those books over there). Thus, when they replace the noun they are pronouns, and carry a written accent mark; when they are used with the noun, in front of it, they are adjectives and do not carry a written accent mark.

Here are some more examples:

Mario, esta pluma es mía; ésa es de Dulce María, y aquélla es de Miguel Ángel. (Mario, this pen is mine; that one is Dulce María's, and that one over there is Miguel Ángel's.)

—*Cecilio, ¿este carro es el tuyo?* (Cecilio, is this your car?)

—*No, el carro mío no es ése, es aquél.* (No, that is not my car; it is that one over there.)

—*¿De quiénes son estas flores?* (Whose flowers are these?)

—*Estas flores son para mi madre, ésas son para la tuya, y aquéllas son para tu abuela.* (These flowers are for my mother, those are for yours, and those over there are for your grandmother.)

Relative pronouns

The relative pronouns replace a noun that has been named previously, an antecedent. For example: *Los niños que vimos anoche son mis sobrinos* (The children that we saw last night are my nephews). Here we have two sentences: one, *Los niños que vimos anoche* (The children that we saw last night), and the other, *son mis sobrinos* (are my nephews). In this case, the relative pronoun *que* replaces *los niños* (the children) who were named before.

The relative pronouns in Spanish are:

que	This refers to persons or things and serves for the singular or plural (that, which, who, or whom).
cual	It is used with the definite article in all of its forms: el/la/los/las, often to clarify or determine the gender and the number of *que*: *el cual, la cual, los cuales, las cuales* (who, that, whom, which, the one that, the ones that, the one who, the ones who).
quien	It is only used referring to persons, and it uses the plural *quienes* (who, or whom).
cuyo	Besides being a relative pronoun, it is also a possessive, and it has feminine and plural forms: *cuyo, cuya, cuyos, cuyas* (whose, of which).

In interrogative and exclamatory phrases, the relative pronouns always carry a written accent mark, and are called interrogative pronouns: *¿Qué has comprado?* (What have you bought?); *¿Cuál prefieres?* (Which one do you prefer?); *¿Quién nos llamó?* (Who called us?); *¡Qué lástima!* (What a pity!)

Indefinite Pronouns

The indefinite pronouns are those that vaguely designate persons or things without determining them. The main ones are: *alguien* (somebody, someone), *algo* (something, anything), *nada* (nothing, anything), *cualquiera* (either, referring to two or more persons and things); *quiera* (any one, referring to two or more things); *quienquiera* (whoever). *Cualquier* is a shortened form of *cualquiera* used before nouns, and it means any. It is invariable in its gender.

Here are some more examples:

Esa mujer, a la cual conozco muy bien, es muy simpática. (That woman, whom I know very well, is very nice.)

Tienes que ser tú mismo quien les hable. (It has to be you who speaks to them.)

Esos hombres, de cuyos nombres no me acuerdo, trabajan con mi padre. (Those men, whose names I can't remember, work with my father.)

Necesito a alguien que me ayude. (I need someone/somebody to help me.)

¿Quieres algo de comer? (Do you want something/anything to eat?)

Lo que haces es mejor que nada. (What you do is better than nothing.)

Pregúntale a cualquiera. (Ask anybody/anyone.)

Quienquiera que lo haya hecho (Whoever may have done it)

BRAIN TICKLERS
Set # 43

Ejercicios

A. Traduce la forma correcta del adjetivo demostrativo según se da en paréntesis:
1. (This is) el maestro de mis hermanos.
2. (That) camisa no te queda bien.
3. A mí me gustan más (those) pantalones que los otros.

4. Por favor, alcánzame (those over there) platos.
5. (These) exámanes son muy difíciles.

B. Traduce la forma correcta del pronombre demostrativo según se da en paréntesis:
  1. Dame (that one) y quédate con los otros dos.
  2. No es (this one) el que pedí, sino el de color azul.
  3. (That one over there) es el vestido que nos gusta a todos.
  4. Los más caros son (those) cerca de ti.
  5. Llévate (those over there) que son las plantas que más le gustan a tu padre.

C. Los adjetivos y pronombres. Traduce la forma correcta de cualquiera de los dos según se dan en paréntesis:
  1. Referring to *relojes*:
     (This) reloj es de oro; (that one) es de plata.
  2. Referring to *maletas*:
     (Those over there) maletas son las mías; (those) son las de Isabel.
  3. Referring to *autobuses*:
     (That one) autobús te lleva a Nueva York; (that one over there) te lleva a Chicago.
  4. Referring to *cuadros*:
     (That one over there) cuadro lo pintó Dalí; (that one) lo pintó Goya.
  5. Referring to *botas*:
     Me gustan (these) botas porque son negras; no me gustan (those over there) porque son grises.

D. Interrogative pronouns. Traduce la forma correcta según se da en paréntesis:
  1. ¿(What) vas a hacer mañana?
  2. ¿(What) hora es?
  3. De esos dos que tienes en la mano, ¿(which one) te vas a comprar?
  4. Hace rato que estoy mirando a ese muchacho. ¿(Who) es él?
  5. ¿(Which ones) de esos carros son los más bonitos?

E. Translate this sentence into Spanish.
   Those three teachers, whose names I forgot, teach history.

F. Write four Spanish sentences using for each: a demonstrative adjective; a demonstrative pronoun; a relative pronoun; and an indefinite pronoun.

Answers are on page 226.

MÁS ES MEJOR
MORE IS BETTER

Nouns

el alcalde	mayor
el senador	senator
el congresista	congressperson
las elecciones	elections
el votante	voter
el ministro/secretario	minister/secretary
el voto	vote
la boleta electoral	ballot
el candidato político	political candidate
el partido político	political party
el colegio electoral	electoral college
el decreto	decree
la máquina de votar	voting machine
el estatuto	statute
el gobernador	governor
la primaria	primary
el proyecto de ley	bill
el gobernante	governor/ruler
el cargo público	public office
el funcionario público	public official
los derechos civiles	civil rights
los derechos humanos	human rights
el juramento	oath
la orden de arresto	arrest warrant
el arma	weapon
la celda	cell
la prueba	proof
el cargo	charge
el interrogatorio	interrogation
el sospechoso	suspect

el demandante	plaintiff
el demandado	defendant
la demanda	lawsuit
el indulto	pardon
el cómplice	accomplice
los antecedentes penales	criminal record
la denuncia	complaint
el testigo	witness
el ladrón	thief
el asesino	murderer
la libertad condicional	parole
la apelación	appeal

Verbs

votar	to vote
elegir	to elect
legislar	to legislate
postularse	to run (for public office)
nominar	to nominate
asignar	to assign
juramentar	to swear
gobernar	to govern
ejercer presión para conseguir algo	to lobby
acusar a un funcionario público	to impeach
arrestar	to arrest
denunciar	to report/denounce
testificar	to testify
soltar	to release
perseguir	to chase
dudar	to doubt
robar	to steal/rob
acusar	to accuse
alegar	to allege
apelar	to appeal
entregarse	to surrender
admitir	to admit

HABLA POPULAR
EVERYDAY SPEECH

Below are some very common Spanish verb idioms/expressions:

caer bien	to sit well
cantar las cuarenta	to tell someone off
caminar con la frente alta	to walk tall
estar de capa caída	to be down
hablar sin rodeos	to get to the point
echar culpas	to blame someone for something
hacerse de la vista gorda	to turn the other way
meterse en camisa de once varas	to get into trouble
no pegar un ojo	to be awake all night
no pintar nada	to be a zero
no saber nada	to know nothing/be ignorant
sabérselas todas	to know everything
ser un pollo con moquillo	to be good-looking but over the hill
tener mala pata	to not have luck
ser más bueno que el pan	to have a good heart
ser un as	to be the best at something/an ace
ser un Jaimito/sabiondo	to be a smart alec
sentar cabeza	to settle down
coger el toro por los cuernos	to grab the bull by the horns
crisparse de nervios	to get your nerves up
darse contra la pared	to hit the wall

Practice with idioms

From the list of idioms/expressions above, choose any five and make up a Spanish sentence with each.

BIEN VALE LA PENA
IT'S WELL WORTH IT

Telling the time in Spanish

Key words you should know:

la hora	time/hour
el minuto	minute
el segundo	second
y	plus
menos	to
el cuarto	quarter
quince	fifteen
en punto	o'clock sharp
pasada/pasadas	past
media	half
treinta	thirty
son las/es la	it is
el reloj	watch/clock
el reloj de pulsera	wristwatch
el reloj de pared	wall clock
el reloj despertador	alarm clock
la aguja del reloj	hand of the clock
el minutero	minute hand
el segundero	second hand
am	A.M.
pm	P.M.

Questions

¿Qué hora es?	What time is it?
¿A qué hora…?	At what time…?

Notice the use of *hora* for time. *Hora* means hour, not time. In both instances, *¿Qué hora es?* and *¿A qué hora?* you always reply this way:

With any time, **except one**, you say:

son las/a las   it is/at

Referring to **one only**, you say:

es la/a la   it is/at

Some examples:

María, ¿qué hora es?	Mary, what time is it?
Son las cuatro en punto.	It is four o'clock.
Juan, ¿qué hora es?	John, what time is it?
Es la una en punto.	It is one o'clock.
Pedro, ¿a qué hora vas a la escuela?	Peter, at what time do you go to school?
Voy a las ocho de la mañana.	I go at eight in the morning.
Rosa, ¿a qué hora vas al trabajo hoy?	Rose, at what time do you go to work today?
Voy a la una de la tarde.	I go at one in the afternoon.

Notice the use of *¿A qué hora?* in the question, meaning *At what time?*, and how you answer: *a la* or *a las* (at).

When it is past the hour up to the half hour, you use *y*, which means *past*, as in:

Son las dos y veinte.	It is twenty past two.
Es la una y diez.	It is ten past one.

From the half hour to the next hour, you use *menos*, which means *to*, as in:

Son las tres menos cinco.	It is five to three.
Es la una menos cuarto.	It is a quarter to one.

You could also say it, as in English, although it is much longer:

Son las dos y cincuenta y cinco.	It is two fifty-five.
Son las doce y cuarenta y cinco.	It is twelve forty-five.

Therefore,
> *y* after the hour up to the half hour
> and
> *menos* after the half hour to the next hour.

And,
> *it is* can be either *es la* (only for one) or *son las* (for any other time);
> *at* can be either *a la* (only for one) or *a las* (for any other time).

Remember: *son las, es la, a las, a la.*

Here is additional vocabulary relating to time:

mañana   morning

Mañana can be a noun or an adverb, meaning morning (noun) or tomorrow (adverb). Used as a noun, it needs the article, whether definite or indefinite, *la* or *una*.

tarde   afternoon

As with *mañana*, *tarde* can be a noun or an adverb. As a noun it means *afternoon*, and it needs the article; as an adverb, it means *late*, no article.

la noche   night

In Spanish, before dark is *tarde*, and *noche* is from dark up to midnight. In reality, it is any time after 12 midnight.

temprano	early
el mediodía	noon
la medianoche	midnight
la madrugada	early morning/dawn/daybreak
el atardecer	dusk
el anochecer	nightfall
el amanecer	daybreak/dawn

BRAIN TICKLERS
Set # 44

Ejercicios

A. Traduce la palabra o las palabras entre paréntesis:
1. Te veo en (five minutes).
2. Pregúntale (the time) a Margarita.
3. La clase empieza en unos (seconds).
4. Me gusta tu (watch).
5. Llámalo en (half hour).

B. Match the description in column A with the word in column B:

Column A	Column B
1. It is used for past the hour.	a. menos
2. It means half.	b. y
3. It means o'clock.	c. media
4. It is used for to the hour.	d. en punto

C. Write out the time in Spanish beginning with *son las* or *es la*:
1. 8:24   3. 12:30   5. 6:00 o'clock
2. 10:15   4. 1:40

D. Contesta estas preguntas en oraciones completas:
1. ¿Qué hora es en este momento?
2. ¿Tiene tu reloj minutero?
3. ¿Hay un reloj en tu clase? ¿Qué hora marca?
4. ¿A qué hora te levantas todas las mañanas?
5. ¿Tu clase de español es por la mañana o por la tarde?

Answers are on pages 226–227.

¡Ojo!—Watch Out!

In Spanish, in the morning, in the afternoon is: *por la mañana, por la tarde*. Notice the use of *por* instead of *en*.

Telling the weather in Spanish

Weather in Spanish is *el tiempo*. This word, *tiempo*, as we saw earlier, is a problematic word for you because it can mean different things: time, hour, weather. When it refers to the time of the day, you already know that it is *hora*. When it refers to time in general, it is *el tiempo pasa muy rápido* (time goes by very fast), *en aquel tiempo yo era muy inocente* (at that time I was very innocent), *no me gusta perder el tiempo* (I don't like to waste time). *Tiempo* is also used with this same meaning in many expressions, such as: *a tiempo* (on time), *al mismo tiempo* (at the same time), *con tiempo* (in good time). It is also the word for weather, as in *¿Cuál es el tiempo para mañana?* (What's the weather for tomorrow?), *Con mal tiempo no podemos salir* (With bad weather we can't go out). However, when you use this word describing the condition of the weather, the verb to use is *hacer* and always in the third person singular> *hace*. For example:

Question

¿Qué tiempo hace hoy? (What's the weather today?)

Answer

Hace frío. (It is cold.)
Hace calor. (It is hot.)
Hace viento. (It is windy.)
Hace sol. (It is sunny.)

Notice that in English you use a totally different verb, also in the third person singular: *to be> it is.*

Of course, we can describe the weather in many other ways, saying, *It is raining, It is snowing, It is drizzling.* Here, as with the verb *hacer*, you also use the verb in the third person singular, and if you say it at the very same time that the weather condition is happening, you use the present participle to indicate that it is occurring as you speak. In such cases, the verb in Spanish is *estar*, plus the present participle, or you can simply use the main verb, to rain, to snow, to drizzle, in the third person singular. Here are some examples:

It is raining.   *Está lloviendo.* or *Llueve.* (from *llover*> to rain)
It is snowing. *Está nevando.* or *Nieva.* (from *nevar*)
It is drizzling. *Está lloviznando.* or *Llovizna.* (from *lloviznar*)

Is there any difference between the verb itself in the third person singular and the use of the helping verb *to be* and the past participle?

Yes, there can be a difference, in this way:

It is raining.   *Está lloviendo.* or *Llueve.*
In Florida it rains every day.   *En la Florida llueve todos los días.*

In other words, in Spanish *llueve* could mean that it is raining right now, or it can refer to a rainy condition unrelated to the time it is occurring. In English, you could say *It is raining* or *It rains*, but you would not say *Is it raining? Yes, it rains.* In Spanish, it is correct and it conveys the same meaning.

Additional weather-related vocabulary

la estación	season
la primavera	spring
el otoño	fall
el verano	summer
el invierno	winter
el clima	climate
el clima cálido	hot climate
el clima templado	mild climate
el clima frío	cold climate
la temperatura	temperature
el pronóstico del tiempo	weather forecast
la condición del tiempo	weather condition
el buen tiempo	good weather
el mal tiempo	bad weather
el hielo	ice
la niebla/la neblina	fog/mist
el rayo	bolt/ray
el relámpago	bolt of lightning
la atmósfera	atmosphere
la humedad	humidity
nublado	cloudy
húmedo	humid
lluvioso	rainy
nevoso	snowy
soleado	sunny
la nevada	snowfall
el copo de nieve	snowflake
la gota de lluvia	raindrop
el huracán	hurricane
la tempestad	storm
la brisa	breeze
el ventarrón	strong wind
aclarar	to clear up
escampar	to stop raining
mojarse	to get wet
empaparse	to get soaked

helarse	to freeze (over)
nublarse	to get cloudy
la bola de nieve	snowball
el hombre de nieve	snowman
claro	clear
obscuro	dark

¡Ojo!—Watch Out!

Llover and *nevar* are irregular verbs in the present indicative and also in the present subjunctive:

	Present indicative	Present subjunctive
llover	*llueve*	*llueva*
nevar	*nieva*	*nieve*

However, the present participle is regular for both: *llover> lloviendo, nevar> nevando*, and so are the past participles: *llover> llovido, nevar> nevado*. With the present participle, as we said, you use *estar* as a helping verb, *está lloviendo, está nevando*, always in the third person singular. The past participle is always used with *haber* to form the present perfect, also the third person singular: *ha llovido* (it has rained), *ha nevado* (it has snowed). No matter what the verb tense is, whether simple or compound, the third person singular form is always used: *habrá llovido* (it will have rained), *había llovido* (it had rained), etc.

Important note: *Calor* (heat) is a noun, not an adjective, which is *caliente* (hot), as in: *El café está caliente* (The coffee is hot). Here's an example of *calor* used as a noun:

No me gusta el calor. (I don't like the heat.)

BRAIN TICKLERS
Set # 45

Ejercicios

A. Traduca la palabra o las palabras entre paréntesis:

1. No me gusta el día porque (it is not sunny).
2. Cuando fui a Chicago (it was very windy).
3. Es una lástima; en estos momentos (it is raining).
4. En el Polo Norte siempre (it snows).
5. En Boston hace tanto (wind) como en Chicago.
6. A los esquimales les encanta (the snow).
7. Cuando salimos de casa esta mañana (it was snowing).
8. En los países tropicales (it is very hot).
9. En el norte de España el tiempo es muy (humid).
10. A mí este (weather) no me gusta nada.

B. Match the descriptions in column A with the word/words in column B:

Column A	Column B
1. Cuando el cielo se obscurece y no hace sol	a. abril
2. Es la época del año cuando más llueve	b. nublado
3. Cuando uno se quema mucho por estar bajo él	c. hace viento
4. Quiere decir *it is windy* en inglés	d. el paraguas
5. Lo que usamos para protegernos de la lluvia	e. el sol

C. Contesta estas preguntas en oraciones completas:
  1. ¿Qué te gusta más, cuando hace frío o cuando hace calor?
  2. ¿Cómo es el clima donde tú vives?
  3. ¿Tú miras el pronóstico del tiempo en la televisión todos los días? ¿A qué hora?
  4. ¿Está nevando ahora?
  5. ¿Vas a trabajar cuando cae una tormenta de nieve?
  6. Cuando llueve, ¿no te importa mojarte?
  7. ¿Qué es lo primero que haces cuando pronostican que se avecina un huracán?
  8. ¿Cómo se pone el cielo antes de llover?
  9. ¿Y cómo se pone el cielo cuando escampa?
  10. A mí no me gusta el viento. ¿Te gusta a ti?

Answers are on page 227.

DILO COMO YO
SAY IT LIKE I DO

Diphthongs/Diptongos

Here is where English and Spanish truly diverge, go in different directions.

A diphthong in Spanish is a combination of a weak and strong vowel, or two weak vowels, in one same syllable. The weak vowels in Spanish are *I* (also *y*) and *u*, and the strong are *a*, *e*, *o*. You must know this well, and remember it in order to better understand what follows.

Golden Rule: In Spanish you can *never* separate a diphthong, *ever*, not in writing, not orally, unless one of the two weak vowels happens to have a written accent mark over it—then, and only then, is when that diphthong can be separated. If the written accent mark happens to be over any of the strong vowels, the diphthong remains intact, together. And, when there are no written accent marks over any of the vowels, whether weak or strong, the stress is placed always over the strong vowel.

Here are two examples:

cierto   This word has two syllables: *cier* and *to*. In the
           first syllable there is a diphthong: *ie* (the *i* weak,
           the *e* strong). There are no written accent marks.
           The stress must then go on the *e*, so you pro-
           nounce it: *ciER-to*.

día   This word also has two syllables, only because
           there is a written accent mark over the *í* (weak
           vowel) and, therefore, the diphthong is split, both
           when you say it or write it. In other words: *dí-a*.

The problem with the diphthongs in English, and the reason
why it is so different from Spanish, is that you almost always
split the diphthongs, not in writing, but orally. Take this word:

piano   You split this word into two syllables, right at the
           diphthong, and say *pi-ano*. In Spanish, that word,
           a cognate, would also have two syllables but you
           would split it differently: *pia-no*, keeping the
           diphthong together. A big difference indeed.

There are just a few exemptions, words that traditionally or
because of their etymology do not break or split a diphthong,
such as in *cruel* and *ruido*, pronounced *cru-el* and *ru-i-do*. But,
again, there are just too few for you to be concerned.

How many diphthongs are there in Spanish? Altogether there
are 14 diphthong combinations and each one follows precisely
what we have said before. In other words, each one adheres to
the rules as explained.

¡Ojo!—Watch Out!

The strong vowels, *a, e, o,* when together, each forms a syllable by itself; in other words, they are not fused together as
in the case of the diphthongs. For example: *floreo* (*flo-re-o*),
aéreo (*a-é-re-o.*)

BRAIN TICKLERS
Set # 46

Ejercicios

A. Say each one of these words out loud, keeping in mind the correct pronunciation of all the diphthongs. We are splitting the words into syllables to make it easier for you:

b*ai*-le	ac*ei*-te	he-r*oi*co	r*ui*-señor
r*au*-do	d*eu*-da	lim-p*ia*	m*ie*-do
ri-p*io*	c*iu*-dad	len-g*ua*	f*ue*-go
con-ti-n*uo*			

B. Now say these other words out loud:

búho	traspiés	decía	subirías	¡huy!
averigüéis	Julián	navío	púa	oído

C. How many syllables would you say these words have:
1. búho
2. decía
3. navío
4. púa
5. oído

Answers are on page 227.

ALMA HISPÁNICA
HISPANIC SOUL

Federico García Lorca

He is among the world's greatest and best-known poets and writers throughout the world. One of the saddest losses during the Spanish Civil War, his life was cut short at the very young age of 38. He was an idol to most and an innocent victim in a country gone insane during one of its darkest periods. He is, undoubtedly, one of the most studied and admired literary figures in U.S. colleges, a testimony to his popularity and genius, perhaps because in 1929, he came to New York where he became deeply identified with Harlem and wrote *Poeta en Nueva York—Oda al Rey de Harlem* (Poet in New York—Ode to the King of Harlem).

He was born in Granada in 1898 (or 1899), and adored his mother, a gifted pianist. His father owned a farm not too far away from Granada. García Lorca attended Sacred Heart University, where he studied law but later gave it up, dedicating himself to his work in poetry and theater. He was greatly influenced by popular culture, particularly flamenco and gypsy themes, which is mirrored in most of his writings. The *Romancero Gitano* (Gypsy Ballads) catapulted him to world fame. He was a key figure of La Barraca, a traveling theater that performed in public squares all over Spain, and that produced some of his finest tragedies: *Bodas de Sangre* (1933), *Yerma* (1934), and *La Casa de Bernarda Alba* (1936). While at his country home in 1936, at the beginning of the Spanish Civil War, he was arrested by Franco's soldiers and later killed with the butt of a rifle then shot numerous times. Soon after, his books were burned in the Plaza of Granada and banned in all of Spain. No one knows to this day what happened to his body or where he was buried, if he was at all.

The writings of García Lorca

From the *Romancero Gitano*.

Verde que te quiero verde.
Verde viento. Verdes ramas.
El barco sobre la mar
y el caballo en la montaña.
Con la sombre en la cintura
ella sueña en su baranda,
verde carne, pelo verde,
con ojos de fría plata.
Verde que te quiero verde.
Bajo la luna gitana,
las cosas la están mirando
y ella no puede mirarlas.

To better understand the poem, here is the meaning of some key words:

sombra	shadow	carne	flesh
cintura	waist	luna	moon
baranda	banister	cosas	things

Review

In your opinion, what is the meaning of the use of the word *verde* in this poem?

PLUMA EN MANO
PEN IN HAND

El Descubrimiento de América/
The Discovery of America

Se cree (It is believed) que los vikingos fueron los primeros europeos que llegaron a América, y se da como fecha probable el año 1000 guiados por Leif Eriksson. Por descubrir se entiende (it is understood) dar a conocer, compartir con otros lo que se

ha (what has been) descubierto. De nada vale que yo descubra algo si me lo callo (if I keep it quiet), si no vas más allá (if it doesn't go beyond) de mi persona. Esto precisamente fue lo ocurrido con el supuesto viaje de los vikingos. No fue, además, un viaje de descubrimiento ni de exploración, guiado exclusivamente por tales metas (objectives), sino más bien un viaje al azar (at random), un viaje casual. Puede ser (It could be) también que antes de los vikingos otras culturas hubiesen arribado (had arrived) a América, por ejemplo de Asia pero, de haber sido así (had it been so), nadie se enteró, quedó en la nada (led to nothing), en el anonimato total.

La persona que dio a conocer América (made America known) al mundo de aquella época, el occidental y en oriental, fue Cristóbal Colón, impulsado por el apoyo que le dio la corona española. América podía haberse quedado (could have remained) como estaba y quizás, bien pensado (on second thought), hubiera sido mejor, pero el destino de los pueblos es uno que nadie puede cambiar. Lo que ha de pasar, pasará; lo que ha de ser, será (what is to happen, happens; what is meant to be, will be). O sea que, para bien o para mal (for better or

221

for worse), el verdadero descubridor de América fue el almirante Colón. Pero Colón no viajó solo; el fue el de la idea, el que tuvo el plan, pero para llevarlo a cabo (to carry it out) tuvo que contar con marineros experimentados y con dineros para sufragar los gastos. Esos marineros, esos dineros, todos esos recursos (resources), se los dio España en momentos en que el país necesitaba más ser ayudado (be helped) que ayudar. España, enfrentaba por entonces (at the time) mil problemas internos que la llevaron muy cerca de la ruina total y, sin embargo, se dejó llevar (went after) por la quimera (illusion) de un desconocido, de un hombre al que los geógrafos de Salamanca consideraron un simple loco. Ciertamente fue más la reina Isabel que su consorte el rey Fernando, interesado principalmente en explorar África, más a la mano, más conocida (better known), que las distantes tierras de un mundo imaginario. En esto demostró el rey cariño y respeto por su mujer y decidió apoyarla (back her up).

Zarpó (Sailed) Colón con sus tres carabelas del puerto de Palos el 3 de agosto de 1492, y al cabo de (at the end of) tres meses, el marinero Rodrigo de Triana divisó (sighted) en el horizonte la tierra soñada el 11 de octubre, desembarcando al día siguiente. Ese momento, ese instante, selló (sealed) para siempre el futuro de la humanidad y abrió un mundo y unas perspectivas que nos cambiarían a todos para siempre. Y la pregunta es esta: ¿Qué sería del mundo de hoy sin América? ¿Qué hubiera pasado con la Unión Soviética, hoy Rusia, con la Europa nazi, con la amenaza (threat) que se nos avecina (that is approaching us) con la China? ¿Quién frena (slows down), quién detiene, quién nos protege, quién impulsa los derechos humanos y la causa de la libertad y democracia? América, sólo América; hoy la del norte, mañana la del sur, y en un tiempo quizá no muy lejano (distant), las dos unidas en una sola. Gracias Cristóbal Colón, gracias reina Isabel.

BRAIN TICKLERS
Set # 47

Ejercicios

A. Choose five words/idioms from the list
   below and write a Spanish sentence
   with each:

probable	de nada vale	metas
cultura	nadie	época
pueblo	quimera	

B. Taken from the passage, give the
   infinitive forms of the following verbs:
   1. cree
   2. descubra
   3. entiende
   4. impulsado
   5. viajó

C. Write three sentences in Spanish about the discovery
   of America.

D. All of the verbs below are regular. Give the future
   tense indicative of each according to the person given
   in parentheses:

   1. llegar (yo):
   2. descubrir (él):
   3. callar (nosotros):
   4. explorar (ellos):
   5. ser (ella):
   6. dar (yo):
   7. cambiar (usted):
   8. viajar (vosotros):
   9. enfrentar (él):
   10. considerar (nosotros):

   Answers are on page 227.

ASÍ SOMOS
THIS IS WHO WE ARE

Hispanic countries, capitals, and nationalities. All names are given in Spanish

Country	Capital	Nationality
Argentina	Buenos Aires	argentinos
Bolivia	La Paz	bolivianos
Chile	Santiago	chilenos
Colombia	Bogotá	colombianos
Costa Rica	San José	costarricenses
Cuba	La Habana	cubanos
Ecuador	Quito	ecuatorianos
El Salvador	San Salvador	salvadoreños
España	Madrid	españoles
Guatemala	Guatemala	guatemaltecos
Honduras	Tegucigalpa	hondureños
México	Ciudad México	mexicanos
Nicaragua	Managua	nicaragüenses
Panamá	Panamá	panameños
Paraguay	La Asunción	paraguayos
Perú	Lima	peruanos
Puerto Rico	San Juan	puertorriqueños/ portorriqueños
República Dominicana	Santo Domingo	dominicanos
Uruguay	Montevideo	uruguayos
Venezuela	Caracas	venezolanos

Notes:

- Names of countries and capitals are capitalized. Nationalities are not.
- To make the names of nationalities feminine, change the *o* to *a*, except *costarricense* and *nicaragüense*, which are the same for both. In the case of *español*, to make it feminine, add *a> española*.
- Some names of countries use the article *el>* El Ecuador, El Paraguay, El Perú, El Uruguay (with or without capital E), except La República Dominicana.
- Most of the countries are spelled the same in Spanish and English, with the exception of La República Dominicana (Dominican Republic), and España (Spain) and, of course, in English, without the written accent mark in the case of México, Panamá, Perú. As for the capitals, they are also spelled the same in both languages, with the exception of La Habana (Havana), and Ciudad México (Mexico City) and, of course, in English, without the written accent marks in the case of Bogotá, San José, Ciudad México, Panamá, La Asunción. Notice also the use of the *ñ* in salvadoreños, españoles, hondureños, panameños, puertorriqueños/portorriqueños, and the use of *ü* in nicaragüenses.
- In Hispanic America, the largest city in every country is also the capital.

BRAIN TICKLERS—THE ANSWERS

Set # 42, page 201

Piénsalo bien

A.
1. It replaces a noun. Example will vary.
2. 5:
   personal pronouns
   possessive pronouns
   demonstrative pronouns
   relative pronouns
   indefinite pronouns

B.
1. Nosotros
2. ellos
3. tú?
4. ustedes
5. Yo
6. su
7. mía – suya/de ustedes
8. Nuestro
9. Mis
10. conmigo
11. mi
12. contigo
13. mí
14. te llamo?
15. Él – ella

C.
1. Es la madre de Leticia.
2. Me encanta mi trabajo.
3. Es nuestro deber hacerlo.
4. Nos alegra ir contigo.
5. No quiero ir con ellos.

Set # 43, page 204

Piénsalo bien

A.
1. Éste es
2. Esa
3. esos
4. aquellos
5. Estos

B.
1. ése
2. éste
3. Aquél
4. esos
5. aquellas

C.
1. Este – ése
2. Aquellas – ésas
3. Ése – aquél
4. Aquel – ése
5. estas – aquéllas

D.
1. ¿Qué
2. ¿Qué
3. ¿cuál
4. ¿Quién
5. ¿Cuáles

E.
Esos tres maestros, cuyos nombres no me acuerdo, enseñan historia.

F. Answers will vary.

Set # 44, page 211

Bien vale la pena

A.
1. cinco minutos
2. la hora
3. segundos
4. reloj (de pulsera)
5. media hora

B.
1. b   2. c   3. d   4. a

C.
1. Son las ocho y veinticuatro.
2. Son las diez y cuarto/quince.
3. Son las doce y media.
4. Son las dos menos veinte./
   Es la una y cuarenta.
5. Son las seis en punto.

D. Answers will vary.

Set # 45, page 216

Bien vale la pena
A.
 1. no está soleado
 2. hacía mucho viento
 3. está lloviendo
 4. nieva
 5. viento
 6. la nieve
 7. estaba nevando
 8. hace mucho calor
 9. húmedo
10. tiempo
B.
1. b   2. a   3. e   4. c   5. d
C. Answers will vary.

Set # 46, page 219

Dilo como yo
A. Pronunciation
B. Pronunciation
C.
1. 2   2. 3   3. 3   4. 2   5. 2

Set # 47, page 223

Pluma en mano
A. Answers will vary.
B.
1. creer   4. impulsar
2. descubrir   5. viajar
3. entender
C. Answers will vary.
D.
 1. llegaré
 2. descubrirá
 3. callaremos
 4. explorarán
 5. será
 6. daré
 7. cambiará
 8. viajaréis
 9. enfrentará
10. consideraremos

El arte es maravilloso

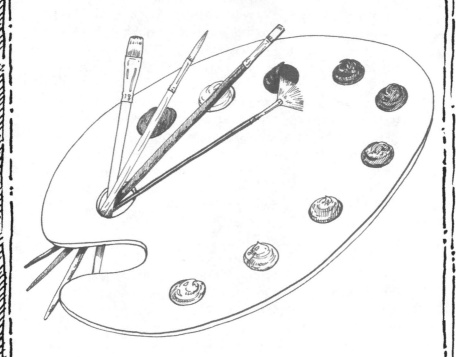

Art is wonderful

El ser humano siempre ha sentido la necesidad *imperiosa* de expresarse, y lo hace con *la palabra viva*, con la pluma, o con *el pincel*. Estos *medios* le valen para comunicar sus más íntimos *pensamientos y sentimientos*, con el deseo y esperanza de que gusten y le sean *comprendidos*, de que otros vean la vida y la interpreten de la misma forma.

En los países hispánicos el arte se ha manisfestado siempre de forma extraordinaria, desde los tiempos más antiguos hasta nuestros días, sobre todo *las artes plásticas*, como son la cerámica, *el grabado*, la escultura, *la joyería* y la pintura. Todas las civilizaciones, la Inca, la Maya, la Azteca se han caracterizado por poseer grandes artistas, por expresiones artísticas de distinta índole. *Desgraciadamente*, muchas de ellas *se han perdido*, quedando sólo *huellas* de una grandiosidad que *se perdió* en el pasado. *Al llegar* los españoles se fundieron, la occidental con la indígena, con la autóctona, produciendo verdaderas obras de arte expresadas mayormente en *la artesanía* popular. Así, en lugares como México, Perú, Guatemala, donde esa fusión entre las dos culturas *cobró más fuerza*, el arte del pueblo, el más puro y verdadero, ha estado siempre *a la cabeza* de los demás. En México, la ciudad de Taxco, entre otras, es donde se hace más visible, más aparente dicha expresión artística en todos *los órdenes*, principalmente en *la orfebrería*, es decir, trabajos *labrados* en oro o plata. En Chile, *por otro lado*, estos trabajos se hacen en *cobre*, mineral que abunda en ese país, y en la Argentina es en cuero o piel por la abundancia de *ganado* que hay allí en la región de Las Pampas. El oro, la plata, *la madera*, el hierro, el cuero, *el barro*, son los materiales usados por excelencia, *sin descontar* otros muchos. *Asombra* a veces los *tallados* que *se han hecho y hacen*, aun en *piedra*, como los hacían todas las culturas aborígenes y de los que permanecen hoy verdaderas *joyas* arquitectónicas aunque casi en ruinas, como son las pirámides y templos de las tres culturas *mencionadas*.

En la ciudad de Bogotá, Colombia, se halla el Museo del Oro en el que se pueden admirar maravillosos objetos tallados en oro que datan de los tiempos pre-Colombinos. La cerámica es otro trabajo *artesanal* de *gusto* exquisito como, por ejemplo, los llamados de Talavera en México, todos pintados *a mano* con un estilo único, *a semejanza de* los de España, los de Talavera de la Reina, en Toledo, de gran influencia árabe y que los misioneros españoles trasladaron a América. *Y ya* que mencionamos a

Toledo, vale destacar *la armería* toledana, sobre todo *las espadas* de limpio *acero* consideradas las mejores del mundo desde hace *siglos.*

Las *bellas artes*, entre las que se encuentra la música, y muchas de las artes plásticas mencionadas, entre las que se encuentran también *el grabado* y a joyería, le dan un carácter *inigualable e inolvidable* al mundo de habla española. *Por estar* más cerca, *vale la pena* visitar la infinidad de museos de toda clase que hay en México, empezando por el Museo Nacional de Arquitectura y el Museo Nacional de Antropología, *sin tomar a menos* los muchos que hay en casi todas sus ciudades. *Pero bueno,* para apreciar el arte hispánico, no es realmente necesario visitar un museo, aunque siempre es recomendable, pues Hispanoamérica en sí *es toda ella* un museo vivo de su historia y pasado. Las ciudades de La Habana, Cartagena, en Colombia, Santo Domingo, Cajamarca, en Perú, *entre otras muchas*, son testimonios *imperecederos* de una de las grandes culturas de la Humanidad. *A los que les guste* el arte, un viaje por la América hispana le resultará una experiencia difícil de olvidar y en el que aprenderá cosas *nunca soñadas.*

Vocabulario básico

imperiosa	pressing
la palabra viva	living word
el pincel	paintbrush
medios	means
pensamientos y sentimientos	thoughts and feelings
comprendidos	understood
las artes plásticas	plastic arts
el grabado	engraving
la joyería	jewelry making
Desgraciadamente	Unfortunately
se han perdido	have been lost
huellas	traces
se perdió	was lost
Al llegar	On arriving
la artesanía	craftwork/craftsmanship

cobró más fuerza	was more intense
a la cabeza	on top
los órdenes	all aspects
la orfebrería	goldsmith trade/ silversmith trade
labrados	carved
por otro lado	on the other hand
cobre	copper
ganado	cattle
la madera	wood
el barro	clay
sin descontar	without leaving out
Asombra	One is amazed
tallados	carvings
se han hecho y hacen	have been made and continue to be made
piedra	stone
joyas	jewels
mencionadas	mentioned
artesanal	craftwork
gusto	taste
a mano	by hand
a semejanza de	similar to
Y ya que	And since
la armería	armor
las espadas	swords
acero	steel
siglos	centuries
bellas artes	fine arts
inigualable e inolvidable	incomparable and unforgettable
Por estar	For being
vale la pena	it's worth
sin tomar a menos	without undermining
Pero bueno	But, well
es toda ella	it is itself
entre otras muchas	among many others
imperecederos	everlasting
A los que les guste	Those liking/appreciating
nunca soñadas	never dreamed

BRAIN TICKLERS
Set # 48

Ejercicios

A. By looking at these words you should know what they mean. Write their meaning on a separate sheet of paper:

1. la necesidad
2. comunicar
3. forma
4. cerámica
5. escultura
6. pintura
7. caracterizado
8. abundancia
9. aborígenes
10. objetos

B. Traduce la palabra o las palabras entre paréntesis:
1. Yo siempre (have felt) ganas de viajar.
2. Yo tengo (the desire and hope) de que algún día habrá paz en el mundo.
3. (Unfortunately) el costo de vida ha subido mucho.
4. En el Museo Metropolitano de Nueva York hay muchas (masterpieces) de todas las culturas y épocas.
5. Los (carvings) en piedra son muy típicos de las culturas aborígenes americanas.
6. A mi me encantan las joyas de (gold and silver).
7. (The pyramids and temples) de los Incas, Aztecas y Mayas son impresionantes.
8. (The swords) toledanas son las mejores del mundo.
9. Mi viaje al Cañón del Colorado fue (unforgettable).
10. (For being) muy cerca de donde yo vivo, voy con frecuencia a Nueva York.

C. Contesta estas preguntas en oraciones completas:
1. ¿Por qué se han caracterizado siempre las culturas Inca, Maya y Azteca?
2. ¿En qué países fue mayor la fusión de las principales culturas americanas con la cultura española?
3. ¿En qué ciudad de México se hacen algunos de los mejores trabajos de orfebrería?

4. ¿En qué ciudad de Hispanoamérica se encuentra el Museo del Oro?

5. ¿Adónde debe viajar toda persona a la que le guste el arte?

D. Basado en el pasaje anterior, dinos si cada una de estas afirmaciones es *verdadera o falsa*:

1. La ciudad de Taxco está en Ecuador.   V   F

2. En Chile no se hacen trabajos de artesanía de cobre.   V   F

3. La cerámica de Talavera de la Reina en Toledo tiene una gran influencia árabe.   V   F

4. En México hay grandes museos de arquitectura y antropología.   V   F

5. La ciudad de Cajamarca está en el Puerto Rico.   V   F

E. Da el equivalente de estas palabras en español:

1. testimony
2. to possess
3. pure
4. iron
5. almost
6. influence
7. character
8. there
9. pre-Columbian
10. to mention

Answers are on page 250.

¿Sabías que? Tahiti was first explored by Domingo de Boenechea in 1772–1775, who named it *Isla de Amat* in honor of Manuel de Amat, Viceroy of Peru.

PIÉNSALO BIEN
THINK IT THROUGH

The conjunction. La conjunción

Be aware. Some conjunctions are difficult, especially those consisting of more than one word. They go far beyond the simple *y* (and) and *o* (or), as you will soon see.

Frequently, sentences are linked or related to each other grammatically by relative pronouns, as well as by other words used with that specific function. These other words are called *conjunctions*. Examples: *El maestro hablaba y el estudiante escuchaba* (The teacher spoke and the student listened); *Queríamos salir pero estaba lloviendo* (We wanted to go out, but it was raining). Here, *y* (and) and *pero* (but) are conjunctions. When one or more sentences are linked by relative pronouns or conjunctions, they are called compound sentences, and they can be either *coordinated sentences* or *subordinated sentences*.

When one sentence does not depend on the other, when the meaning is complete in itself, it is called a *coordinated sentence*. When it does depend on another sentence to complete its meaning, it is called a *subordinated sentence*. Here are examples of each one:

Coordinated sentences:
Queremos comprar el carro pero no tenemos dinero.
(We want to buy the car, but we have no money.)

Here, each one of the sentences: *Queremos comprar el carro* and *no tenemos dinero*, can stand on its own with its own complete, separate meaning.

Subordinated sentences:
Te lo hago saber a ti para que estés enterado. (I am telling you so you know.)

Here, obviously, *para que estés enterado* (so you know) would have no meaning without *Te lo hago saber* (I tell you). In other words, the second sentence depends on the first to complete the meaning.

There are a host of conjunctions in Spanish classified into two main categories (coordinants and subordinants, according to how one or the other relates to the sentences they unite). Some are just one word; some are a combination of words, making it difficult to distinguish between the two, especially when translating them into English. The translations of some of the following conjunctions are not complete, meaning that there are additional ways of translating them. We are just providing the basic translation for each, especially regarding conjunctions consisting of more than one word.

Here are some common one-word conjunctions:

y/e	and	(use *e* before a word beginning with *i* or *hi*)
o/u	or	(use *u* before a word beginning with *o* or *ho*)
pero/mas	but	
sino	but rather/on the contrary	
si	if	
ni	neither, nor	
que	that	
aunque	although	
porque	because	
luego	therefore/then	
pues	well	
porque/pues	because	
como	as, since	
menos	but	
antes	before	
así/como/siquiera	although, though, whether	
excepto	except	

Here are some common multiple-word conjunctions:

a causa de	because of
puesto que	since, although
no obstante	nevertheless/nonetheless
por lo cual/así pues/por tanto	therefore
de modo que	so/so that
siempre que/con tal de que	provided that, whenever
sin embargo	however
a fin de que	in order that, so that
con el fin de que	with the purpose of
ya que/bien/mal que	since

¡Ojo!—Watch Out!

Sometimes, conjunctions can be found within the same sentence, not related to another one, as in *La madre y el hijo* (the mother and the child), *Me desagrada éste o aquél* (I dislike this one or that one).

BRAIN TICKLERS
Set # 49

Ejercicios

A. Traduce la palabra o las palabras entre paréntesis:
1. Los libros (and) los cuadernos están sobre la mesa.
2. El padre de Lucila (or) el de Matilde nos van a acompañar.
3. Lo entendemos todo. (However) nos lo debes explicar una vez más.
4. No tengo puesto el reloj (because) lo perdí ayer.
5. (Before) de que se haga tarde, me llamas.
6. Te iré a buscar (provided that) vayas solo.
7. Estudiaremos todo el fin de semana (in order that) saquemos buenas notas.
8. No nos ayudó, (but rather) se fue a la fiesta de Jacinto.
9. Compré la entrada (so that) pudiéramos ir juntos.
10. (Nevertheless) lo voy a comprar porque es muy bueno.

B. The following paragraph contains several conjuctions. Underline each one that you find and rewrite them giving their meaning in English:

Celebramos el 4 de julio con una comida campestre. Fueron los jefes míos y los de mi compañera Adela. Al poco rato de estar allí, aunque estábamos bajo una tienda de campaña, comenzó a llover y nos empapamos de pies a cabeza. Pero, aún así, la pasamos muy bien. Sin embargo, uno de los jefes se enfermó de pronto y tuvimos que llevarlo a su casa a la carrera. Los demás, ya que estábamos allí, continuamos con la fiesta hasta entrada la noche. A eso de la medianoche, le dije a mi novio: —O me llevas a casa o me quedo a dormir aquí, puesto que es muy tarde y estoy muy cansada.

Answers are on page 250.

MÁS ES MEJOR
MORE IS BETTER

Nouns

el pintor	painter
el dibujante	artist/draftsman/draftswoman
la acuarela	watercolor
el lienzo	canvas
el caballete	easel
el aguarrás	turpentine
el dibujo	drawing
la galería de arte	art gallery
la tinta	ink
la exposición de arte	art exhibit
el escultor/tora	sculptor
la escultura	sculpture
el tallador/dora	carver
el artesano	artisan/craftsman/-woman
el premio	award
el borde	border
el fondo	background
el marco	frame
la naturaleza muerta	still life
la caricatura	caricature/cartoon
el caricaturista	caricaturist/cartoonist
el orfebre	silversmith/goldsmith
el acrílico	acrylic
el carboncillo	charcoal
el retrato	portrait
la fotografía	photograph
el diseño	design
la porcelana	porcelain
el yeso	plaster
la sombra	shadow
la perspectiva	perspective
el paisaje	landscape
el grabado	engraving

Verbs

pintar	to paint
dibujar	to draw

exponer	to exhibit
tallar	to carve
plasmar	to give expression to
esculpir	to sculpt
premiar	to award
diseñar	to design
retratar	to paint a portrait/to photograph
enmarcar	to frame
fotografiar	to photograph
enyesar	to plaster

¿Cuánto sabes? Do you know the last names of these two world-famous contemporary Spanish painters?

Pablo _____ and Salvador _____.

Answer: Picasso and Dali.

HABLA POPULAR
EVERYDAY SPEECH

Here are more common Spanish verb idioms/expressions:

ser un Quijote	to be a dreamer
andar de coronillas	to be running around
abrirse paso	to get ahead
caerse de la mata	to be obvious
coger la baja	to get over (someone)
botar la pelota	to hit a home run
dar donde duela	to hit hard
estar como una cabra	to be crazy
lavar el cerebro	to brainwash (someone)
hacerle a alguien un número ocho	to get someone into trouble
levantarse con el pie izquierdo	to get up on the wrong side of the bed
ir viento en popa	to do well/at full speed
matar dos pájaros de un tiro	to kill two birds with one stone
mirar de reojo	to look at someone out of the corner of your eye

dejarse llevar — to be easygoing
pensar en las musarañas — to think nonsense
no pintar nada — to get ignored
romperse el lomo — to work too hard
ser una gallina — to be a coward/chicken

More Practice with Idioms

From the list of idioms/expressions above, choose any five and write a Spanish sentence with each.

> **¿Sabías que?** Today, the United States leads the world in agriculture. Much of this is owed to the Spanish Franciscan missionaries who pioneered some of the main agricultural industries, such as citrus, peaches, and vineyards.

BIEN VALE LA PENA
IT'S WELL WORTH IT

Colors. Colores

Note: Colors can either be nouns or adjectives. As a noun, they need the article, which is always masculine, *el*, for example, *me gusta más el rojo* (I like the red one better). As an adjective, they must agree in gender and number with the noun. Here are the basic colors:

blanco	white	
negro	black	
gris	gray	(same for masculine and feminine)
rojo	red	
azul	blue	(same for masculine and feminine)
verde	green	(same for masculine and feminine)
marrón/carmelita	brown	(always *marrón/carmelita* for both masculine and feminine. For the plural of *marrón*, add –*es*, and take out the accent mark, as you are adding another syllable. For brown, you could also use *café* for the masculine and feminine.)

rosado	pink	
plata	silver	(always *plata* for both masculine and feminine. You could use *plateado/plateada*.)
dorado	gold	
amarillo	yellow	
morado	purple	
violeta	violet	(same for masculine and feminine)
cobre	copper	(same for masculine and feminine)
mostaza	mustard	(same for masculine and feminine)
crema	cream	(same for masculine and feminine)
anaranjado	orange	

Some of the words commonly used with colors are

claro	light (not clear)
obscuro	dark
llamativo	bright
apagado	dull
opaco	opaque
desteñido	faded
semi+color	semi+color

¡Ojo!—Watch Out!

When you say *la mesa es roja* (the table is red), *la mesa* is the subject, so the adjective *roja* (red) must agree with it in gender and number. When you say *el color de la mesa es rojo*, *el color* (the color) is the subject and the adjective must agree with it, thus *rojo*.

BRAIN TICKLERS
Set # 50

Ejercicios

A. Contesta estas preguntas en oraciones completas:
1. ¿De qué color es la camisa/blusa que llevas puesta hoy?
2. ¿Y de qué color son los zapatos que llevas puestos hoy?
3. Las manzanas por fuera (outside) pueden ser _____ o _____.
4. El color del sol es _____.
5. Los árboles en el verano son siempre de color _____.

B. Match the definition in column A with the word in column B:

Column A	Column B
1. Es el color de la luna.	a. amarillo
2. Es el color de la noche.	b. blanco
3. Es el color de las franjas (stripes) en la bandera de Estados Unidos.	c. negro
	d. rojas y blanco
4. Es el color del acero (steel).	e. gris
5. Es el color de la banana.	

C. Write five sentences in Spanish using for each one of the following colors:
1. verde   3. plata   5. violeta
2. marrón   4. amarilla

Answers are on page 251.

¿**Te acuerdas?** The demonstrative *éste* is a demonstrative pronoun, and *este* a demonstrative adjective when it is placed before a noun.

DILO COMO YO
SAY IT LIKE I DO

The syllable. La sílaba

Here we will deal with dividing words into syllables.

Generally, a syllable in Spanish is formed by a consonant and a vowel, although a vowel by itself can also form a syllable, as in: *igual> i-gual, acero> a-ce-ro*. A consonant by itself can't form a syllable in Spanish. When a consonant is between two vowels, it forms a syllable with the second vowel, as in: *rebanada> re-ba-na-da, mecánico> me-cá-ni-co*.

Here is step one:

In Spanish, the consonants *ch, ll, rr*, are double consonants and can't be separated. They must form a syllable with a vowel, as in: *noche> no-che, pollo> po-llo, carro> ca-rro*. Never, *never* separate these double consonants in Spanish.

Step two:

There are also combinations or groups of consonants that can't be separated in Spanish. These are

consonant groups	examples	consonant groups	examples
bl	pueblo> pue-blo	fr	africano> a-fri-ca-no
br	cabra> ca-bra	gl	regla> re-gla
cl	aclamar> a-cla-mar	gr	lograba> lo-gra-ba
cr	recreo> re-cre-o	pl	plaza> pla-za
dr	padre> pa-dre	pr	apretar> a-pre-tar
fl	flaco> fla-co	tr	retroceso> re-tro-ce-so

Step three:

When there are two consonants in a row, one after the other, the first consonant forms a syllable with the preceding vowel, and the second with the following vowel, as in: *observar> ob-ser-var, inmovilidad> in-mo-vi-li-dad*. The same occurs if both consonants happen to be the same, as in: *ennoblecer> en-no-ble-cer*.

When there are three consonants in a row, the first two form a syllable with the preceding vowel, and the third with the following vowel, as in: *perspectiva> pers-pec-tiva, obstinado> obs-ti-na-do.*

When there is a group of three or more consonants, and the last two are *bl, br, cl, cr, dr, fl, fr, gl, gr, pl, pr, tr,* they form a syllable with the following vowel, and the others with the preceding vowel, as in *temblor> tem-blor, infracción> in-frac-ción.*

An important reminder for the division of words into syllables in Spanish: You must keep in mind what we said in the previous lessons about the diphthongs and triphthongs—when they can be separated and when they cannot.

BRAIN TICKLERS
Set # 51

Ejercicios

A. Separate the following words into syllables:
1. aeroplano:
2. castañuela:
3. Constantinopla:
4. vejaminoso:
5. extranjero:
6. aplazamiento:
7. gravedad:
8. insomnio:
9. artritis:
10. callejuela:
11. arboleda:
12. río:
13. riachuelo:
14. escarabajo:
15. atropellamiento:
16. hagáis:
17. simpatiquísimo:
18. tembleque:
19. abismal:
20. astronómico:

B. In the paragraph below, underline the 13 words that have one of the consonant groups previously indicated; then divide each word into syllables and give a total syllable count for each of the words. You don't need to pay any attention to the meaning of any of the words. Two of the words are repeated twice, so use only one of each, giving you a total of 13 words.

Yo me veo en mi casa, metido en un ancho cuarto, sentado sobre un arcaz de pino, calladito, con los pies colgando, mirando cómo mi madre va arreglando la ropa blanca. De trecho en trecho, en la ancha estantería, penden unos cartelitos que indican lo que en aquella parte de la tabla está colocado... Mi madre va removiendo los rimeros y espantando las terribles polillas; luego abre las grandes arcas y van sacando de ellas trajes antiguos de seda que crujen dulcemente, manguitos en pequeños cilindros verdes, un miriñaque, una caja vieja, de la que extrae una mantilla negra.

Azorín

C. Also, in that same paragraph, five words are written with *ll*, two with *ch*, and two with *rr*. Write these words, divide each into syllables, and give a syllable count for each.

D. Also, in the same paragraph, there is a word with an accent mark over a weak vowel. Write this word, divide it into syllables, and give a syllable count.

Answers are on page 251.

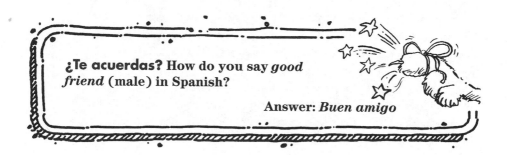

¿Te acuerdas? How do you say *good friend* (male) in Spanish?

Answer: *Buen amigo*

ALMA HISPÁNICA
HISPANIC SOUL

Benito Pérez Galdós

Benito Pérez Galdós is considered by many the greatest Spanish writer after Miguel de Cervantes, a big claim that can only be ascertained by the readers themselves. What can be said, without any hesitation, is that he was Spain's greatest writer of the nineteenth century, with a broad and profound vision of the individual and the society of his time. He was born in Las Palmas, Canary Islands, in 1843, and died in Madrid in 1920. His literary production centers on *los Episodios Nacionales* (National Episodes), the contemporary novel, and the theater; however, he was above all a novelist. He was a very prolific writer, having completed throughout his career 46 volumes of the *Episodios Nacionales*, 34 novels, 24 plays, and another 24 volumes of articles and other works, a phenomenal literary production rarely equaled. He studied law without liking it, and soon abandoned it to dedicate himself to his writing, especially after returning from a trip to France in 1868. His realism and his vast and complex creation of characters stand out as the basis for his work.

The writings of Benito Pérez Galdós.

Episodios Nacionales (extract)

...Así *atravesamos* la Mancha, triste y solitario país, donde el sol está en *su reino* y el hombre parece obra exclusiva del sol y del *polvo*; país entre todos famoso desde que el mundo entero *hase* acostumbrado a suponer la inmensidad de sus *llanuras* recorrida por el caballo de Don Quijote... Don Quijote no se comprende sino en la grandeza de la Mancha... Don Quijote no hubiera podido existir y habría muerto *en flor*, tras la primera salida, sin asombrar al mundo con las grandes *hazañas* de la segunda. Don Quijote necesitaba aquel horizonte, aquel *suelo* sin caminos, y que, sin embargo, *todo él* es camino, aquella tierra sin direcciones, pues por ella se va a todas partes, sin ir determinadamente a ninguna.

To help you understand the passage, here is the meaning of some key words:

atravesamos	crossed
su reino	its kingdom
polvo	dust
hase>se ha	*ha* (has), from the helping verb *haber*
llanuras	prairies
en flor	young/full of life
hazañas	deeds
suelo	soil
todo él	all of it

¿Sabías que? *La Mancha* (which literally means *the stain*, in English) is a vast region of Spain, northeast, west, and south of Madrid, composed of the provinces of Toledo, Cuenca, Ciudad Real, Guadalajara, and Albacete. The capital of the region is Toledo. It borders with other major regions: Aragón, Extremadura, Andalucía, Murcia, and Castilla y León.

PLUMA EN MANO
PEN IN HAND

Sobre la amistad/About friendship

Difícil es en la vida encontrar (to find) un buen amigo. Todos tenemos muchos conocidos, gente que vemos de vez en cuando, aquí y allá (here and there), a la que saludamos (greet) y con las que charlamos casualmente. Si se me preguntase: ¿Cuánta gente conoces? Contestaría muchísimas, cientos de personas a lo largo de mi vida. De algunas (some of them) me acuerdo, de la mayoría ni idea tengo de quiénes fueron, dónde y cuándo las conocí. Pasaron por mi vida sin saber que pasaron, como dijo el poeta. Pero los amigos son algo muy distinto, y si se me preguntase: ¿Cuántos amigos tienes? Los podría quizás contar con los dedos de la mano, y aún quitando uno o dos. Éstos son los que no se olvidan, los que están muy cerca de nuestros corazones, los que han influenciado grandemente nuestro pensar y proceder (conduct). Un buen amigo nunca nos abandona y se mantiene firme a nuestro lado en las buenas y en las malas (in good and bad times), cuando necesitamos ayuda (help) y cuando no, cuando precisamos (need) un buen consejo (advice) que nos ayude a salir de un problema. A cambio (In exchange) de todo esto, de tanto cariño y comprensión (understanding), nada pide, nada exige (demands), sino saber que estando él en una situación similar, le paguemos con la misma moneda (we do likewise).

En mi caso, mi mejor amigo fue un muchacho cubano. No porque lo conocía desde hacía mucho tiempo, sino por la gran muestra de amistad (friendship) que me dio un día cuando yo menos lo esperaba (least expected it). Ocurrió así (It happended this way): Estando en la plaza del Capitolio en La Habana, allá por (around) 1955, escuchando un concierto (concert) de un pianista extranjero, tuve sin proponérmelo (unintentionally) un altercado (argument) con un grupo de muchachos revoltosos (rowdy) que se me habían acercado (that had approached me). Súbitamente, empezaron a volar puñetazos (punches). Yo en el suelo, y todos ellos encima (on top) de mí hasta que casi perdí el conocimiento (consciousness). En ese momento se les abalanzó alguien (someone leaped on them) y me los quitó de encima. Asustados (Frightened) y sorprendidos, salierom huyendo (they all fled) y desaparecieron (disappeared) en la muchedumbre (crowd). El muchacho cubano me tendió la mano (held out his hand) y me ayudó a levantarme. —¿Estás bien?—, me preguntó. Su nombre era Cecilio, y desde ese día nos hicimos (we became) amigos inseparables.

BRAIN TICKLERS
Set # 52

Ejercicios

A. Choose five words/idioms from the list below and write a Spanish sentence with each:

amistad   de vez en cuando
acordarse   nunca   altercado
tender la mano
perder el conocimiento   muchedumbre

B. Taken from the passage, give the infinitive forms of the following verbs:
1. vemos
2. saludamos
3. preguntase
4. empezaron
5. salieron

C. Write a brief composition in Spanish about your best friend. How you met him/her, where, and the reason why you consider him/her your best friend. Use no less than five sentences.

Answers are on page 251.

ASÍ SOMOS
THIS IS WHO WE ARE

The Burial of the Count of Orgaz

In a small church, in the city of Toledo, Spain, there is one of the most famous paintings in the world: *El Entierro del Conde de Orgaz*, or The Burial of the Count of Orgaz, done by Domenicos Theotocopoulos, a Greek born in Candia, in the Island of Crete, called El Greco by the Spaniards. For a while, El Greco lived in Venice where he met Titian, his mentor. In 1570, he went to Rome, where he met Michelangelo. Around 1576 he went to Spain, where he was in the service of Philip II. He then moved to Toledo in 1580, where he lived until his death. In Toledo he rented the palace of the Marquis of Villena, which is now the Museum of El Greco. Here he had an affair with an aristocrat, Jerónima de las Cuevas, with whom he had an illegitimate son, Jorge Manuel, who later became an architect.

The painting of The Burial of the Count of Orgaz, an oil on canvas with a dimension of 16×11 feet 10 inches (487×350 cm), hangs in the vestibule of the church of Santo Tomé. The top of the painting, which is round, was meant to fit onto a wall of that shape. The painting depicts the burial of the count, a devout Catholic known for his piety. His soul, in the figure of a small child, is shown ascending to heaven, while his body is being placed into a coffin. The spirit of St. Augustine is on the right, and that of St. Stephen is on the left. Also in the painting is a small child, believed to be El Greco's son, and the painter himself looking out toward the viewer, immediately above St. Stephen. Depicted also in the painting is a group of elegantly dressed Spanish gentlemen showing great sorrow about the death of the Count. The church of Santo Tomé is located near the house of El Greco and the synagogue of el Tránsito. The church was built in the twelfth century and rebuilt in 1300.

BRAIN TICKLERS—THE ANSWERS

Set # 48, page 233

A.
1. necessity
2. to communicate
3. form
4. ceramic
5. sculpture
6. painting
7. characterized
8. abundance
9. aborigines
10. objects

B.
1. he sentido
2. el deseo y la esperanza
3. Desafortunadamente
4. obras maestras
5. tallados
6. oro y plata
7. Las pirámides y los templos
8. Las espadas
9. inolvidable
10. Por estar

C.
1. por poseer grandes artistas
2. México, Perú, Guatemala
3. Taxco
4. Bogotá
5. la América hispana

D.
1. F   2. F   3. V   4. V   5. F

E.
1. testimonio
2. poseer
3. puro/pura
4. el hierro
5. casi
6. la influencia
7. el carácter
8. allí
9. pre-Colombiano
10. mencionar

Set # 49, page 237

Piénsalo bien

A.
1. y
2. o
3. Sin embargo
4. porque
5. Antes
6. con tal de que
7. a fin de que
8. sino
9. de modo que
10. No obstante

B. Answers will vary.

Set # 50, page 242

Bien vale la pena
A.
1. Answers will vary.
2. Answers will vary.
3. rojas – verdes
4. amarillo
5. verde
B.
1. b   2. c   3. d   4. e   5. a
C. Answers will vary.

Set # 51, page 244

A.
1. a-e-ro-pla-no
2. cas-ta-ñue-la
3. Cons-tan-ti-no-pla
4. ve-ja-mi-no-so
5. ex-tran-je-ro
6. a-pla-za-mien-to
7. gra-ve-dad
8. in-som-nio
9. ar-tri-tis
10. ca-lle-jue-la
11. ar-bo-le-da
12. rí-o
13. ria-chue-lo
14. es-ca-ra-ba-jo
15. a-tro-pe-lla-mien-to
16. ha-gáis
17. sim-pa-ti-quí-si-mo
18. tem-ble-que
19. a-bis-mal
20. as-tro-nó-mi-co

B. Exercise for teacher and students to do.

C. Exercise for teacher and students to do.
Sample answer is:
Word: mantilla
Syllable break: man-ti-lla
Number of syllables: 3

D. Answers will vary. Sample answer is:
Word: estantería
Syllable break: es-tan-ter-í-a
Number of syllables: 5

Set # 52, page 248

Pluma en mano
A. Answers will vary.
B.
1. ver
2. saludar
3. preguntar
4. empezar
5. salir
C. Answers will vary.

Deportes para todos los gustos

Sports for all tastes

No todos tenemos el mismo gusto e igual pasa *tratándose* de los deportes. De ahí, que exista una enorme variedad de deportes para que cada cual *escoja* el que más le guste. Cada país o región del mundo tiene su deporte favorito: en Estados Unidos es el béisbol, *el baloncesto*, y el fútbol americano; en Europa y en la América hispánica es el fútbol o soccer, quitando al Caribe donde *se juega* más el béisbol o *pelota*. Otros deportes preferidos por todo el mundo son el golf, el tenis, el voleibol, el boxeo, *la natación*, el hockey sobre hielo, y en España y en algunos países hispánicos *la corrida de toros*. Estos son algunos de los deportes tradicionales, pero en los últimos años *han surgido* infinidad de otros aunque no son tan populares como los citados, entre ellos *el paracaidismo* y el surfing. Ahora bien, no es igual *gustarle a uno* un deporte, como espectador, que saberlo jugar bien, para lo cual se requiere una *habilidad o destreza* especial *y que* por lo general *nace* con la persona. Siendo niños y adolescentes todos jugamos uno que otro deporte pero más como ejercicio que otra cosa o *como un medio de* divertirse, de *pasar un buen rato*, de entretenerse.

Jugar un deporte también requiere contar con el equipo necesario, *como son* el uniforme, *calzado* especial y otros accesorios que dependerán de la clase de deporte *de que se trate*. Por ejemplo, en el béisbol serán la pelota, *el guante*, el bate, *la máscara*, o en el tenis la raqueta y la pelota. También se requiere un lugar especial en donde jugar, un campo, una *cancha*, una *pista*, una *piscina*. Y si el deporte es profesional, un estadio *bien dispuesto* y lo suficientemente grande para acomodar a miles de espectadores. Jugar un deporte también nos ayuda a ejercitarnos, a mantener nuestro cuerpo *sano y en forma*, y también a *llevarnos bien* con otras gentes.

Como queda dicho, el béisbol es uno de los pasatiempos favoritos de los norteamericanos, principalmente cuando se juega la Serie Mundial, en la que compiten dos equipos ganadores de la ligas Nacional y la Americana. Se juegan en total siete juegos y será el campeón el equipo que gane cuatro de los juegos. Realmente no sabemos por qué se le llama Serie Mundial pues en realidad no participa en ella otro país *que no sea* Estados Unidos. Claro que en muchos de los equipos famosos, como los Yankees, muchos de los jugadores o peloteros son extranjeros, mayormente hispanos, pero esto *en sí* no la hace mundial. Las Olimpiadas sí son mundiales en *el más amplio sentido*, pues en ellas intervienen un gran número de países de todo el mundo. Aquí no compiten países, por ejemplo, Italia contra Portugal, *sino más bien* individuos que a su vez representan a distintos países. *Al que queda* en *primer lugar* se le entrega un *medallón* de oro, al del segundo lugar, una de plata, y al del tercer lugar, una de cobre.

Vocabulario básico

tratándose	regarding
escoja	chooses
el baloncesto (also básquetbol)	basketball
se juega	is played
pelota	ball/baseball
la natación	swimming
la corrida de toros	bullfights
han surgido	have emerged
el paracaidismo	parachuting
gustarle a uno	that one likes
habilidad o destreza	skill
y que	and that
nace	is born
como un medio	as a way
de pasar un buen rato	to have a good time
como son	such as
calzado	shoes
de que se trate	we are dealing with
el guante	glove
la máscara	mask
cancha	court
pista	track
piscina	pool
bien dispuesto	well suited/equipped
sano y en forma	healthy and in good shape
llevarnos bien	get along well
Como queda dicho	As has been said
que no sea	other than
en sí	in itself

en el más amplio sentido	in the broadest sense
sino más bien	but rather
Al que queda	The one finishing (in)
primer lugar	first place
medallón	medal

¿Sabías que? Around 1524, the northeastern coastline of North America, stretching from New Jersey to Rhode Island, was named *Land of Esteban Gómez* (according to the Ribero map). Gómez was a Portuguese explorer in the service of Spain. On his voyage, he had seen Cape Cod, Massachusetts Bay, and the mouths of the Connecticut, Delaware, and Hudson rivers. He called the Hudson *Río San Antón.*

BRAIN TICKLERS
Set # 53

Ejercicios

A. Traduce la palabra o las palabras entre paréntesis:
   1. (Talking about) del tiempo, el frío no me gusta.
   2. (Baseball) es el deporte más popular en Estados Unidos.
   3. (Some) de los deportes que más se juegan son el tenis y el golf.
   4. No hay nada como bañarse en (a pool) cuando hace mucho calor.
   5. En el equipo de los Yankees, muchos de los (players) son hispanos.

B. Contesta estas preguntas en oraciones completas:
   1. ¿Qué deporte es el más popular en los países hispánicos?

2. ¿En qué países hispánicos hay corridas de toro?
3. ¿Tienes tú alguna habilidad especial para algún deporte?
4. Entre todos los deportes, ¿cuál te gusta más?
5. ¿Cuáles son dos de los accesorios que necesita un pelotero?

C. Basado en el pasaje anterior, dinos si cada una de estas afirmaciones es *verdadera o falsa*:

1. En el Caribe no se juega la pelota.	V	F
2. Para jugar bien un deporte no se necesita ninguna habilidad especial.	V	F
3. El estadio de los Yankees está en el Bronx.	V	F
4. Las Olimpiadas nacieron en la India.	V	F
5. El paracaidismo es un deporte reciente.	V	F

¿Cuánto sabes? *El campeón* in Spanish is a *male champion*. How would you say in Spanish a *female champion*?

Answers are on page 270.

PIÉNSALO BIEN
THINK IT THROUGH

The preposition. La preposición

Some common prepositions in Spanish:

con	with
de	of, from
desde	from, since, after
durante	during
en	in, on
entre	between, among
hacia	toward
hasta	until, up to
según	according to
sobre	on, upon, above, over

There are others, but these are the ones you should know well.

In addition, there are many, hundreds, of prepositional phrases, both in Spanish and English, that very often present a problem in terms of translating them into English, especially when Spanish uses a preposition and English doesn't, as in: *alrededor de>* around, *antes de>* before, *acerca de>* about. If you leave the prepositions out in any of those phrases, they would be adverbs, not prepositions, as in:

Prepositional phrase:

> *La iglesia está alrededor*   The church is around
> *de la esquina.*   the corner.

Here, the prepositional phrase is *alrededor de* (around). Notice in Spanish the use of the preposition *de*.

Used as an adverb:

> *No hay nadie alrededor.*   There is nobody around.

When not used in a prepositional phrase, the function of a preposition is simply to connect words and also to express the relationship between them, as in: *Manuel es de Barcelona* (Manuel is from Barcelona), *El reloj es de Pablo* (The watch is Paul's).

Prepositional phrases in English are also very difficult to translate into Spanish. Take, for example, the verb *to go*, and see how it changes meaning according to the various prepositions. In these cases, the use of the preposition results in a totally different word in Spanish.

To go in English generally is *ir* in Spanish. However, look at these prepositional phrases used with verbs:

to go in	*entrar* (en)
to go out	*salir* (a, de)
to go up	*subir* (a)
to go down	*bajar* (a)
to go after	*perseguir* (a)
to go against	*oponerse* (a)
to go by	*pasar* (por)
to go off	*marcharse* (a, de)
to go on	*proseguir* (various ways of using it in Spanish)
to go under	*hundirse* (en)

As you can see, none of those verbs in Spanish have anything to do with *ir* (to go), and the prepositions in Spanish generally do not correspond to English. In these cases, what you would most likely do is to translate the English phrase literally, thus saying, for example, for *to go up*: *ir arriba*, or in a sentence, *El niño va arriba al baño* (The child goes up to the bathroom), instead of *El niño sube al baño*, which is the common way of saying it in Spanish. Unfortunately, you have no other alternative but to memorize such phrases in Spanish, especially the common ones.

To help you out, we are giving you below some other common phrases using the prepositions *a* and *de*:

a followed by infinitives:

ayudar a	to help to	*La ayudo a estudiar.* (I help her study.)
aprender a	to learn to	*Queremos aprender a bailar.* (We want to learn how to dance.)
decidirse a	to decide to	*Se decidió a tomar el examen.* (He decided to take the exam.)
contribuir a	to contribute to	*Voy a contribuir a preparar la fiesta.* (I am going to contribute to preparing the party.)

de followed by infinitives:

acordarse de	to remember to	*No me acordé de cerrar la puerta.* (I didn't remember to close the door.)
cansarse de	to get tired of	*Estamos cansados de estudiar.* (We are tired of studying.)
acabar de	to have just	*Juan acaba de regresar de un viaje.* (John has just returned from a trip.)
olvidarse de	to forget to	*Me olvidé de llamarla.* (I forgot to call her.)

BRAIN TICKLERS
Set # 54

Ejercicios

A. Traduce la palabra o frase entre paréntesis:
1. (Maria's dress) es el más bonito.
2. No me gusta salir (with) ellos.
3. (We have just finished) la lección.
4. Nos vemos (before) del juego de pelota.
5. Para (go down) al sótano tienes que usar esa puerta.

B. Write a sentence in Spanish with each of the following:
   1. entre   3. alegrarse de   5. alrededor
   2. hasta   4. salir a

¿Te acuerdas? When using a verb in the command form, the direct object pronoun must always be placed _____.

Answers are on page 270.

MÁS ES MEJOR
MORE IS BETTER

Nouns

la anotación/puntuación	score
el campeonato	championship
el partido	match, game
el juego	play, game
el gol	goal
el partidario	supporter
el fanático	fan
el ciclismo	cycling
el campeón/la campeona	champion
el árbitro	umpire
el entrenador/la entrenadora	coach

la pesca	fishing
la bicicleta	bicycle
el punto	point
el campo de deportes	playing field
la carrera	race
la lucha libre	wrestling
el levantamiento de pesas	weight lifting
el arco y la flecha	bow and arrow
el casco	helmet
los bolos	bowling
el empate	a tie

Verbs

nadar	to swim	perder	to lose
correr	to run	tirar	to throw
saltar	to jump	cazar	to hunt
coger	to catch	pescar	to fish
anotar	to score	bucear	to swim underwater
ganar	to win		

HABLA POPULAR
EVERYDAY SPEECH

Here are more common Spanish verb idioms/expressions:

matarlas callando	to deceive
estar más muerto que vivo	to be more dead than alive
estar ciego como un murciélago	to be as blind as a bat
ser un MacPato	to be very wealthy
tragárselas todas	to be naïve
bañarse como un gato	to take a quick bath
pensar con la cabeza, no con los pies	to think with your head, not your feet
verse en un aprieto	to find oneself in a tight spot
perder los estribos	to lose your cool/composure
tratar con guantes de seda	to treat someone gently/ with kid gloves
ser un hacha	to be very skillful
tener malas pulgas	to have a bad temper
volver a las andadas	to behave as usual
vagar como un alma en pena	to wander aimlessly

BIEN VALE LA PENA
IT'S WELL WORTH IT

Courtesy phrases. Frases de cortesía

Some common Spanish courtesy phrases:

¡Hola!	Hello!
¡Gracias!	Thank you!
¡Muchas gracias!	Many thanks!
¡de nada!/¡No hay de qué!/ ¡No es nada!	You're welcome!
¡Por favor!	Please!
¡Con gusto!/¡Encantado!	With pleasure!
¡Gusto en conocerlo!	Nice to meet you!
¡Con mucho gusto!	With much pleasure!
¡El gusto es mío!	The pleasure is mine!
¡Perdón!	Excuse me!/Pardon me!
¡Con permiso!	Excuse me!
¡Bienvenido!	Welcome!
¡Adiós!	Goodbye!
¡Hasta luego!/¡Hasta la vista!	See you later!
¡Nos vemos!	See you!
¡Que esté bien!	Be well!
¡Cuidese!	Take care!
¡Muy agradecido!	I am very grateful!
¡Que pase un buen día!	Have a nice day!
¡Encantado de verle!	Nice to see you!
¡Lo siento!	Sorry!
¡Cuánto lo siento!	I am very/so sorry!
¡La culpa es mía!	It is my fault!
¡Perdone la molestia!	Sorry to bother you!
Saludos a	Regards to
¡Felicidades!/¡Enhorabuena!	Congratulations!
¡Buen viaje!	Have a nice trip!
¡Qué pena!/¡Qué lástima!	What a shame/pity!
¡Me encanta!	I love it!
¡Que le aproveche!	Enjoy your meal!
¡Es usted muy amable!	You're very kind!
¡Por supuesto!/¡No faltaba más!	Of course!
¡Buenos días!	Good morning!
¡Buenas tardes!	Good afternoon!

¡Buenas noches!	Good evening!/Good night!
¡Mis mejores deseos!	My best wishes!
¡Salud!	Cheers!/To your health!
¡Mi más sentido pésame!	My deepest condolences!

BRAIN TICKLERS
Set # 55

Ejercicio

Completa los espacios en blanco con la frase de cortesía según se da en paréntesis:

1. (Many thanks!) ¡_____ por el regalo!
2. ¡Hasta luego y (nice to meet you!) _____!
3. ¿Te compraste un carro nuevo? (Congratulations!) ¡_____!
4. (You're welcome!) ¡_____! Lo hice con mucho gusto.
5. Tengo mucho sueño. (Good night!) ¡_____!

¿Te acuerdas? Hispanics generally have two last names; the first is the _____ and the second is the _____. The abbreviation of Señor is _____, of Señora _____, and of Señorita _____.

Answers are on page 270.

DILO COMO YO
SAY IT LIKE I DO

The synalepha or linking of words.
La sinalefa o enlace de palabras

This is a very common occurrence but only in spoken Spanish. The synalepha is the fusion into one syllable of vowels belonging to separate words, and resulting in the notion to the untrained ear that the speaker is speaking too fast, eating up letters. Let's see how the synalepha works.

Take this sentence as an example:

Siempre te esperamos.

Grammatically, this sentence, counting all three words, has a total of seven syllables:

siem-pre-te-es-pe-ra-mos

However, phonetically, it has only six because of the linking of *ee*:

siempre-tees-pe-ra-mos

Here is another example:

dale agua>   grammatically, four syllables: *da-le-a-gua;* phonetically, three syllables because of the linking of *ea*: *da-lea-gua*

There are cases, however, in which the synalepha does not occur because of the way certain vowels are pronounced—less open or more open—as in these examples: *aoa, aie, euo, oia,* and others. This, however, should not concern you at this time; we just want you to be aware of the synalepha, especially when you hear native speakers talk. It is not that they speak too fast, but because of the synalepha.

Following are some common examples of the synalepha:

How is written	How is said
fiesta especial	*fies(**ta es**)pecial*
para mi hermano	*para(**mi her**)mano*
puede influir	*pue(**de in**)fluir*
sin tu esfuerzo	*sin(**tu es**)fuerzo*
si hubiera venido	*(**si hu**)biera venido*
uno a uno	*u(**no a u**)no*
entraba ahora	*entra(**ba aho**)ra*

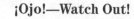

¡Ojo!—Watch Out!

You must anticipate that when listening to a native speak Spanish it would not be the same as listening to your teacher in class. A teacher will always make the effort to speak slowly so you can understand him or her better, and may repeat a sentence more than once. In the real world, people just express themselves spontaneously, letting the language flow naturally, as it should.

ALMA HISPÁNICA
HISPANIC SOUL

Ana María Matute

Her fiction is one of the most searing expressions of the turbulent time of the Spanish Civil War. Ana María Matute ignites every page in her books with memories of a youngster caught up in the midst of human passion and cruelty, of the struggle between two ideologies that tore apart an entire nation for three long years. She lived it, experienced it, and it crushed her heart, which she could only revive by expressing her most intimate feelings of suffering and anguish. She is widely hailed as one of Spain's greatest contemporary novelists, very well known and respected. Many of her works have been translated into several languages, including English. In 1966 and 1967, she was a visiting professor at Indiana University in Bloomington, where she taught advanced courses in Spanish literature.

Ana María Matute was born in Barcelona in 1926. Among her most famous novels are: *Los Abel* (1948), *Fiesta al noroeste* (1952), *Los hijos muertos* (1958), and *Los soldados lloran de noche* (1977). Two of her semiautobiographical novels are *La trampa* (1973), and *Luciérnagas* (1993).

The writings of Ana María Matute.

Excerpt from *Los soldados lloran de noche*

No te enfades. Escucha, *sigo el hilo*: entré, y estaba él ahí, sobre la mesa, doblado. Parecía dormido, pero cuando le di un *empujoncito* en el hombro se derrumbó hacia la derecha, y cayó como un saco. Pobre señor, tenía el corazón *gastado*. Porque sabes, hijito, las vísceras, como las máquinas, se gastan, se estropean, se atrancan... El médico dijo que era una *angina de pecho*. Lloré mucho, te lo juro. Había rosas por todas partes, encarnadas, como a él le gustaban, y fui y traje todas las que pude, se las eché encima y me dije: es lo último que puedo hacer por ti, porque mi pobre guitarra no la oirás jamás.

To help you better understand this passage, here is the meaning of some key words:

no te enfades	don't get upset
sigo el hilo	I continue with my train of thought
empujoncito	little push
gastado	wasted
angina de pecho	angina (heart attack)

PLUMA EN MANO
PEN IN HAND

La corrida de toros/Bullfighting

Se dice que más que un deporte la corrida de toros es un arte, y quizá la gente en parte tenga razón (they are right). Es un arte por el espectáculo en sí, por la vestimenta (attire) o traje de luces  del torero y por su donaire (gracefulness). También puede considerarse un deporte por haber dos contrincantes parejos (even): el torero o matador y el toro. Cualquiera de los dos tiene las de ganar o perder (win or lose), aunque al torero lo ayudan grandemente los banderilleros*, a pie (on foot), o a caballo que poco a poco van debilitando (weakening) al animal, que le van mermando (reducing) la vida. El torero tiene habilidad, experiencia, quizá más agilidad, pero mucha menos fuerza (strength) que el toro que con sólo un roce (rubbing/brush) lo puede tumbar al suelo (knock him to the ground) y con sus cuernos (horns) o peso mandarlo al otro mundo (send him to the other/next world), con capa y todo (with cape and all).

Según la historia, la corrida de toros tuvo su origen en los tiempos prehistóricos de los iberos (Iberian), en los que el toro bravo (fierce bull) se consideraba algo así (something like) como semi-sagrado. En la isla de Creta se reverenciaba al toro y en los libros se habla de haberlo sacrificado en honor de la justicia. Pero fue en tiempos de Roma cuando el espectáculo, o sea, la corrida, se hizo popular. Nada de extrañar (nothing to be surprised about) pues tales (such) espectáculos públicos y sanguinarios (bloody) eran grandes diversiones en la sociedad romana. Durante la Edad Media la corrida se hizo (became) popularísima, sobre todo entre la alta sociedad o aristocracia, aunque el torear (to fight – the bull) se hacía a caballo y no a pie.

A pesar de ser un arte o deporte muy polémico, principalmente entre los anglosajones (Anglo Saxons), sigue ocupando un lugar de primerísimo orden en los pueblos hispánicos y con majetuosas plazas de toros (bullrings).

*banderilleros: men on horseback or foot carrying barbered darts (called *banderillas*) that are stuck into the bull's neck.

BRAIN TICKLERS
Set # 56

Ejercicios

A. Choose five words from the list below and write a Spanish sentence with each:

el deporte	tener razón
tener las de ganar	tumbar al suelo
algo así	en honor de
hacerse	polémico

B. Taken from the passage, give the infinitive forms of the
following verbs:
1. Se dice   4. se hizo
2. ayudan   5. se hacía
3. reverenciaba

C. Write a composition in Spanish about how you feel about
bullfighting in general. Use no less than five sentences.

Answers are on page 270.

ASÍ SOMOS
THIS IS WHO WE ARE

The legend of El Dorado/Eldorado

Gold, gold, gold—anything gold has been an obsession of
humans since the beginning of time. In the sixteenth century,
with the discoveries of Mexico and later of Peru, Europeans
sought the precious metal for personal wealth and power, just
as we do today. In terms of desiring it, of wishing to possess it,
there is absolutely no difference between them and us—we
live for it and die for it, fight wars, and go to the farthest
confines of the earth to find it. It seems that the magic of
gold is eternal.

The legend or myth of El Dorado is a logical consequence
of the mentality of sixteenth-century Western Europe. Spain,
England, France, Holland, among other nations, vied for power,
and gold was the conduit to grab it and thus rule the world.

The legend of El Dorado originated in South America and
may have been based on fact. In the region of New Granada
(today's Colombia), there was an Indian
tribe on the shores of Lake Guatavitá
whose *cacique* or chief, during a
ceremony, covered his body with gold
dust stuck to his skin with some kind of
glue. From a distance, he appeared to
be made of solid gold. Then he boarded
a boat with many pieces of gold and
precious stones that were offered to the

gods, jumped in the water, and washed away the gold dust. Following the conquest of Quito by Benalcázar, an Indian from the region informed captain Luis de Daza about the Indian chief and his custom, and the Spaniards went searching for the *Golden Man,* or *el Hombre Dorado.* Soon after, the man was forgotten but the myth took wings, being now not a man but an entire country where gold was plentiful. Although El Dorado, or Eldorado, was never found, it served a greater purpose, which was the discovery and exploration of vast South American lands, just as happened in North America with Coronado and the Seven Cities of Cíbola and the city of Quivira.

The first expedition that specifically set out to look for El Dorado was one by Philip Hutten to the coast of Venezuela in 1541, which lasted five years. It was followed by one by Hernán Pérez de Quesada, also in 1541, along the shores of the Amazon River, and by Gonzalo Pizarro (1541–1543). Many years later, in 1560–1561, Pedro de Ursúa y Lope de Aguirre also set out from Peru to find it. The English explorer, Walter Raleigh, joined the group of El Dorado explorers in 1595 but was also unsuccessful.

The elusive El Dorado has remained hidden since the myth surfaced 500 years ago, although it may have resurfaced under a different disguise—the California Gold Rush? the Diamond Mines of South America or Brazil? the City of New York?

BRAIN TICKLERS—THE ANSWERS

Set # 53, page 256

A.
1. Tratándose
2. La pelota
3. Algunos
4. una piscina
5. jugadores

B.
1. fútbol
2. España, México y Perú
3–5. Answers will vary.

C.
1. F   2. F   3. V   4. F   5. V

Cuánto sabes?
Campeona

Set # 54, page 260

Piénsalo bien
A.
1. El vestido de María
2. con
3. Acabamos de terminar
4. antes
5. bajar

B. Answers will vary.

¿Te acuerdas?
After the verb (attached)

Set # 55, page 263

Bien vale la pena
1. Muchas gracias
2. gusto en conocerlo/a!
3. ¡Felícitaciones!
4. ¡De nada!
5. ¡Buenas noches!

¿Te acuerdas?
father's name – mother's
maiden name.
Sr.–Sra.–Srta.

Set # 56, page 267

Pluma en mano
A. Answers will vary.

B.
1. decir
2. ayudar
3. reverenciar
4. hacer
5. hacer

C. Answers will vary.

La naturaleza es vida

Nature is life

¿Puede haber algo más *placentero* que pasarse un día en el campo, fuera del *bullicio y ajetreo* de la ciudad, del *amontonamiento* de gentes, de sonidos estridentes y *inoportunos*. Allí, tirado *debajo de un árbol, dejando que* la brisa matinal *nos acaricie* la piel, respirando aire puro y sano, oyendo *el silbar* de los pájaros que *aceleran* el vuelo para *posarse* en alguna *rama* en la que *reposar*. El rumor de las tranquilas aguas de un *arroyuelo* o del *salpicar* de algún salto de agua, *el crujir* de las altas hierbas con *el azote* del viento.

Esto representa *a cabalidad* un día de campo que pasamos mi familia y yo en un pueblo de Castilla la Vieja, en la región llamada el Bierzo. Era un sábado en el mes de julio. Llegamos a las 10 de la mañana y nos situamos *a tiro de piedra* del río Burbia. A pesar de ser verano, hacía su poco de frío y más fría aún estaba el agua. Pero, *así y todo*, nos fuimos metiendo poco a poco en el río hasta que el agua *nos dio por el cuello*. Allí *retozamos*, jugamos, hicimos *maromas, nos zambullimos* varias veces. Aguas más cristalinas *no había visto* en mi vida, *ni siquiera* las de las bellas playas del Caribe, la de Varadero en Cuba, por ejemplo, o las de Viña del Mar en Chile, o la de Luquillo en San Juan Puerto Rico. *Debía haber sido* por la soledad de aquel *paraje* del Bierzo, no visitado por turistas ni aun por *los pueblerinos*.

Después del baño, *nos desplomamos* todos en la hierba, y mis primas prepararon la comida que se había llevado en dos grandes *cestas: salchichón*, chorizo, *tortilla española, queso manchego*, buenas *hogazas de pan*, y vino. Comimos con las dos manos y, acto seguido, medio adormecidos, *nos zampamos* una siesta olímpica. A eso de las 7 de la tarde, más contentos y satisfechos que un monarca, regresamos a casa. El campo, ¡oh el campo!, con su *embrujo*, con su serenidad, con su limpidez de cielo y tierra… Un día en el campo, haciéndole compañía a la naturaleza; *no hay nada igual*.

Vocabulario básico

placentero	enjoyable
bullicio y ajetreo	noise and hustle and bustle
amontonamiento	crowding
inoportunos	inopportune
debajo de	under
árbol	tree
dejando que	letting
nos acaricie	caresses us
el silbar	whistling
aceleran	speed up
posarse	to perch
rama	branch
reposar	rest
arroyuelo	brook
salpicar	to splash
el crujir	rustling
el azote	whipping
a cabalidad	faithfully
a tiro de piedra	next to/within a stone's throw
así y todo	even so
nos dio por el cuello	got up to our neck/was neck high
retozamos	frolicked
maromas	antics
nos zambullimos	we dived
no había visto	I had not seen
ni siquiera	not even
Debía haber sido	It could have been
paraje	place
los pueblerinos	townspeople
nos desplomamos	we collapsed
cestas	baskets
salchichón	sausage (similar to salami)
tortilla española	Spanish omelet
queso manchego	Manchego cheese
hogazas de pan	loaf of bread
nos zampamos	to wolf down
embrujo	spell
no hay nada igual	there's nothing like it

BRAIN TICKLERS
Set # 57

Ejercicios

A. Traduce la palabra o las palabras que se dan en peréntesis:
1. No hay nada más (enjoyable) que un día en el campo.
2. Sueño con estar (under) un frondoso árbol.
3. Yo siempre cumplo (faithfully) con mi trabajo.
4. Si Carlos no salió bien en el examen, (it could have been) por estar enfermo.
5. Una vez probé la (Spanish omelet) y me gustó muchísimo.

B. Contesta estas preguntas en oraciones completas:
1. ¿Te gusta a ti el campo? ¿Por qué?
2. ¿Te has bañado alguna vez en un arroyuelo o río?
3. ¿Has probado alguna vez *chorizo español*? ¿Te gustó?
4. ¿Qué árbol te gusta más?
5. ¿Qué piensas tú de la naturaleza en general?

C. Basado en el pasaje anterior, dinos si cada una de estas afirmaciones es *verdadera o falsa*:
1. En el campo siempre hay bullicio y ajetreo. V F
2. A los pájaros les encanta posarse en una rama. V F
3. La playa de Varadero está en la costa de Perú. V F
4. La capital de Estados Unidos es muy visitada por turistas. V F
5. Después de comer mucho, todos nos adormecemos un poco. V F

¿Cuánto sabes? ¿Puedes mencionar dos de las playas más famosas de México?

Answers are on page 286.

PIÉNSALO BIEN
THINK IT THROUGH

The interjection. La interjección

The interjection doesn't constitute a part of speech, as the noun, verb, or adjective do. In fact, it constitutes a sentence all by itself. It is used to express an emotion, such as surprise: *¡oh!*, pain: *¡ay!*, amazement: *¡bravo! ¡caramba!* (Good heavens!) *¡ándale!* (Get going!) If I say *¡ah!*, it would mean pretty much what I could express by using a whole sentence, such as: *Me encanta la buena noticia* (I love good news), *Me admira tu valentía* (I admire your courage). *¡Ni a la fuerza!* (No way!)

The meaning of most interjections largely depends on the intonation, on how they are expressed. For example, *¡ah!* can mean either surprise or a threat, as in: *¡Ah, fantástico!*, *¡Ah, si pasa algo, yo no respondo!* (Ah, if anything happens, I will not be held responsible!). There are other interjections, however, that have a fixed meaning, such as: *¡Ojalá!*, expressing a hope, or *¡Bravo!*, expressing amazement or satisfaction.

Also, there are many nouns, verbs, adjectives, and adverbs that can be used as interjections, such as *¡Madre!* (My goodness!) *¡Ojo!* (Watch out!), *¡Vaya!* (Well done!, Fantastic!), *¡ya!* (Right now!/Enough!), etc. Likewise, many phrases or expressions can also be used as interjections, such as: *¡Ni loco!* (No way!), *¡Que si me gusta!* (Of course, I like it!), etc. Notice that in all of these examples the intonation is what makes them interjections.

BRAIN TICKLERS
Set # 58

Ejercicios

A. Here are five interjections. According to their meaning, complete the sentence with your own words:
  1. ¡Ojo, _____!
  2. ¡Ya _____!
  3. ¡Caramba, _____!
  4. ¡Ni a la fuerza _____!
  5. ¡Ándale, _____!

B. Here are some uses of interjections. Circle each one and give a basic English translation:
1. ¡Ay, Dios mío, que mala suerte tengo!
2. ¡Vaya con tu insistencia! ¿No ves que no puedo?
3. ¡Sí y no! No te puedo dar una respuesta específica.
4. ¿Ganaste el partido? ¡Bravo, eres un campeón!
5. Cuando vayas a la playa, ¡ojo con los tiburones!

C. Write three sentences in Spanish using your own interjections:

Answers are on page 286.

MÁS ES MEJOR
MORE IS BETTER

Nouns

la hoja	leaf
el tronco de árbol	tree trunk
el lago	lake
la montaña	mountain
la colina	hill
la roca	rock
el paisaje	landscape
la hoguera	campfire
el campesino	country person
la tienda de campaña	tent
el bicho	bug
el bosque	woods
la raíz	root
la paja	straw
el terremoto	earthquake
el arco iris	rainbow
el derrumbamiento	landslide
la marea	tide
el desfiladero	ravine/gorge
el barranco	gully/ravine
el pantano/la ciénaga	swamp
la bruma	mist
la semilla	seed
la cuerda	rope
la sabia	sap

la leña	firewood
el fuego	fire
el valle	valley
la piedra	stone
el arroyo	creek
la planta	plant

Verbs

acampar	to camp
florecer	to flower/bloom
despejar	to clear up
trepar	to climb
deslizarse	to glide
remar	to row/paddle
encender	to light up/turn on
apagar	to put out/turn off
sembrar	to plant
cortar	to cut
clavar	to hammer
ir de caminata	to hike
quemar	to burn

¿Sabías que? The first Catholic church in North America was built by Friar Francisco de Pareja in St. Augustine, Florida, in 1560.

And the Smith Chair, specifically meant for the study of Spanish, was established at Harvard University in 1815. Abel Smith, a graduate of the institution, donated $20,000 for this purpose.

HABLA POPULAR
EVERYDAY SPEECH

Here are more common Spanish verb idioms/expressions:

pasar por alto	to overlook
estar emberrenchinado	to be mad/upset
dar el gato por liebre	to trick somebody
arrancar los motores/ ponerse las pilas	to get going
pasar las de Caín	to go through a tough situation

enredar la pita	to get entangled/complicated
dárselas de sabio	to pretend to know it all
quedarse en babia	to not understand something
dormir a pierna suelta	to sleep well
fruncir el ceño	to frown
ser testarudo	to be stubborn
ser un simplón	to be empty-headed
tener algo en la punta de la lengua	to have something on the tip of your tongue
ser un bocón	to have a big mouth

BIEN VALE LA PENA
IT'S WELL WORTH IT

Augmentatives and diminutives.
Aumentativos y diminutivos

The difference between *pequeño* and *pequeñito* is the size. *Pequeño* means small, and *pequeñito* means very small. Those are adjective examples, and, as adjectives, they agree in gender and number with the noun. Regarding nouns:

hombre>	man	
hombrón/hombrote>	big man	endings: -ón and -ote
hombrecito>	small man	ending: -ito

Besides indicating size, at times the augmentative and diminutive suffixes denote certain disdain or mockery. For example, if I say, *hombracho,* or *mujerzuela,* using the suffixes *-acho* and *-uela,* I am talking disdainfully about a man and a woman. In other words, there are various kinds of suffixes applied to both nouns and adjectives, and they can denote either size or disdain. They can also denote certain affection or esteem. Look at these examples:

Carlos	means Charles
Carlitos	means little Charles
Carliños	means something like loving little Charles
chico	means small
chiquito	means very small
chiquilín	means something lovably small

In short, augmentative and diminutive suffixes can denote, besides size, affection or disdain.

The most common augmentative suffixes in Spanish are

masculine	feminine	examples	
-ón	-ona	caserón	big house
-azo	-aza	perrazo	big dog
-acho	-acha	hombracho	big man
-ote	-ota	grandote	very big

The most common diminutive suffixes in Spanish are

-ito	-ita	muñequita	little doll
-illo	-illa	nubecilla	little cloud
-ico	-ica	gatico	little cat

Here are a few other examples of augmentatives and diminutives:

Noun	Augmentative	Diminutive
niño	niñote	niñito
animal	animalazo	animalito
mujer	mujerona	mujercita
amigo	amigazo	amiguito
carro	carrote	carrito
paquete (package)	paquetón	paquetico
comida	comelona	comidita
fiesta	fiestón	fiestecilla
árbol	arbolazo	arbolito
bicho (bug)	bichote	bichito
lata (can)	latona	latica
carretera (highway)	carreteraza	carreterilla

BRAIN TICKLERS
Set # 59

Ejercicio

Give the augmentative and diminutive for the following nouns, using *-ote* and *-ito* or the feminine form if required:

Noun	Augmentative	Diminutive
1. hermano	_____	_____
2. cama	_____	_____
3. mata	_____	_____
4. luna	_____	_____
5. rato	_____	_____

Answers are on page 286.

DILO COMO YO
SAY IT LIKE I DO

Footnote to Spanish pronunciation

As said earlier, Spanish is basically one language, both in the way that it is spoken and written. However, the Hispanic world is very vast and complex, having been profoundly influenced by many cultures and races, just as Spain was through its early history up to the fifteenth century. Logically, all of those influences have impacted the language through the acquisition of new words, intonation, and rhythm of the spoken language. What this means is that you can't expect every single Hispanic person to express himself/herself exactly the same, which may present a bit of a challenge to you when you're talking to a native speaker, watching Spanish-language television, or listening to Spanish radio. Your ear has to get used to/adapted to various language nuances, just as happens here in the United States between speakers from Boston and Mississippi, or with speakers from England, Australia, or India. They all speak basically the same language, but it just sounds different. Besides that, Spanish pronunciation presents numerous phonetic barriers or challenges that can add to your uneasiness and frustration. But you shouldn't get discouraged! You have the interest and willingness to learn, and that's what really counts. Just be aware of the differences and be prepared. Remember that eventually you will overcome them, as well as some other roadblocks that you may find along the way.

Key Spanish letter sounds to watch out for:

b-v	d-t	h	j
ñ	q	rr	z

¿Te acuerdas? Spanish uses two words for congratulations! One is *¡felicidades!* and the other one is *¡enhorabuena!*

ALMA HISPÁNICA
HISPANIC SOUL

José Hernández

José Hernández (1834–1886) is all about the gaucho, the legendary man of the *pampas*, the forgotten and underestimated man who lived a life of his own, always asserting his own personality and roots. This was the gaucho until José Hernández took it upon himself to bring him out from obscurity and hail his unique human traits through his work *Martín Fierro*. The long poem is divided into two parts: *La Ida* (1872) and *La Vuelta* (1879), and is directed both to the intellectual and to the gaucho himself. There are two distinct messages for each: to proclaim justice for the gaucho, and to awaken in the gaucho a sense of self-worth in order to better his condition. It has been called an epic poem by some critics, while for others it is more of a popular poem, deeply rooted in the oral tradition of the *pampas* and the gaucho. Hernández was active in politics and stood up against several of the regimes of the time, including the government of Alsina, and participated in the battles of Cepeda and Pavón. In 1880, he was elected president of the Argentinian Congress and provincial senator in 1881, reelected in 1885. While president of the Congress, he campaigned for the project of federalization, which resulted in establishing Buenos Aires as the capital of the country.

The writings of José Hernández.

From *Martín Fierro*.
First Part: La Ida.

1

Aquí me pongo a cantar
al compás de la vigüela,
que el hombre que lo desvela
una pena extraordinaria
como la ave solitaria
con el cantar se consuela.

2

Pido a los santos del Cielo
que ayuden mi pensamiento;
les pido en este momento
que voy a cantar mi historia
que refresquen la memoria
y aclaren mi entendimiento.

3

Vengan santos milagrosos,
vengan todos en mi ayuda,
que la lengua se me añuda
y se me turba la vista;
pido a mi Dios que me asista
en una ocasión tan ruda.

6

Cantando me he de morir,
cantando me han de enterrar,
y cantando he de llegar
al pie del Eterno Padre:
desde el vientre de mi madre
vine a este mundo a cantar.

To help you better understand this poem, here is the meaning of some key words:

vigüela> vihuela	early guitar
desvela	doesn't let one sleep
ave	bird
consuela	consoles, comforts
refresquen	refresh
aclaren	clear up
entendimiento	mind
que la lengua se me añuda	I get tongue-tied
se me turba la vista	my sight gets blurry
ruda	tough
desde	from
vientre	womb

Review

Answer these questions in English:

1. Why is the man asking for help?
2. What is he saying about his singing?

PLUMA EN MANO
PEN IN HAND

El Boquerón/The Boquerón

En San Salvador, la capital de El Salvador, muy cerca de la ciudad, se encuentra un volcán, ya extinguido, que es una de las vistas naturales más impresionantes del país, aunque no tanto, claro está, como el volcán Izalco, el más conocido y que aún sigue echando humo y bramando (spewing smoke and roaring). Aunque el nombre propio del volcán es San Salvador, se le conoce (it is known) generalmente por el nombre del Boquerón, realmente una gigantesca boca que espanta (frightens) sólo de verla.

Lo visitamos por primera vez hace muchos años con un grupo de amigos, todos avecindados (residing) en El Salvador. No sé la causa, pero al llegar allí quisimos pretender ser osados aventureros y descender al fondo (bottom) del cráter, a una distancia de la cima (top) de unos cinco kilómetros. Dispuestos a hacer alarde (show off) de valentía y arrojo, comenzamos el descenso abriéndonos paso (making way) entre matorrales y pisando ceniza movediza (ash like quicksand). De pronto, a mitad del camino, y resollando (breathing heavily) como bueyes, mi hermana resbaló (slipped) y se asió (grabbed/held onto) del tronco de un pequeño árbol que a su lado estaba, quedándose con él en la mano con raíz y todo. Si no hubiera sido por la pronta ayuda que sin vacilar (without hesitation) le dimos, mi hermana se hubiera caído dando vueltas (tumbling) al fondo del cráter. Superado el susto, proseguimos nuestra marcha y llegamos al fondo. Allí nos quedamos pasmados (shocked) con los ojos abiertos observando aquella maravilla de la naturaleza.

Después de un merecido reposo, y como ya se hacía tarde y empezaba a obscurecer, emprendimos el viaje de regreso subiendo la cuesta (uphill) con mucho más trabajo que al bajar, y nos encontramos en el camino a un señor llevando sobre sus hombros una pesada carga de leña (firewood). – ¿Y usted, cómo lo hace? – Lo hago, señor, para vender la leña en el mercado del pueblo y así poder alimentar a mi familia. Asombroso, realmente asombroso. Aquel hombre, que tenía sobre sesenta años de edad, subía y bajaba el volcán tres veces al día para al final recibir unos cuantos colones por su esfuerzo.

En los días siguientes visitamos también el Izalco, los Chorros, los Planes de Renderos, desde donde se nos presentaba en toda su amplitud la ciudad de San Salvador. Este país es, sin duda alguna, uno de los más pintorescos y atractivos de Centroamérica y, si le sumamos la gente y sus costumbres, difícil es encontrarle igual.

BRAIN TICKLERS
Set # 60

Ejercicios

Choose five words from the list below and write a Spanish sentence with each:
nombre propio avecindados osados
ceniza pasmados reposo carga
pintoresco

B. Taken from the passage above, give the infinitive forms of the following verbs:
1. espanta   3. resollando 5. subiendo
2. quisimos   4. caído

C. Write a composition in Spanish about a trip you made to the countryside. Use no less than five sentences.

¿Cuánto sabes? Here is a little project for you: Do you know what the words *pampa* and *gaucho* mean? Look them up on the web and give your answer.

Answers are on page 286.

ASÍ SOMOS
THIS IS WHO WE ARE

The City of Buenos Aires

It is called the *Paris of the Americas* and in many aspects it well deserves the name. Buenos Aires is indeed one of the greatest cities, not only in the Americas, but in the world. Magnificent buildings, spacious avenues and boulevards, well-manicured and well-kept public parks and squares. Tidy, exceedingly clean, inviting. The city is well-known for its restaurants, shopping, and, of course, its nightlife. Like most major Hispanic cities, it comes alive after midnight with thousands of people strolling through the streets, filling the movie theaters, eateries, nightclubs, the many museums and art galleries, or just sitting out at a sidewalk café, chatting about the news of the day. The city was made for walking since most sites to see are within easy reach. The Plaza de Mayo, where mothers gather every Thursday to pray for relatives missing during the 1980 military rule, has been the heart of the city since 1580. It is surrounded by the Catedral Metropolitana, finished in 1862, where General José de San Martín is buried, the Banco de la Nación, the Casa Rosada (Government House), and El Cabildo (Town Hall.) Other interesting sites are the Museo Nacional de Bellas Artes, with art relics dating back to the 12th century, the Teatro Colón, for the finest opera and ballet, the Obelisco, rising over 70 meters high, the Parque de la Costa, for shows and dancing, and the Barrio de San Telmo, specially on Sundays from 10 to 6, where tango comes alive by Argentina's finest performers. Calle Florida is the place for shoppers, packed with trendy and very chic stores sure to please the most demanding tastes.

Buenos Aires is a city built mostly by immigrants, just like New York. Spanish, Italian, Portuguese, German, and British immigrants left their native countries in search of opportunity, of a new way of life, fell in love with the city and settled there. Each one of these cultures contributed in large measure to the development of Buenos Aires and of Argentina in general.

When and by whom was Buenos Aires founded? The city was founded in 1536 by Pedro de Mendoza who named it *Nuestra Señora del Buen Aire*, or Our Lady of the Good Air. It was later abandoned in 1541 and replaced by La Asunción, but eventually, due to the strategic location of its harbor, was re-settled by Juan Torres de Vera in 1580. The people from Buenos Aires are called *porteños* because of Buenos Aires's port or harbor.

BRAIN TICKLERS—THE ANSWERS

Set # 57, page 274

A.
1. placentero
2. debajo de
3. a cabalidad
4. pudo haber sido
5. tortilla española

B. Answers will vary.

C.
1. F   2. V   3. F   4. V   5. V

¿Cuánto sabes?
Answers will vary. Sample answer is: Acapulco y Cancún.

Set # 58, page 275

Piénsalo bien

A. Answers will vary. Sample answer is: ¡Ojo, no te lastimes!

B. Answers will vary.

C. Answers will vary.

Set # 59, page 280

Bien vale la pena

A.
1. hermanote – hermanito
2. camota – camita
3. matota – matita
4. lunota – lunita
5. ratote – ratito

Set # 60, page 284

Pluma en mano

A. Answers will vary.

B.
1. espantar
2. querer
3. resollar
4. caer
5. subir

C. Answers will vary.

¿Cuánto sabes?
Answers will vary.

APPENDIX A

Spanish online reference sources.

Recommended online reference sources for Spanish language and Hispanic culture.

Real Academia de la Lengua Española

www.rae.es
By far the best online reference sources for all matters pertaining to the Spanish language. All explanations are given in Spanish; often includes examples.

www.yourdictionary.com
Good reference source for Spanish grammar. All explanations are given in English.

www.wikipedia.org
One of the best reference sources for all matters pertaining to the Spanish language and Hispanic culture.

www.donquijote.org
Good reference sources for Spanish games.

www.wordreference.com
Good reference source for English/Spanish words, sayings, idioms, etc.

www.babylon.com
Very good reference source for Spanish to English, English to Spanish translations.

www.thefreedictionary.com
Very good reference source for English to Spanish translations.

www.yahoo.es
Very good reference source for Spanish grammar in general, and in particular for spelling of Spanish words.

www.urbandictionary.com
Very good reference source for American idioms; often includes Spanish equivalents or translation of terms and phrases.

www.etymonline.com
Very good source for English/Spanish etymologies.

APPENDIX B

Spanish Model Verb Conjugation.

Included are the full conjugations of regular verbs ending in
-*AR*, -*ER*, and -*IR*. Note that the imperfect subjunctive has two
forms, and that the future indicative and the conditional simple
are formed by keeping the whole infinitive to which the endings
are added. The "pretérito anterior" is not included as it is
seldom used. Same applies to the "future perfect" of the
subjunctive as it is only used in literary language.

Names of tenses/moods in English and Spanish

English	Spanish
infinitive	infinitivo
gerund	gerundio
past participle	participio pasado
indicative	indicativo
conditional	potencial/condicional
subjunctive	subjuntivo
command/imperative	imperativo
present	presente
preterite/past	pretérito/pasado
imperfect	imperfecto
future	futuro
present perfect	pretérito perfecto
past perfect	pretérito pluscuamperfecto
future perfect	futuro perfecto
conditional perfect	potencial/condicional perfecto

Other verb-related words:

mood	el modo
verb	el verbo
verb tense	el tiempo verbal
verb root	la raíz verbal
verb ending	la terminación verbal
simple tense	el tiempo simple
compound tense	el tiempo compuesto

–Ar

Infinitive	cantar
Gerund	cantando
Past participle	cantado

Indicative

Present	Preterite	Imperfect	Future
canto	canté	cantaba	cantaré
cantas	cantaste	cantabas	cantarás
canta	cantó	cantaba	cantará
cantamos	cantamos	cantábamos	cantaremos
cantáis	cantasteis	cantabais	cantaréis
cantan	cantaron	cantaban	cantarán

Present Perfect	Past Perfect	Future Perfect
he cantado	había cantado	habré cantado
has cantado	habías cantado	habrás cantado
ha cantado	había cantado	habrá cantado
hemos cantado	habíamos cantado	habremos cantado
habéis cantado	habíais cantado	habréis cantado
han cantado	habían cantado	habrán cantado

Conditional	Conditional Perfect
cantaría	habría cantado
cantarías	habrías cantado
cantaría	habría cantado
cantaríamos	habríamos cantado
cantaríais	habríais cantado
cantarían	habrían cantado

Command

canta
cante
cantemos
cantad
canten

Subjunctive

Present	Imperfect	Present Perfect
cante	cantara/cantase	haya cantado
cantes	cantaras/cantasses	hayas cantado
cante	cantara/cantase	haya cantado
cantemos	cantáramos/cantásemos	hayamos cantado
cantéis	cantarais/cantaseis	hayáis cantado
canten	cantaran/cantasen	hayan cantado

Past Perfect
hubiera/hubiese cantado
hubieras/hubieses cantado
hubiera/hubiese cantado
hubiéramos/hubiésemos cantado
hubierais/hubieseis cantado
hubieran/hubiesen cantado

–Er

Infinitive	comer
Gerund	comiendo
Past participle	comido

Indicative

Present	Preterite	Imperfect	Future
como	comí	comía	comeré
comes	comiste	comías	comerás
come	comió	comía	comerá
comemos	comimos	comíamos	comeremos
coméis	comisteis	comíais	comeréis
comen	comieron	comían	comerán

Present Perfect	Past Perfect	Future Perfect
he comido	había comido	habré comido
has comido	habías comido	habrás comido
ha comido	había comido	habrá comido
hemos comido	habíamos comido	habremos comido
habéis comido	habíais comido	habréis comido
han comido	habían comido	habrán comido

Conditional	Conditional Perfect
comería	habría comido
comerías	habrías comido
comería	habría comido
comeríamos	habríamos comido
comeríais	habríais comido
comerían	habrían comido

Command

come
coma
comamos
comed
coman

Subjunctive

Present	Imperfect	Present Perfect
coma	comiera/comiese	haya comido
comas	comieras/comieses	hayas comido
coma	comiera/comiese	haya comido
comamos	comiéramos/comiésemos	hayamos comido
comáis	comierais/comieseis	hayáis comido
coman	comieran/comiesen	hayan comido

Past Perfect
hubiera/hubiese comido
hubieras/hubieses comido
hubiera/hubiese comido
hubiéramos/hubiésemos comido
hubierais/hubieseis comido
hubieran/hubiesen comido

–Ir

Infinitive	vivir
Gerund	viviendo
Past Participle	vivido

Indicative

Present	Preterite	Imperfect	Future
vivo	viví	vivía	viviré
vives	viviste	vivías	vivirás
vive	vivió	vivía	vivirá
vivimos	vivimos	vivíamos	viviremos
vivís	vivisteis	vivíais	viviréis
viven	vivieron	vivían	vivirán

Present Perfect	Past Perfect	Future Perfect
he vivido	había vivido	habré vivido
has vivido	habías vivido	habrás vivido
ha vivido	había vivido	habrá vivido
hemos vivido	habíamos vivido	habremos vivido
habéis vivido	habíais vivido	habréis vivido
han vivido	habían vivido	habrán vivido

Conditional	Conditional Perfect
viviría	habría vivido
vivirías	habrías vivido
viviría	habría vivido
viviríamos	habríamos vivido
viviríais	habríais vivido
vivirían	habrían vivido

Command

vive
viva
vivamos
vivid
vivan

Subjunctive

Present	Imperfect	Present Perfect
viva	viviera/viviese	haya vivido
vivas	vivieras/vivieses	hayas vivido
viva	viviera/viviese	haya vivido
vivamos	viviéramos/viviésemos	hayamos vivido
viváis	vivierais/vivieseis	hayáis vivido
vivan	vivieran/viviesen	hayan vivido

Past Perfect
hubiera/hubiese vivido
hubieras/hubieses vivido
hubiera/hubiese vivido
hubiéramos/hubiésemos vivido
hubierais/hubieseis vivido
hubieran/hubiesen vivido

APPENDIX C

Some Irregular gerunds and/or past participles in Spanish.
Regular forms are excluded and marked "–."

Infinitive	Gerund	Past participle
abrir (to open)	–	abierto
caer (to fall)	cayendo	–
competir (to compete)	compitiendo	–
componer (to compose/ repair)	–	compuesto
creer (to believe)	creyendo	–
cubrir (to cover)	–	cubierto
decir (to say/tell)	diciendo	dicho
descubrir (to discover)	–	descubierto
devolver (to give back)	–	devuelto
digerir (to digest)	digiriendo	–
dormir (to sleep)	durmiendo	–
escribir (to write)	–	escrito
freír (to fry)	friendo	frito
hacer (to do/make)	–	hecho
huir (to flee/escape)	huyendo	–
imprimir (to print)	–	impreso
ir (to go)	yendo	ido
leer (to read)	leyendo	–
mentir (to lie)	mintiendo	–
morir (to die)	muriendo	muerto
oír (to hear)	oyendo	–
pedir (to ask for)	pidiendo	–
poder (to be able to/can)	pudiendo	–
poner (to put)	–	puesto

preferir (to prefer)	prefiriendo	–
reír (to laugh)	ridiendo	–
resolver (to solve)	–	resuelto
romper (to break)	–	roto
satisfacer (to pay/settle)	–	satisfecho
seguir (to follow)	siguiendo	–
sentir (to feel)	sintiendo	–
sugerir (to suggest)	sugiriendo	–
traer (to bring)	trayendo	–
venir (to come)	viniendo	–
ver (to see)	viendo	visto
vestir (to dress)	vistiendo	–
volver (to return)	–	vuelto

APPENDIX D

Spanish word order exercise.

Put the following ten sentences in the right word order following the basic Spanish sentence structure:

Subject + Predicate + complement of the Predicate

Keep in mind that the subject can also have a complement. The first word has a capital letter and the last has a period.

visita niña La abuelos en a Buenos Aires. sus

_____

Right order: La niña visita a sus abuelos en Buenos Aires.

juegan amigos Los parque. baloncesto el en

_____

Right order: Los amigos juegan baloncesto en el parque.

comida la perro en cocina. El come la

_____

Right order: El perro come la comida en la cocina.

al ayuda maestra La estudiante la con tarea.

_____

Right order: La maestra ayuda al estudiante con la tarea.

dimos lo Se ella su a casa. en

_____

Right order: Se lo dimos a ella en su casa.

Juan muy novia La es bonita de inteligente. e

_____

Right order: La novia de Juan es muy bonita e inteligente.

gusta No me puerco el ni pescado. el ni

_____

Right order: No me gusta ni el pescado ni el puerco.

fiesta en mi hermana. bailando la Estamos mucho de

_____

Right order: Estamos bailando mucho en la fiesta de mi hermana.

hecho tarea todavía. han la No

_____

Right order: No han hecho la tarea todavía.

reunión. mañana venga la a que Ojalá

_____

Right order: Ojalá que venga mañana a la reunión.

APPENDIX E

Matching exercise.

Match each item in column A with the corresponding item in Column B.

Column A

1. the auhor of "Don Quijote"
2. the capital of Spain
3. the meaning of the verb "soñar"
4. the direct object pronoun "it"
5. the indirect object pronoun "them"
6. the meaning of "se" added to the end of a Spanish infinitive
7. the main auxiliary verb in Spanish
8. the ending of a regular past participle for "AR" verbs in Spanish
9. the possessive pronoun "my" singular
10. the demonstrative adjective "this" masculine singular
11. pronunciation of the "h" in Spanish
12. fourth letter of the Spanish alphabet
13. famous Chilean writer
14. main square in Mexico City
15. an adverb of time in Spanish
16. an adjective in Spanish
17. "I have" in Spanish
18. "they have opened the door" in Spanish
19. The gerund of "leer"
20. a huge mountain range in South America
21. the number "26" in Spanish
22. ancient Mexican civilization
23. a diphthong in Spanish
24. the only nasal sound in Spanish
25. "I am hungry" in Spanish

Column B

a. silent, mute
b. han abierto la puerta
c. veintiséis
d. Los Andes
e. Miguel de Cervantes
f. haber
g. temprano
h. Gabriela Mistral
i. Aztecs
j. ai
k. ado
l. tengo hambre
m. to form a reflexive verb
n. ñ
o. El Zócalo
p. tengo
q. leyendo
r. Madrid
s. lo/la
t. mi
u. contento
v. les
w. to dream
x. este
y. ch

1. e 2. r 3. w 4. s 5. v 6. m
7. f 8. k 9. t 10. x 11. a 12. y
13. h 14. o 15. g 16. u 17. p
18. b 19. q 20. d 21. c 22. i
23. j 24. n 25. l

APPENDIX F

Vocabulary exercise—Juego "El Ahorcado" (Hangman)

Write in the blanks each of the letters in the right order corresponding to each Spanish word. Use accent marks where needed. Don't forget that double consonants (*ll*, *rr*) count as one letter in Spanish.

___ ___ ___ ___ ___ ___ ___ ___   elephant

___ ___ ___ ___ ___ ___ ___ ___ ___ ___   railroad

___ ___ ___ ___ ___ ___ ___ ___ ___ ___   airport

___ ___ ___ ___ ___ ___ ___ ___ ___ ___   Christmas Eve

___ ___ ___ ___ ___ ___ ___ ___ ___   highway

___ ___ ___ ___ ___ ___ ___ ___   rainy

___ ___ ___ ___ ___ ___ ___ ___ ___ ___ ___   university

___ ___ ___ ___ ___ ___ ___ ___ ___ ___ ___ ___   catastrophic

___ ___ ___ ___ ___ ___ ___   chemistry

___ ___ ___ ___ ___ ___ ___   scarf

___ ___ ___ ___ ___ ___ ___ ___   nice/pleasant

Answers in order of appearance: elefante, ferrocarril, aeropuerto, nochebuena, carretera, lluvioso, universidad, catastrófico, química, bufanda, simpático

APPENDIX G

Dividing words into syllables/The orthographical accent

Following is a list of 18 Spanish words. Some need accent marks, others don't. Listen to your teacher as he/she reads each word twice and 1) divide the word into syllables; 2) place the accent mark if needed on the correct syllable.

español
es-pa-ñol

contemporaneo
con-tem-po-rá-ne-o

clase
cla-se

estudiante
es-tu-dian-te

dandoselo
dán-do-se-lo

refrigerador
re-fri-ge-ra-dor

Mexico
Mé-xi-co

costumbre
cos-tum-bre

repleto
re-ple-to

Camagüey
Ca-ma-güey

cafeteria
ca-fe-te-rí-a

caballero
ca-ba-lle-ro

trabalenguas
tra-ba-len-guas

fisiologico
fi-sio-ló-gi-co

sombrero
som-bre-ro

suramericano
sur-a-me-ri-ca-no

guantes
guan-tes

camara
cá-ma-ra

INDEX

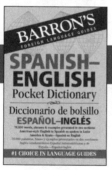